D0572546

# THE GRILLING MANUAL

## 264 ESSENTIALS FOR COOKING WITH FIRE

weldon**owen**

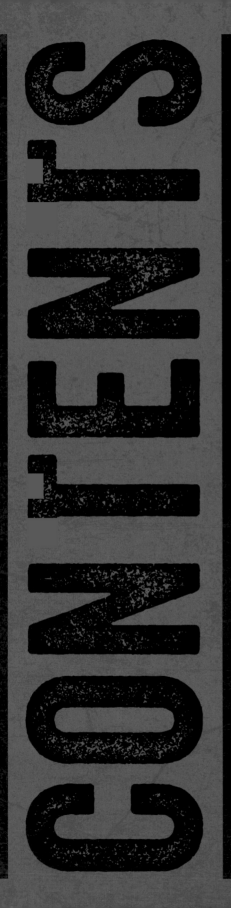

# CONTENTS

# TOOLS & TECHNIQUES

## PORK

## LAMB

## POULTRY

## SEAFOOD

## SIDES & DRINKS

# INTRODUCTION

**G**rilling is as much about culture as it is about technique. Whether what you're cooking is ruggedly primal or surprisingly sophisticated, the casual nature of cooking with fire makes it a universal pleasure. The simple techniques and communal atmosphere of a barbecue bring people together, whether for an impromptu dinner of burgers on a summer night or an all-day pig roast with all the trimmings.

Food roasted over an open flame was one of humanity's first culinary triumphs, and even today you can accomplish wonders with only an open flame and a succulent cut of your favorite meat. However, today's outdoor cooks have an incredible range of tools and appliances at their disposal, allowing us to grill whole fish, perfect pizzas, and delightful desserts as well as the usual suspects.

A growing interest in global grilling techniques adds to this lexicon, allowing backyard cooks to bring Korean bolgogi, Jamaican jerk chicken, Thai satay skewers, and more to the table alongside the more familiar pulled pork and barbecued ribs.

Armed with specialized gear and a world of recipes, modern grillmasters are equipped with everything they need to make that flame-cooked dinner as fancy or as simple as time, taste, and ingredients allow. Part of the fun is navigating the process.

The 264 tips, recipes, and techniques that follow cover everything about that process: all the basics, such as the pros and cons of cooking over gas or charcoal, indirect- and direct-heat cooking, choosing your fuel, and mastering your fire; and expert-level specifics, such as choosing a smoking wood, picking the right brine ingredients, and perfecting open-fire cookery. Learn the details of each cut of meat, master the art of flavor combinations, and take everything from the butcher to the table.

Recipes run the gamut from flash-grilled steak to tea-smoked duck breasts, from barbecued pizza to grill-roasted s'mores, with chapters devoted to beef, pork, lamb, poultry, and seafood, and liberally peppered with an arsenal of tools, techniques, rubs, marinades, sauces, sides, and drinks.

You have everything you need to know about grilling at your fingertips, so it's time to get started. Fire it up and enjoy!

TOOLS & TECHNIQUES

# 001 Cook with Fire

Starting a fire and cooking with it is both intrinsically primal and wonderfully practical. These days, cooking with fire has evolved to include a range of grilling and smoking options that begins with the selection of a charcoal or gas grill, and the accessories and tools that let you hone your technique. Here are the most popular options for the modern caveman.

**CHARCOAL GRILLS** When it comes to cooking with charcoal, you have a number of options to choose from. You can burn regular or hardwood charcoal briquettes or lump charcoal, and you can select from a wide range of grills—from small disposable picnic grills to a party-size ranch kettle model. Whatever your fancy, look for a well-built, high-grade steel grill that comes with a lid and at least two vents to control airflow and temperature. In the United States, perhaps the most quintessential grill model is the standard 22-inch (55-cm) kettle. It efficiently and quickly grills cuts of meat and seafood over a hot or medium-hot charcoal fire and can also be converted to accommodate longer-cooking foods that require low

temperatures. Smaller charcoal grills, such as square or rectangular Japanese-style hibachis, are easily portable and perfect for grilling on the balcony or patio.

**GAS GRILLS** Gas grills run the gamut from a no-frills cart to a gadget-filled mini kitchen. They can be fueled by propane, making them at least somewhat portable, or connected to a home's natural-gas line. The gas flames heat stainless steel or enameled baffles, a rack of heat-absorbent ceramic briquettes, or a bed of lava rock underneath the grill rack. Don't know where to start? Here's the skinny: Two burners are a must, but if you plan to utilize an indirect cooking method (useful for many of the recipes in this book), three burners will make your life easier and give you better control. Don't get hung up on BTUs—35,000 should be plenty. Instead, examine how the heat is diffused: angled metal plates covering the burners are particularly effective and reduce flare-ups. Look for cooking racks that are either plain stainless steel or stainless steel with a powder-paint finish. If your grill has an infrared burner, know that it will cook hotter than regular gas. Some models also have a "searing station" burner that produces an extra-hot heat for searing meat and vegetables prior to longer cooking on the grill.

**SMOKER GRILLS** If what you want is low, slow cooking and lots of smoky flavor, look no further. Egg-shaped ceramic *kamado*-style smoker grills, such as the popular Big Green Egg, are prized for their unique heat retention and the distinctive flavor from the lump hardwood charcoal they burn for fuel. More traditional smokers—which can be round, vertical, or bullet shaped—can be fired by gas or charcoal, usually with the addition of water-soaked wood chunks to provide their signature flavor. Most include a water pan in order to help keep the temperature low and the food nice and moist.

**INDOOR GRILLS** Are you outdoor-challenged? Never fear, there's a range of options for indoor grilling enthusiasts as well. Grill pans are excellent and widely available; they make cooking on your stovetop a snap. When it comes to materials, cast iron is the ideal choice for your grill pan; it's easy to use, provides a good sear, and the pans are virtually indestructible (see item 010). If you're in a rush, look for preseasoned models, which are already prepped and ready for stovetop cooking.

# 002 Gear Up!

You can spend a lot of time, effort, and money collecting an array of high-tech accessories to craft a magazine-perfect grilling setup. Or you can round up the essentials listed here, and get grilling. Neither way is right nor wrong, but one gets burgers on your plate a lot faster.

**KEEP CLEAN** You'll need a long-handled wire brush for cleaning the grill: brass bristles are best for porcelain-enamel grates, steel for cast iron grates. Use the brush on the grate when it's hot, both before and after cooking. Try a smaller, more angled brush with a stainless steel scraper for cleaning between the grate bars.

**FLIP OUT** A sturdy set of long-handled stainless steel tongs is the best choice for turning most grilled foods. To flip burgers or turn items that might fall apart if handled roughly, a medium-length stainless steel spatula offers optimal control. Handles should be well insulated.

**CHECK THE DIGITS** An instant-read meat thermometer takes the guesswork out of cooking time. Simply insert the probe into the thickest part of the protein, away from any bone, and in seconds it registers the temperature. It's also important to keep track of the temperature inside the grill, especially when you'll be cooking food over a long period of time—but specialized grill thermometers that attach to the grate can be wildly inaccurate. A good oven thermometer is a better choice. A laser thermometer is even more reliable but can cost a bundle.

**BRUSH UP** Cotton mop–style basting brushes look good during barbecue contests, but can be tough to clean. Serious grill masters opt for silicone-bristle brushes instead.

The rubber bristles hold sauce well and clean up with ease. Most are safe to toss in the dishwasher.

**STAY SAFE** Burned fingers don't look good on anyone—especially the cook. Keep an oven mitt or pot holder made of heavy quilted cotton close by to protect your hands from the grill's intense heat. Look for mitts that are ribbed with silicone for superior grip. Leather gloves made for grilling or using with fireplace tools are also useful.

**STICK UP** A set of 8-inch (20-cm) metal skewers are good to have on hand if satay or kebabs are frequently on the menu. The metal conducts heat nicely, so food cooks quickly and evenly. If you opt for wood skewers, soak them in water for at least 30 minutes before using.

**GRILL MORE** Grill baskets are awesome for delicate foods that are difficult to turn or that could fall through the cooking grate, such as asparagus, fish fillets, and onions. Screens and plates have similar uses. A screen is wire mesh supported by a metal frame; a plate is a sheet of metal that is perforated with small holes and helps prevent flare-ups. Both are used in the same way: Place the screen or plate over direct heat, brush with oil, and let heat for a minute or two to minimize sticking before adding the food to be cooked.

**USE A CHIMNEY** This triumph of simple engineering (see item 013) allows you to light charcoal fire without lighter fluid, which can leave an unpleasant chemical aftertaste. Chimneys come in a range of sizes; one with a 7.5-inch (19-cm) diameter that's 12 inches (30 cm) tall will fit the bill for most medium to large kettle grills.

**DON'T BE A DRIP** You can set a metal drip pan on the grill bed of a charcoal grill under large cuts of meat and poultry to capture dripping fat and juices, preventing flare-ups. It's also indispensable for making gravy. Try any disposable aluminum pan as long and as wide as the item being grilled and about 2 inches (5 cm) deep.

**SMOKE OUT** Smoker boxes are heavy, vented metal containers that hold wood chips or herbs to create a flavoring smoke when using a gas grill (see item 017). Don't have a smoke box? A perforated piece of heavy-duty aluminum foil folded into a rectangular envelope also does the job nicely.

**SPIN CONTROL** A rotisserie is a large spit that's powered by an electric motor. It slowly rotates at a constant speed above the fire bed, making it a good choice for grilling a large roast or whole bird. When choosing a rotisserie, look for a model with a strong, reliable motor and a sturdy counterweight system.

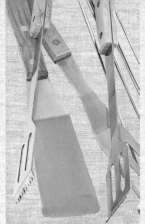

# 003 Add to Your Arsenal

You might have thought you were set with your basic collection of grilling tools (see item 002). Think again! There's a gadget for just about anything you can cook over a fire—from s'more roasters to whole-fish baskets. If your definition of "must have" is on the gourmet side, you might want (or need!) some of these.

**PIGTAIL** Times was, every cowpoke cook had one of these crafted by the local blacksmith. A cast-iron rod with its tip bent into a U shape, it's just the thing for turning heavy steaks on the grill over an open fire, and modern cooks don't even need a neighboring smithy.

**PIZZA STONE** The same pizza stone that works in your oven can work on the grill, but you can opt for one specifically designed for grilling, too. These stones are usually made of a thicker, more durable grade of ceramic to withstand the grill's heat. Many also include a slight lip or a metal framework that keeps them from resting directly on the grill rack, as well as side handles for easy lifting.

**CHAPA** Unlike regular cast iron griddles, this Argentine grilling essential is manufactured from solid, rolled steel, which maintains a nice, consistent cooking temperature and has a smooth, nonstick cooking surface similar to that of a wok. Argentine outdoor cooks often rest it over a wood fire, but it works nearly as well over a bed of glowing hot lump charcoal. It can be used just as you would a griddle— for everything from searing steaks to cooking griddle breads.

**S'MORE ROASTER** Pop a few marshmallow-and-chocolate-bar-stuffed graham crackers into one of these and you'll produce the type of fire-roasted s'mores that most kids can only dream about.

## QUESADILLA MAKER

This round grill rack makes a mean quesadilla, and also works wonders on grilled flatbread, pita bread, and pizza dough.

**CEDAR PLANKS** Grill-ready cedar planks are easy to find in any home-supply or culinary store, providing an awesome way to add smoky flavor to fresh fish as well as chicken, pork, and vegetables cooked on the grill. Just soak the plank in water, put the food to be cooked on top of it, and place it on the grill rack for long, indirect-heat smoking.

## FISH BASKET

This fish-shaped rack, especially when nicely greased, keeps delicate fish skin intact and prevents the tender fillets from sticking to the grill rack.

**POPCORN POPPER** Pop up old-fashioned corn over the grill rack or an open flame with equal ease. Variations include the enameled kettle style with a perforated top, shown here, and a heavy-duty aluminum bowl topped with a mesh dome to trap the popping kernels.

## SANDWICH IRON

Available in all sorts of shapes and sizes—from square and rectangular to molded seashells, this long-handled wonder lets you cook pies or hot sandwiches over an open fire or glowing coals, or place it right on the grill rack atop a charcoal or gas fire.

# 004 Have It Both Ways

Hybrid grilling is often the best of both methods—searing foods over direct heat to accomplish that wonderful caramelized outer crust, then finishing over indirect heat for lengthy cooking without burning. Bone-in chicken pieces are a hybrid cooking success story. The chicken can be nicely browned and crisped over direct heat, then moved to a cooler part of the grill away from the heat where the interior can cook to perfection without over-browning on the outside.

# 005 Feel The Flames

Direct-heat grilling is probably the method that springs to mind when you think of a simple cookout, whether you know this term for it or not—burgers and franks on a grill, sizzling over the flames. Food is placed on a grill grate directly over the heat source. Cooking directly over hot coals or on a gas grill's preheated burner lends foods a nice sear, creating a flavorful caramelized crust and, with good temperature monitoring, a quickly cooked interior. Direct-heat grilling can be done with or without a lid, although the use of a lid will reduce the airflow that could foster flare-ups when fatty meats and oil-marinated vegetables drip juices onto the heat source. When using direct heat to cook thicker cuts of meat and other large food items, you often get the best results by turning down the heat after the initial searing, in order to prevent burning. Many foods cooked over direct heat are seasoned, sauced, or marinated before or during their time on the grill, making for a messier affair. Sauces, especially those laden with sugar or oil, are best applied to food toward the end of its time over direct heat so as to avoid burning. Try direct-heat grilling for steaks, chops, burgers, fish fillets, boneless chicken, sausages, and most vegetables.

# 006
## Go the Indirect Route

Much like oven roasting, grilling with indirect heat relies on reflected heat that circulates around the food, cooking it more slowly and reducing the likelihood of burning.

**CLEAR A SPACE** On a charcoal grill, coals are pushed to the sides, leaving the center grill rack open for cooking without the searing quality of direct heat. On a gas grill, one or more of the burners should be turned off, allowing a space for food to cook that captures the heat from the burners without being placed directly over them.

**PUT A LID ON IT** Indirect-heat cooking works best with a grill that is covered—throughout a cooking time that can be much longer than that required for direct-heat grilling. Savvy grill masters who understand indirect heat know to keep extra coals at the ready (even better if they're already glowing) to replenish those being diminished during the often long and slow cooking process. Try indirect-heat grilling for beef roasts, leg of lamb, thick-cut pork chops, pork loins, whole chickens, bone-in chicken pieces, whole fish, and anything that is heavily sauced.

# 007
## Smoke and Steam

For basic smoking, the cooking heat is provided by both smoke and steam. In a grill, the setup is usually about the same as for indirect-heat grilling. The difference comes in the form of water-soaked wood chips added to the coals (or to a smoker box in a gas grill) to create smoke. The moist chips also create steam, which is often significantly bolstered by a drip pan filled with water set underneath the food to be smoked, either in the center of a bed of coals or between burners in a gas grill. Get ready for a long, slow cook at a low temperature, and be sure to keep adding more coals to a charcoal fire and more soaked wood to the heat source to keep the smoke and heat at a nice and steady pace. Smoking works great for brisket, ribs, pulled pork, and turkey.

# 008 Iron Things Out

Cast iron is an amazingly sturdy, long-lasting, and versatile material for pots and pans. Pots and pans made from cast iron are an outdoor cook's best friend, as you can place a skillet right on the grate or suspend a cookpot right over the coals without fear of damaging it. Cast iron pots can be hung over an open fire, buried in a pit of coals, and perched atop a gas grill or charcoal barbecue. Use frying pans for cooking shellfish or simmering sauces; dutch ovens are the top choice for long-simmering dishes such as stews. These pots and pans need a little special care (see next page), but the tradeoff is that, when treated right, you can use them every day—and they'll not only last you a lifetime, but your children and their children, too.

# 009 Season a Cast Iron Pot

One of cast iron's allures, and an attribute that contributes to its durability, is the wonderful black-pot patina that builds over time with repeated use. This time-earned patina, initiated with a careful seasoning of your pots before you use them, provides your cast iron with a rust-proof, nonstick, and flavor-enhancing coating that works better the more you use it. Building and maintaining the patina is a snap if you know how to do it.

**STEP 1** Preheat an oven to 450°F (232°C). While it's heating, wash the pot with hot, soapy water, and rinse and dry it well.

**STEP 2** Put the pot in the oven for 10 minutes, then take it out and let it cool.

**STEP 3** Reduce oven temperature to 300°F (149°C). Use cooking oil to grease all surfaces of the pot, inside and out (and the handle, too).

**STEP 4** Put it back in the oven for an hour. (Crack a few kitchen windows open. It's going to smoke and smell like burned metal. Don't worry, this is normal.)

**STEP 5** Remove the pot and let it cool, then wipe away any excess oil. Store with a paper towel inside. Newly seasoned cast iron will sport a shiny caramel color that turns black with use, especially if you use it to cook a few greasy dishes the first few times you use it after seasoning.

# 010 Make It Last a Lifetime (Or Two)

Every time you use a cast iron pot or pan, be sure to clean it properly and refresh the seasoning.

**WASH UP** Wash the pan with warm, soapy water just as you would any of your other pots (yes, you can, in fact, use soap). Next, rinse it well and dry it thoroughly with a paper towel or a clean cloth.

**GET HOT** To reseason, pour a bit of oil into the pan and place it over medium heat on the stovetop or in the oven at 450°F (232°C) until it starts to smoke. Remove it from the heat, rub the oil around with a paper towel, and let it cool.

**STAY DRY** Remember, water is the enemy of cast iron. To make sure your pan never rusts, simply dry and oil it faithfully after every use. If rust somehow sneaks up on your pan, use a scouring brush to scrape it off, then rinse, dry, and reseason with oil.

# 011 Choose Your Charcoal

Not all charcoal is created equal. Each variety has a little something different to offer—flavor, heat, burn time, or some combination thereof. Standard briquettes are made by baking together a mixture of charcoal ingredients, while both hardwood and lump charcoals are created with a traditional process called slow pyrolysis—in which wood is heated in an oxygen-free pit until it's completely charred. Makers may use oak, hickory, or mesquite wood, each of which delivers subtle variations in flavor.

**STANDARD BRIQUETTES** Usually composed of compressed bits of charcoal, coal, and sawdust, as well as binders and burning agents, this economical option delivers a nice, even heat and steady burn rate. Watch out for brands that are pumped full of toxic ingredients like nitrates, petroleum, sand, or clay, as well as any of the self-starting varieties. Some briquettes include smoking woods in the mix; look for those laced with hickory, oak, and mesquite for added flavor.

**NATURAL LUMP CHARCOAL** Made from a variety of hardwoods, this burns hotter, cleaner, and longer than traditional briquettes, offering a distinct wood smoke flavor to the food it cooks. Lump charcoal can be used more than once; closing the grill dampers at the end of cooking time will eventually extinguish its heat. Any remaining charcoal can be relit when you have your next cookout. Lump charcoal is a good choice for ceramic grill smokers that cook and smoke foods over low heat for long periods of time.

**NATURAL HARDWOOD CHARCOAL** Fragrant woods add a subtle smoke and flavor to foods during cooking. Since it burns much hotter than briquettes and retains the heat longer, natural hardwood is a better choice for both quick direct-heat cooking and lengthy indirect-heat cooking.

# 012 Buy Enough Briquettes

Is there anything worse than running out of charcoal mid-cookout? How much you'll need depends on how much you're cooking, of course, but also on your cooking method.

**DIRECT HEAT** For straight grilling over direct heat, assuming an hour or so of cooking time is all you need, figure on 20–40 briquettes (1½–2 lb/750 g–1 kg) for four people, or 40 briquettes (3 lb/1.5 kg) for eight.

**INDIRECT HEAT** If you're cooking over indirect heat, add another 40 briquettes directly to the fire after about 1½ hours, or start more briquettes in your chimney starter and add them to the fire after about 2 hours.

**BACKUP HEAT** When hefty items such as beef brisket, roast turkey, or bone-in pork loin are on the menu, it's often necessary to keep the coals lit and at a steady temperature for many hours. Be sure to have plenty of coals on hand to feed the fire and keep the heat consistent. You should replenish the coals every 1½ hours or so by adding about half the amount you started with to your fire. You can also keep a chimney starter full of lit coals at the ready, using sturdy tongs to transfer glowing coals to your grill fire as needed.

# 013 Light Up

You have a few options for lighting your coals. In most circumstances, a chimney starter is hands down the best choice, unless you're working with a large amount of charcoal, or larger lumps than usual. If what you've got is standard charcoal, hardwood briquettes, or smaller chunks of lump charcoal, go for the chimney. A tall metal cylinder with vents on the bottom and an open top, it uses the fact that heat rises to light your coals, and it can ignite enough of them at once to grill your whole meal.

**USE A CHIMNEY** Lightly stuff a couple of sheets of newspaper into the bottom of the cylinder (under the grate). Don't use too much paper or you will smother the fire. Then pour the briquettes or hardwood chunks over the grate, filling the chimney, then light the paper (A). The fire will burn upward and ignite your fuel. You'll know it's working when you look at the starter sideways and see the heat rising. In 15–20 minutes, the coals should be covered with gray ash and glowing.

**START IT UP** When large amounts of charcoal or larger chunks need to be ignited, a chimney starter may be too small to get the job done. In those cases, it may be more efficient to use an electric starter wand or clean-burning fire starters. To do this, start by mounding the charcoal in the bottom of your grill. Open all the vents to increase the airflow, giving the fire plenty of oxygen. Place the wand or starters into the center of the coals (B) and turn on the wand or light the starters. In about 10 minutes, the surrounding coals should be edged with white ash. Mound more coals from the sides on top of the lit coals. In another 10–15 minutes, most of the coals should be lit and edged in white.

**GET READY TO GRILL** When the coals on top of the heap are rimmed with white ash but still black in the centers (C), it's time to get down to business. If you're using a chimney starter, pour the lit coals from the cylinder onto the charcoal rack at the bottom of your grill. Spread the mound of glowing coals into an even layer with a pair of heavy tongs. Place the grill rack on top and let it heat before you add the food.

# 014 Check Your Heat

Of course there are thermometers for this kind of thing, but it's easier and more fun to use this simple way of measuring your charcoal fire's heat. Hold your hand about 3 inches (7.5 cm) above the fire and count off the seconds: one Mississippi, two Mississippi, three Mississippi, and so on, until the fire feels so hot you need to move your hand. Here's the key (and the matching temperatures to check your results). To control the heat while you're grilling for a longer period of time, move the food closer to or farther away from the fire, or adjust the grill's vents. Position them so they're more open for greater heat, more closed for less.

| SECONDS COUNTED | HOW THAT FIRE? | TEMPERATURE | READY TO COOK? |
|---|---|---|---|
| 1–2 | Hot | 450–500°F (230–260°C) | Perfect for most barbecuing and smoking. |
| 2–4 | Medium-hot | 400–450°F (200–230°C) | Almost there! |
| 4–5 | Medium | 350–400°F (180–200°C) | Be patient! |
| 6–7 | Medium-low | 300–350°F (148–180°C) | Still no. |
| 7–9 | Low | 250–300°F (120–148°C) | Not yet! |

# 015 Don't Go There

Some woods emit strong, resinous, even noxious smoke. Be sure you know what you're adding to your cooking fire, and don't use these woods for anything other than a campfire. Even then, avoid inhaling their smoke. The trees to stay away from are all conifers (pine, fir, spruce, redwood, cedar, cypress, and their close relatives) as well as elm, eucalyptus, sassafras, sycamore, and liquid amber.

# 017 Pick Smoking Woods for Flavor

Experienced fire masters choose a wood for smoking much as they would select spices, with an appreciation for how each type lends its own particular nuance to the finished dish. Like spices, woods can also be blended to create subtle new flavors. Mixing hickory with apple or cherry punches up those mild fruitwoods and adds a nice golden brown finish, while a blend of pecan and peach woods lend a fruit and nut aroma. Just remember: Everything in moderation. Too much smoke and that's all anyone will taste, so try smoking for no more than half the total cooking time.

| MILD SMOKE | Stone fruit (peach, apricot, nectarine, plum) | Light, subtle, fruity flavor. For plum, use only the wood of fruit-bearing trees. | Poultry, pork, fish |
|---|---|---|---|
| | Crabapple | Very mild with subtle fruit flavor, slightly sweet. Can add a nice browned finish to food. | Poultry, pork, game birds |
| | Cherry | Mild and fruity. One of the best. | Poultry, pork, game, beef |
| | Citrus | Nice, mild smoky flavor with mild citrus notes. | Poultry, pork, beef, fish |
| | Cottonwood | Its subtle flavor tends to enhance the flavors of other woods it's added to. Use only seasoned cottonwood. | Poultry, pork, beef, fish |
| | Lilac | Very light, subtle with a hint of floral. | Lamb, seafood |
| | Mulberry | Sweet smell similar to apple. | Chicken, pork |
| | Pear | Nice, subtle smoke, similar to apple. | Chicken, pork |
| MILD TO MEDIUM SMOKE | Birch | Flavor similar to maple. | Salmon, poultry, pork |
| MEDIUM SMOKE | Acacia | Comes from the same family as mesquite. Similar flavor, though not as heavy. | Red meat, vegetables |
| | Alder | Very delicate with a hint of sweetness. | Poultry, pork, light-meat game birds, fish (particularly salmon) |
| | Almond | Sweet smoke flavor; light ash. | Good with all meats, especially chicken and turkey |
| | Ash | Soft, smoky flavor with a nice, subtle sweetness. Fast burning. | Poultry, pork, beef, seafood |
| | Beechnut | Mild, somewhat delicate smoke flavor. Similar to maple. | Poultry, pork, fish |

# 016 Soak It Up

Most experts agree that you don't have to soak your chips in water before adding them to the smoker. But you can always soak them in something more interesting. Chips soaked in a strong red wine will impart a spicy flavor reminiscent of grapevines. Apple juice–soaked chips have a sweet fruitiness; add a shot of rum to the soaking mix to give mild-flavored meat a delicious, caramelized flavor.

| | | | |
|---|---|---|---|
| **MEDIUM SMOKE** | Cedar | Sweet, spicy flavor with very mild smokiness. | Fish |
| | Chestnut | Slightly sweet, nutty smoke flavor. | Chicken, pork, red meat |
| | Guava | Semisweet aroma and flavor. | Poultry, pork, beef, lamb, fish |
| | Hazelnut | Sweet, hazelnut flavor. | Chicken, pork |
| | Hickory | The king of smoking woods. Sweet to strong, heavy bacon flavor. | Pork, ham, beef |
| | Maple | Smoky, mellow, and slightly sweet. | Poultry, pork, small game birds |
| | Sugar Maple | Sweeter than maple, with a subtle maple syrup tone. Mellow, non-overpowering smoke. | Poultry, pork, game birds, fruit |
| | Red Oak | The queen of smoking woods. Heavy smoke flavor. | Ribs, red meat, pork, fish, heavy game |
| | White Oak | Solid, rugged smoke flavor. | Pork, red meat, heavy game, fish |
| | Olive | Fragrant burn with a mild flavor and a hint of sweetness. Similar to hickory but distinctly lighter. Nice in Mediterranean preparations. | Poultry, pork, lamb, seafood |
| | Pecan | One of the best woods for smoking. Sweet and mild with a subtle flavor similar to hickory, but lighter and smoother. | Poultry, pork, beef |
| | Persimmon | Medium piney, smoke flavor. | Good beef, ribs, steaks |
| | Sassafras | Mild, sweet smoke. Great for making jerky. | Poultry, pork, beef, fish |
| **MEDIUM TO STRONG SMOKE** | Grapevines | Tart, rich, and fruity. Provides a lot of smoke. | Poultry, red meat, game, lamb |
| **STRONG SMOKE** | Mesquite | One of the hottest burning woods. Strong, earthy flavor. | Chicken, beef, game, fish |
| | Walnut (English & Black) | Very heavy smoke flavor. Can be bitter if used alone, so usually mixed with lighter woods like almond, pear, or apple. | Red meat, game |

# 018
# Build Your Own Smoker

Heed the nugget of wisdom shared by most true barbecue aficionados: There's no great grilling without lots of smoke. In fact, learning how to harness smoke is essential to bolstering a grill master's repertoire. But hold off before you go spending a bundle on a store-bought smoker; it's easy to make your own. A heavy-duty galvanized trash can, a few easy-to-find implements, and a smidge of DIY grit is all you need.

## YOU'LL NEED

- Large metal trash can
- Circular grill grating (usually sold as an accessory to a kettle grill)
- Electric hot plate
- Bricks or large rocks for stability
- Metal smoker box or other heavy-duty metal container to hold wood chips
- Smoking wood chips
- Grill thermometer

First, make sure the grill grating fits snugly inside the top third of the trash can (or use a few bolts). Using a drill and a metal nibbler, make a small opening in the side of the trash can near the bottom for the hot plate power cord. Next, drill two holes into the can lid, one for the thermometer and one to release just enough smoke so as not to snuff out the fire. Place the electric hot plate in the bottom of the trash can and thread the power cord out through the opening. Set bricks (or rocks) alongside the hot plate to stabilize the can.

Soak smoking wood chips in water 20–30 minutes. Turn the hot plate on and place the soaked wood chips on top. Set the grate inside the can, add your meat or whatever is to be cooked, and set the can lid snugly over the top. Now you're smoking.

Optimal smoking temperature is about 230°F (110°C). Wood chips will smoke about 60–90 minutes before they need to be replaced. Keep an eye on your temperature, and replace wood chips as needed.

# 019 Take It to the Next Level

For smoking perfectionists or those who'd like to take the smoker design up a notch, there are a few ways to improve upon the basic setup.

**GET SOME SUPPORT** Using a ⅜-inch (10-mm) drill bit, drill three holes about 8 inches (20 cm) below the top of the garbage can (or just where the grate naturally rests), equidistantly placed around the circumference of the can. Then slide three 3x⅜-inch (76x10-mm) bolts through those holes and secure with a corresponding washer and nut to support the grill grate.

**FEED THE FIRE** Ensure easy access and replenishing of smoking woods by cutting a hole into the bottom side of the garbage can that is large enough to slip out the smoker box without removing the can lid. Cover the hole during smoking with a triple layer of heavy-duty aluminum foil folded to fit inside the opening.

**GET JUICY** Capture meat juices by folding a disposable metal cooking pan to fit snugly in the garbage can smoker between the meat and the smoke source (but allowing ample room for the smoke to pass from below). A smaller grill grate, or two parallel rods threaded through holes cut into the garbage can, can serve as a more stable surface on which to rest midlevel juice pans.

**CLASS UP THE JOINT** Trash cans a bit too redneck for your refined sensibilities? An empty wine barrel or tall ceramic pot works just as well!

# 020 Think Outside the Bark

Smoking woods are your gateway to a wealth of new and different flavors. But if you stop there, you'll still only have part of the story. Try tossing any or all of these enhancements into your fire for flavor and smoke.

**HERBS** Try sprigs of oregano, sage, thyme, marjoram, rosemary, or basil for a smoky, herbaceous flavor. Rosemary and sage work especially well because of their thicker, more woody stems. The intensive smoke can overpower lighter meats, so use sparingly at first.

**COCONUT HULLS** Dried coconut hulls can add a nice fruity tone to lighter meats such as chicken, pork, and seafood.

**CORN COBS** Providing a nice, slightly sweet, and somewhat fruity smoke, corn cobs lend lots of flavor and are good with pork and poultry.

# 021
## Cook It on a Stick

Start with the glowing embers of a campfire after it's been going for a while, or the smoldering charcoal at the bottom of an open grill. Add a nice, long, green willow twig or another stick that's fresh enough not to burn too easily. Are you thinking what I'm thinking? There's a classic weiner roast, of course. Toasted marshmallows, too. Heck, a couple of resourceful kids could find any number of foods to poke with a twig and cook up over a fire. Just in case you've been growing up a bit too fast, here's a whole pile of ideas about what's good to cook on a stick.

# 022 Balance Your Breakfast

With a little luck and the right set of sticks, you can wow your campsite with a full breakfast cooked over the flames.

**EGGS** Cooking a whole egg over the fire is tricky, but it can be done. Success comes with the right stick—choose one that's both spindly thin and sturdy. Make two small holes on the ends of the egg with your pocketknife. Then, starting at the wider end, gently thread the stick through. Roast it levelly over the fire, turning to ensure even cooking. When the egg white stops leaking from the holes and turns white, the egg is done. If your first attempts fail, take another route: Poke a hole in the egg for steam to escape and nestle it upright in the coals. Done in a jiffy!

**BACON** Want some bacon with that egg? Of course you do! Just wrap a piece around a stick (if the stick has a couple of nubs for traction, all the better), and hold next to the embers. Bacon burns easily, so while you might be in a hurry to get that mouth-watering strip in your mouth, take it nice and slow.

**BREAD** Spiral a single portion of refrigerator breadstick dough around the end of a thick, straight stick, giving the dough a little room to spread out. Toast it slowly over the embers, turning it constantly until golden brown and cooked through. Add some savory flavor with a drizzle of garlic olive oil and a dusting of parmesan cheese, or make it sweet with a coating of sweet butter and a roll in a cinnamon-sugar mixture.

# 023 Roast Your Apple a Day

Apples are another stick-cooked treat that benefits from a generous dredging with cinnamon-sugar. Impale a whole fruit through the stem end into the core. Roast over a smoldering hot fire, turning to cook evenly, until it starts to hiss and sizzle, and begins to loosen its grip on the stick. Take the apple from the fire, let it cool a bit, and carefully remove the skin. Roll the virgin flesh in spiced sugar for extra sweetness. Apples not at hand? Most stone fruits make an easy substitute. Try peaches or pears first.

# 024 Skewer a Fish

You can get pretty fancy cooking large fillets, like salmon, on a plank (see item 202). But for smaller whole fish, like brook trout, the down-and-dirty Boy Scout method does the trick: Simply gut and scale the fish, skewer it with a green stick through the mouth almost to the tail, sprinkle with salt and pepper inside and out, and hold near the fire. Once the side of the fish starts to flake apart, it's done. The more adventurous Scout then toasts up the tail right next to the heat until nice and crispy—just like a potato chip! Yum.

# 025 Grill a Cheese Sandwich

Here's a case where you really need the right stick. Choose a thick one with a nice V-shape upon which you can balance your sandwich over the fire. Put together your basic grilled cheese (A), then set it atop the forked end (B). Once the bottom is crisped and golden, carefully flip it to toast the other side (C).

# 026 Spear a Shrimp

Shrimp-on-a-stick is a variation on the basic "shrimp-on-the-barbie" theme (which usually features skewers and a grill grate), but the idea is pretty much the same. It capitalizes on the shrimp shell which, when left on, keeps the meat nice and moist and offers up some extra flavor too. Skewer a whole shrimp through the belly to cook it, and remove the shell after it's done.

# 027 Construct a Cooking Tripod

If you're the kind of person who gets all pumped up over the prospect of open-fire cooking, you're likely also the type who wouldn't dream of buying a cooking tripod when you can just as easily make one yourself. Construct it out of iron pipe if it's going to stay in one place, or build it with conduit if you're going to take it on the go. Here's what you need for the job.

## TRIPOD

3 sections of iron pipe or conduit, ½ inches (1.3 cm) wide and 4 feet (1.2 m) or longer ■ 3 sturdy eyebolts ■ 2 S-hooks ■ 4 feet (1.2 m) of wire link chain ■ Hammer ■ Pliers

## HANGING GRILL

4 pieces of wire link chain 1½ feet (0.5 m) each ■ 5 S-hooks ■ Round grill grate

**STEP 1** Have the pipe cut at the hardware store to about 4½ feet (1.4 m) long. Open one eye of an eyebolt using pliers. Thread the eyes of the other two eyebolts onto the open one, along with one end of the 4-foot (1.2-m) chain. Use the hammer to pound the open eyebolt shut.

**STEP 2** Put the shafts of the eyebolts into the ends of the pipe legs and stand it up like it will rest over a campfire. Put one of the S-hooks on the chain near the top and use the pliers to close the hook tight over the chain. This will be the adjuster for the height of your cook pot or grill grate.

**STEP 3** If you want to add a hanging grill, thread one end of each 1½-foot (0.5-m) chain onto a single S-hook. Use pliers to crimp the hook closed. Attach the four remaining S-hooks onto the bottom of the chains and then crimp closed. Hook the ends of the chains at equidistant lengths onto the grill grate so it hangs evenly. Crimp the hooks closed over the grate.

**STEP 4** Set the tripod up over your fire pit and ignite your blaze. When the logs have burned down to smoldering embers, hang a cast iron dutch oven or the grill grate from the chain and you're ready to get cookin'!

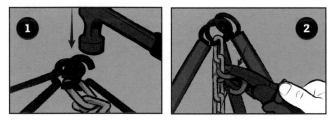

# 028 Add a DIY Rotisserie

Once you've aced the tripod, variations on its use and construction abound! For a rotisserie, set the tripod up to one side of the fire. Set the loop in the tripod chain to a good cooking length. Set a log, a pile of rocks, or a tower of bricks on the other side at the same height from the ground as the end of your cooking chain. Thread the meat to be cooked onto a sturdy metal rod or straight pointed stick. (If you're worried about the meat sliding around on the rod while it's turned, choose a green stick with a branch to one side. Thread your meat onto the stick, bend your branch over the meat, and lash to the other end to secure the meat in place.) Set one end of the rod in the loop of your cooking chain and rest the other on your log, stabilizing the meat over the fire pit.

# 029 Build a Fire Pit

A fire pit can be as simple as a clearing with a pile of logs—or, if you want to get fancy, there are a myriad of possibilities. For the purposes of open-fire grilling, it's a good idea to create a pit with some backbone structure, as well as one with the potential for reflected heat. Here's how to set up the perfect pit.

**STEP 1** Choose a spot that is flat, dry, and clear of structures, building materials, tree branches, and brush. The surface of the pit should be nonflammable (a metal fire ring is ideal).

**STEP 2** Line the bottom and sides of the pit with large stones or bricks to retain and reflect the heat, as well as to keep the fire contained. Build the sides tall enough to support a round grill rack, if you like.

**STEP 3** For fuel, use hardwood, such as oak, hickory, or fruitwood; stay away from softwood like pine or fir. For more even burning, mix the wood with lump charcoal or hardwood briquettes.

**STEP 4** Arrange the logs (and charcoal, if using) with kindling such as twigs and dried grass (or clean-burning charcoal lighters) in a pyramid shape in the pit. Ignite the kindling to light the logs.

**STEP 5** Let the logs burn down 1–2 hours until the embers are covered in ash. Add wood and charcoal to maintain an even heat level, and let them burn down a bit. At this point, your fire is optimal for cooking up a feast.

# 030 Get the Heat Right

When you make a wood fire, you should rarely cook over direct flame. Instead, wait for the logs to burn down and break up into red-hot coals, then into coals covered with whitish ash. The ash stage is the optimum time for cooking—even better when you maintain the fire's heat with pre-lit logs that are glowing red. (Serious fire masters have a separate pit or rugged iron basket for igniting heat-maintaining logs to add to the cooking fire.)

# 031 Go for Hardwood

When stocking the woodpile for your fire pit, good options include oak, maple, and birch, and, for their own distinctive flavors, also hickory and mesquite. Most hardwoods burn long and hot—just what you want for a cooking fire. Fruit and nut woods, such as apple and pecan, add their own whiff of flavoring to the flames. Fast-burning hardwoods (such as ash) don't work as well, and all softwoods (pine, fir, and other evergreens) produce a resinous smoke that doesn't taste good with food.

# 032 Give Gas A Chance

Grilling elitists who insist that charcoal or wood are the only way to go are missing out. Gas grills can fire up within minutes and, with the right tools and techniques, deliver a subtly smoky flavor and blistering heat—comparable to what you might get from charcoal. Some newer models even come equipped with a "searing" burner, offering meats an initial blast of heat for a nicely charred exterior. Here are the basics.

**STEP 1** Ignite the grill, turn all the burners to high, cover, and preheat for 15 minutes.

**STEP 2** Scrub the grates clean with a wire grill brush. Oil the grill rack with an oil-dipped cloth or heavy-duty paper towel.

**STEP 3** For direct-heat grilling, simply adjust the heat to the desired level, place your food on the grate, and cook.

# 033 Choose Your Gas

As if you didn't have enough choices with all the bells and whistles that now accompany most outdoor appliances, there is one that lies at the very core of basic gas grilling technique: natural gas or propane? Most gas grills are already wired for one or the other, so the decision may be made for you. But for those grills that allow you to make a choice, here are some pros and cons to inform your selection.

| PROS | CONS |
|---|---|
| Light, portable tanks mean a lighter, portable grill. | Propane is more expensive. |
| Burns hotter, providing 2500 BTUs (British Thermal Units) per unit volume in comparison to 1000 BTUs provided by natural gas for the same unit size. | It creates a wet heat that can sometimes change the texture of the food being cooked. |
| Environmentally friendly, propane contains no lead, creates low greenhouse gas emissions, and produces only water vapor and carbon dioxide. | Can be slightly more explosive that natural gas because it's heavier than air and stays concentrated for longer periods. |
| You'll never run out of fuel. | You won't be able to move your grill. |
| Usually about one-third of the total cost of propane. | Professional installation is required. |
| Burns more cleanly than propane and is more environmentally friendly. | Natural gas grills are more expensive than propane ones. |

# 034 Smoke with Gas

No matter how you smoke your meats, they're going to be delicious. Here's how to do it with a gas grill.

**STEP 1** Soak wood chips in water for at least 30 minutes, or chunks for at least 1 hour.

**STEP 2** Drain and place soaked chips in a smoker box or piece of perforated aluminum foil. Place the box or foil packet on a burner or designated area of your grill (check your user's manual, if you've got it).

**STEP 3** Ignite the grill, turn the burners to high, cover, and preheat about 15 minutes.

**STEP 4** Scrub the grates clean with a wire grill brush. Oil the grill rack with an oil-dipped cloth or heavy-duty paper towel.

**STEP 5** Cover the grill. When smoke begins to appear, open the grill and set up as if for indirect-heat grilling, placing a small pan of water or other liquid under the food to create steam. Cover and cook.

**STEP 6** Add more wood chips every 30 minutes, or chunks every 45 minutes, for at least the first 2 hours. Refill the pan with liquid as needed.

# 035 Set Up Gas for Indirect Heat

Use indirect heat on a gas barbecue for cooking larger items that need lots of time on the grill, or for those that are more fatty and need to avoid the direct heat that can cause flare-ups.

To cook using indirect heat, turn off the burner directly under the area where the food will be placed—one burner of a two-burner grill, or the center portion of a three- or more burner grill. Place a metal drip pan underneath the area where the food will sit. Then place the food on the grill grate over the pan. Cover and cook.

# 036 Grill Around the World

Limit yourself to the progeny of the American grill and you could be missing out on some of the world's best barbecue. Consider that every culture has been pairing its local ingredients and singular topography with basic fire cooking for millennia, and you know there's something worth discovering. Argentina's rugged and meat-inspired type of outdoor cookery is at home atop the rocky grazing terrain of the Patagonia peninsula; Hawaii's soft, coal-dappled sand pits are the ideal location for slow-roasting wild pig. Local cooks everywhere have adopted the grilling and open-fire techniques that best complement their environment—and cuisine. Cheers to us for living in a world where all can be universally experienced.

**DÖNER KEBAB (TURKEY)** This ubiquitous form of Turkish street food capitalizes on the law of gravity to disperse succulent meat juices over thin slices of meat stacked on a vertical skewer. Lamb is the most popular choice for döner kebab, but you're also likely to see beef and even chicken at restaurants or curbside stands. The pieces of meat are pounded until thin and tender, then seasoned with meat fats and a variety of herbs and spices. Once cooked, the meats are shaved off the spit and served with rice or potatoes, or wrapped in pita bread.

**SATAY (THAILAND)** Highly seasoned skewers cooked on a charcoal or wood fire grill is king on the global grilling hit parade. Most feature tasty, bite-sized pieces of long-marinated meat cooked and sold by roadside vendors. The satay of Thailand and Indonesia is often served with dipping sauces (see item 176). *Chuanr*, usually skewers of lamb or mutton, is tops among China's cheap and ubiquitous street food. Shish kebab, traditionally cooked over an open flame, are smoky, char-tinged skewers (usually of lamb or beef) from Turkey and the Middle East. Yakitori is Japan's version, starring marinated bite-sized chicken skewers that make for an A+ bar snack (see item 167).

**JERK (JAMAICA, THE CARIBBEAN)** An offbeat combo of savory and sweet, jerk is both the star seasoning blend and reigning cooking style in Jamaica and throughout the Caribbean. Allspice and fiery Scotch bonnet peppers are at the root of the seasoning, along with a variety of other potential spices such as cloves, cinnamon, nutmeg, ginger, salt, garlic, and thyme. It is classically rubbed onto meat—especially chicken (see item 178) and pork—then cooked up in a repurposed oil-barrel grill. Modern cooks don't limit themselves to the island-variety kettle grill and apply the seasoning to all types of seafood, lamb, beef, tofu, and vegetables as well.

**ASADO (URUGUAY, CHILE, ARGENTINA)** South America boasts a primal brand of barbecue involving lots of meat and the smoldering logs of an open fire. *Asado* refers to both grilling style and grilling event, most often featuring large slabs of beef (the go-to meat of most of the region) splayed on a metal crossbar (known as a *parrillero*) and set upright next to the low-burning logs of an open fire. The meat cooks low and slow, self-basting in its own juices and forming a nicely charred crust atop especially juicy meat. Like Brazil's *churrasco*, asado originated with the brazen cooking style of the gaucho tradition.

**GOGIGUI (KOREA)** In Korea, grilling is a self-service affair, with diners seated around a small grill at the center of the table where they cook an array of thinly sliced and marinated beef, pork, and chicken. *Bulgogi*—a barbecued beef sirloin—is the most popular form of Korean barbecue, although *galbi* (short ribs, see item 080) and *jumulleok* (marinated short ribs) are also mainstays on the menu.

**SMOLDERING UNDERGROUND OVENS (HAWAII, MEXICO, CHILE)** Some early tropical cultures seemed to forgo basic grill techniques altogether in favor of long-smoldering ashes in sandy or volcanic underground ovens. In Hawaii, ocean-side cooks dig a shallow imu for cooking whole pigs in coals buried on the beach. In Mexico, *barbacoa* refers to meat that is wrapped in large leaves and slow-cooked in a pit over a wood fire or heated volcanic rock. In Chile, native cooks cherish *curanto*—a mix of local shellfish, meats, and potatoes—that is wrapped in leaves and smoked in an earthen pit.

**BRAAI (SOUTH AFRICA)** *Braai* originated in the late 17th century as spit-roasts at fairs held by the Cape's Dutch governor and have since become synonymous with South African barbecue. The typical *braai*—Afrikaans for barbecue or grill—is the South African approach to cooking for a crowd. It's a laid-back affair beginning with a metal grill set over a big wood or charcoal fire and lots of local meats. Popular is *boerewors* (a spiced sausage made of pork and beef), *sosaties* (marinated chicken kebabs), fish from the Cape's southern coast, and beef and lamb from the desert regions.

# 037 Be Safe

Nothing ruins a nice backyard cookout like a visit from the fire department. Grilling is a lot of fun, but don't let that fun distract you from the fact that you are literally playing with fire. Here are a few tips to help you circumvent red-hot disaster and avoid having your hot-dog buns soaked by a fire hose.

**DON'T SPRAY IT** Never spray starter fluid, oil, or any other flammable liquid on already lit charcoal. It won't make the coals ready for cooking any faster, and it might cause a disaster.

**CHECK FOR GAS LEAKS** Check the seal on your propane tank fixtures by coating them with a thin spray of water. The emergence of tiny bubbles or a quiet hiss should help you detect the location of any unwanted holes that should be marked for repair.

**CLEAR THE AREA** Establish a no-fly zone around your grill area. If any small kids or dogs get too close, steer them away from the heat.

**DRESS FOR SUCCESS** Tie back long hair, tuck in loose clothing, and roll your sleeves up nice and tight before reaching over the hot grill.

**START IT RIGHT** Be sure you're using a fire starter that was designed for the kind of grill and charcoal you are using. Store the starters in a safe and secure spot well away from the grill. In addition, when using a chimney starter, be sure to set it down safely—not on a sun-baked lawn, wood deck, or anything else flammable.

**CHOOSE YOUR SPOT** Set up your grill on level ground in an area with plenty of open-air ventilation. Be sure you're well clear of enclosures, overhangs, and anything combustible.

**WATCH IT** It only takes a few minutes for smoke to turn to flame. Never leave your grill unattended while it's in use.

**BE PREPARED** Always have a fire extinguisher and a water hose handy—just in case.

# 038 Do It Right

Whether you've carefully read every page up to this point, or eagerly flipped ahead to get to the many tasty recipes that follow, you're ready to fire up the grill and get cooking. But before you don your "Kiss the Cook" apron and break out the grill tools, let's go back over the most crucial Dos and Don'ts when it comes to cooking with fire.

## DO

**BE PATIENT**
Let your grill fully preheat before you start to cook. Gas grills should power up for 10–15 minutes; charcoal should be ash gray.

**CLEAN YOUR GRATE**
Get in the habit of cleaning the grill grate with a stiff wire brush, then greasing it with a vegetable oil–dipped cloth just before you start to cook. You'll avoid sticking and simultaneously accomplish the sexy grill marks you're after.

**CHOOSE THE RIGHT TECHNIQUE**
Make sure you understand direct- and indirect-heat grilling, and when to use one, the other, or a combination of the two.

**MASTER YOUR HEAT**
Lots of foods like a quick searing, then moderate heat for cooking through. Set up zones for varying heat levels by banking your coals to one side or turning off one or more burners if you're cooking with gas. Learn how to use your vents.

**SEASON WELL**
Some foods, like steak, may only need a sprinkling of salt and pepper, but most like plenty of seasoning and lots of marinade time when they're destined for the grill.

**USE A THERMOMETER**
Check doneness by temperature and by using the touch test (see item 045). Also make good use of your thermometer to check and maintain heat.

**LIGHT A CHIMNEY STARTER**
Done just right, the rising heat method of a chimney starter is the quickest and cleanest way to start a charcoal fire.

**BE CAREFUL**
Don't forget that you're playing with fire, and fire can have a mind of its own. Set up your grill in an open space, keep an extinguisher handy, and watch out for the kids and pets.

## DON'T

**RUSH**
You should be going for the zen experience here. Grab a beer and relax.

**USE A DIRTY GRATE**
You don't want your fish fillet to taste like last week's hamburger.

**COVER THE GRILL EVERY TIME**
A grill cover is great for keeping heat level and snuffing flare-ups, but there are times to cook without one. When grilling fatty or oil-marinated food over direct heat, drips of fat hitting the heat source can make for some bad-tasting smoke. If that's the case, keep the cover off, let the smoke waft away, and only then clamp down the lid.

**SKIMP ON CHARCOAL OR GAS**
A hot fire is a must for good grilling.

**BASTE WITH SUGARY SAUCES**
Wait until the meat is almost done before you baste—even ketchup-based sauces will burn if you brush them on when there's still plenty of grilling time to go.

**CUT INTO YOUR MEAT TOO EARLY**
Don't spare a drop of those delicious juices to check for doneness. Once you've determined that your steak is just right, set it aside for about 10 minutes before you cut into it. A quick rest will allow the juices to redistribute evenly, ensuring the best flavor and juiciness.

**BURN BRIQUETTES INFUSED WITH STARTER FLUID**
These briquettes can add a chemical taste to whatever you're cooking, whether you've got the store-bought kind or doused them yourself.

**SOAK CHARCOAL FLARE-UPS**
Even a judicious spray of water can kick up enough ash to coat your hot dogs. If you're fighting a flare-up, move your food to a cooler part of the grill until the flames subside.

# 039 Keep It Clean

We all love that tempting sizzle when meat juices hit the burners of a hot gas grill, but there's less to admire when it comes to dealing with the aftermath. All that grease, along with a liberal dose of marinades and sauces, and the inevitable, if unintended, sprinkling of errant vegetable pieces can truly gunk up a grill. You can minimize the grime by brushing the grill grate before and after each use. Burning off the meat juices every week or so with a 15-minute blast of intense heat can also help. But to keep your grill in tip-top shape, it really needs to be thoroughly cleaned at least once a year—or every few months if you're a heavy user. Not familiar with all the parts and pieces? Here's a handy guide to make the process an easy one.

**STEP 1** Use a sturdy wire brush to remove the burned-on juices from your grill grates. Turn the grates over and brush the undersides, too.

**STEP 2** Take a look underneath your grill grate and locate the burner protectors, which are usually long metal covers spanning the length of each burner or other heating element. Remove these protectors (most lift out easily). Using a sponge and a pail of soapy water, give them a good scrub.

**STEP 3** Using the sponge, wipe any grime from the burners themselves.

**STEP 4** Remove the plates underneath the burners. Use your grill brush to scrape out the nice layer of char that's likely coating them.

**STEP 5** Slide out the removable tray under the plates. Scrape out all the blackened bits with the brush (or a metal spatula if you need something sturdier), then do your best to wipe the charred debris from the tray bottom.

**STEP 6** Reassemble the grill, putting each layer back in place and in order: tray, plates, burners, protectors, and grates. Ready to grill!

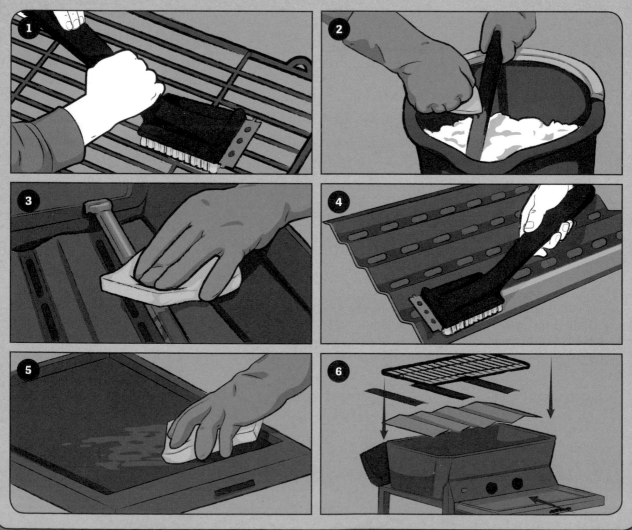

# 040 Chuck Your Ashes

After repeated sessions at the charcoal grill, you'll want to dispose of the pile of ashes accumulating at the bottom. Depending on the type of charcoal you've been using, there are several ways you can go about it.

**DISPOSAL** To safely dispose of charcoal and wood ash, let it cool for a full 48 hours. To speed up the process, sprinkle some water on the ash and carefully stir it in to dampen any residual heat. When the ash has cooled completely, wrap it in a large piece of foil and place in a non-combustible outdoor trash bin.

**RECYCLE AND REUSE** If recycling is more your thing, stick with the ashes of only hardwood charcoal (avoiding briquettes, which can be laden with petrochemicals). In the garden, hardwood charcoal ash can make a great fertilizer for plants that prefer a more alkaline (nonacidic) soil, such as daffodils, asparagus, asters, salvias, and boxwood. It can also increase the carbon content of a compost pile, speeding the breakdown of organic matter. Mulching is another of its garden-friendly uses, acting as a weed barrier and moisture retainer.

# 041 Be a Spin Doctor

Once you start taking apart your grill piece by piece, you'll notice that not all parts see the same amount of action. Rotate the burner plates, burner covers, and grill grates to balance out their wear and corrosion, and to keep your grill running smoothly.

# 042 Clean Your Charcoal Grill

Charcoal grills may have fewer parts than their gas-powered cousins, but that doesn't mean they don't need some care, upkeep, and occasional TLC.

Start with the lid. What may look like a thick layer of rough black paint can begin to peel and reveal its true identity: a blanket of grease and smoke that accumulates after regular use. A vigorous scrub with a stiff wire brush should take care of it. To avoid future buildup, wipe the lid with paper towels or soapy water after each grilling session—when the lid is still warm (but not hot!).

For the body of the grill, scoop the ashes from the bottom, then scrape the surface clean with the wire brush. A steel wool pad and some warm soapy water will make it squeaky clean.

Grill grates can be cleaned with the "heat and scrape" method. Fire up some charcoal in the grill and heat it to its maximum by opening all the vents and keeping the grill at a high temperature 10–15 minutes. Then give it a brisk scouring with a stiff wire brush to remove any excess debris left on the grates.

The ash catcher is your final stop. Remove the ashes, wipe the catcher clean, and you're ready to get back in action.

# 043 Know What to Look For

You don't need a culinary degree to choose a nice piece of beef for the grill—just a little know-how. Educate yourself on quality, grade, and flavor specifics to make the choice a simple one, every time. Here's how to do it with authority.

**START WITH QUALITY** When perusing the butcher counter in search of the perfect cut, look first at color: Good beef should be cherry red to purplish-red, not bright pink or brown. It should also look moist and finely-textured, with light and evenly distributed marbling, and nearly white exterior fat. If you have questions about which cut is best for what you want to cook, ask your butcher! Most are experts and woefully underutilized. You can also check out our guide for all you need to know about specific cuts (see item 047).

**UNDERSTAND THE GRADING SYSTEM** The United States Department of Agriculture (USDA) has up to eight grades it can attach to beef; the most common are prime, choice, and select. The labels reflect different characteristics, such as the degree of fat marbling, color, and maturity. Prime is the highest grade, has the most marbling, and comes from young cattle. Choice beef is the next step down, containing less marbling but still some tender and juicy cuts. Select meats are usually very lean and need lots of marinating and a long, slow cooking process to make them tender.

**DECIDE GRASS-FED VS. GRAIN-FED** People who love grass-fed beef swear by the superiority of its earthy, grassy, gamier flavor and its slightly increased levels of healthy omega-3 fats and nutrients. Whether or not grass-fed beef is worth the uptick in price is a question of personal preference and budget.

# 044 Start Your Countdown to Perfectly Grilled Steak

### FIVE...

**Do a Warm-Up**
Take your steak out of the fridge about 30 minutes before grilling to bring it to room temperature. A freezing-cold steak won't cook evenly.

### FOUR...

**Make It Sizzle**
Heat up the grill grate before putting the steak on. Searing creates that lovely caramelized crust that gives a good steak its robust flavor and crisp exterior texture.

### THREE...

**Hold Steady**
Let your steak develop a seared crust on the grill before moving or flipping it. If you try to lift the meat before it's ready, it'll stick to the grates and mess up your grill marks.

### TWO...

**Master the Touch Test**
No doneness test can quite match a practiced knack for the touch test (see item 045). A thermometer can offer scientific backup as well. Still not sure? Err on the side of caution and remove steaks on the early side of doneness to check. You can always throw the meat back on the grill to cook for a few minutes longer.

### ONE...

**Let It Rest**
It's best to let that sizzling hot steak take a breather before you cut into it. Here's why: As meat cooks, the muscle fibers start to firm up and water gets pushed out. This moisture moves outward toward the surface of the meat (where you'll likely hear it hiss as it drops). When your remove meat from the heat, the moisture still inside needs some time to redistribute back through the flesh. If you cut into it right away, the juices will pool out, leaving the meat quite dry. By letting it rest, the moisture is re-absorbed and the meat remains tender and juicy.

### LIFTOFF!

**Dig In!**
Tasty? Check. Juicy? Check. Crispy on the outside and tender in the center? Check and check.

# 045 Practice the Touch Test

People have been poking themselves for years trying to come up with easy touch tests that correspond to the finger feel of meat in various stages of doneness. Some go for the cheek (rare), chin (medium), forehead (well) method. Others press the outside of the hand between thumb and forefinger. Most cooks, however, agree on the success of this palm technique. Here's how it works: Relax your hand and touch different fingers together to create different levels of firmness in the meaty portion of your palm, below the pointer finger and adjacent to the thumb. When your thumb and forefinger meet, the fleshy part will mimic the feel of a medium-rare steak. When your thumb and middle finger meet, it's medium. Thumb and ring finger make for medium-well, and thumb and pinky mimics well done. Try it out—it's a good cheat sheet for when you need one.

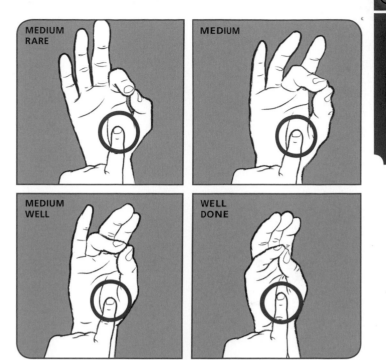

MEDIUM RARE

MEDIUM

MEDIUM WELL

WELL DONE

# 046 Consult a Thermometer

If prodding your steak on the grill with your forefinger seems a less-than-definite ascertainment of doneness, then a good meat thermometer may be the way to go. Here's the catch: Steak will continue to cook once it's taken from the heat, so remove your meat when it's about 5 degrees shy of your temperature goal. Here are temperature ranges for ready-to-serve beef.

**RARE** 125–130°F (52–54°C)

**MEDIUM-RARE** 130–140°F (54–60°C)

**MEDIUM** 145°F (63°C)

**MEDIUM-WELL** 155–160°F (68–71°C)

**WELL** OVER 160°F (71°C)

# 047 Know Your Cuts of Beef

For a lot of us, grilling is synonymous with sizzling steaks and juicy burgers—for good reason (that reason being that they're delicious). Understanding the various cuts of beef available help you not only make the best steaks and burgers, but also explore a wide range of other options.

## CHUCK
**Chuck blade steak, chuck eye steak, arm roast, chuck blade roast, chuck short ribs**

Cuts from this shoulder section of a steer are striated with lots of fat and collagen (connective tissue), which usually equates to a long, slow cooking technique—usually over indirect medium heat when on the grill. An exception to the rule is the flat-iron steak, also know as butlers' steak in the UK and oyster blade steak in Australia, which is one of the most popular cuts of beef for direct-heat grilling. It is cut with the grain from the top blade, often into two thinner steaks with a layer of tough fascia between them removed. Chuck eye is another exception—both are tender and lean, making them a great choice for grilling. Ground chuck, in the form of hamburgers, is another favorite for the grill.

## RIB
**Bone-in rib steak, rib-eye steak, rib-eye roast, standing rib roast, short ribs, back ribs**

The generously marbled meat from this primal cut has a full-bodied flavor. Smaller cuts such as wonderfully juicy and tender rib-eye steak and rib steak are the best choice for the barbecue. Larger cuts—especially the meaty short ribs—like a longer cooking time, getting nice and tender over indirect heat on a medium grill.

## SHORT LOIN
**T-bone steak, porterhouse steak, New York strip steak, tenderloin roast (chateaubriand), tenderloin steak (filet mignon)**

Some of the tastiest steaks for grilling, or any type of cooking, come from this section. The T-bone steak gets its name because it has a bone that is shaped like a T, with a strip steak on one side and a piece of tenderloin filet on the other. Porterhouse steak is similar to T-bone steak but is cut from the rear of the short loin and thus includes more tenderloin steak and less strip steak, where as T-bones are cut closer to the front and contain a smaller section of tenderloin. The strip steak, also known as New York or Kansas City strip, consists of a muscle that does little work, making the meat particularly tender, though not as tender as the nearby rib-eye or tenderloin. Filet mignon is the small, tender cut of beef taken from the end of the tenderloin. Chateaubriand is a small roast, usually about 4 inches (10 cm), cut from the center of the tenderloin.

## SIRLOIN
**Sirloin steak, tri-tip steak, tri-tip roast, ball roast**

This harder-working region yields tri-tip and sirloin steaks. Both are lean cuts of meat that benefit from marinades and low and slow cooking.

## ROUND
**Bottom round roast, top round roast (London broil), rump roast, eye of round**

Meat in this region has little marbling, making it a good choice for burgers or sausages on the grill. Otherwise, it begs for long, slow cooking. Of these rump cuts, London broil is the best choice for the barbecue. Give it a long, flavorful marinade before setting it on the grill.

## FLANK & PLATE
**Skirt steak, plate short ribs, flank steak, hanger steak**

Skirt steak—the traditional meat for fajitas—is a thin, fibrous cut separating the chest from the abdomen. Since it's actually the cow's diaphragm muscle, its hardworking location makes for a chewy piece of meat that needs a lot of tenderizer and a healthy dose of marinade or dry rub before grilling. Flank steak lies on the belly close to the hind legs of the cow. Unlike the fattier skirt steak, the flank is super lean on its own and also benefits from marinades and rubs. Hanger steak gets its name from the fact that it hangs down between the tenderloin and the rib. Known as the "hanging tender" by some old-school butchers, it is the steak of choice for steak frites.

## BRISKET
**Whole brisket, brisket first cut, brisket front cut**

Babying a brisket to perfectly smoked perfection is a religion to avid grill masters (especially those from the Lone Star State!). This tough cut only gains flavor from long, slow cooking. The lengthy grilling process usually includes an overnight brining, a healthy dose of flavorful spices, and hours of indirect-heat smoking. The first cut is the larger and leaner piece, usually sold as brisket. The second cut, or "deckle," has much more interior fat—making it more appealing to some and less so to others. A griller's favorite cut is all about personal preference.

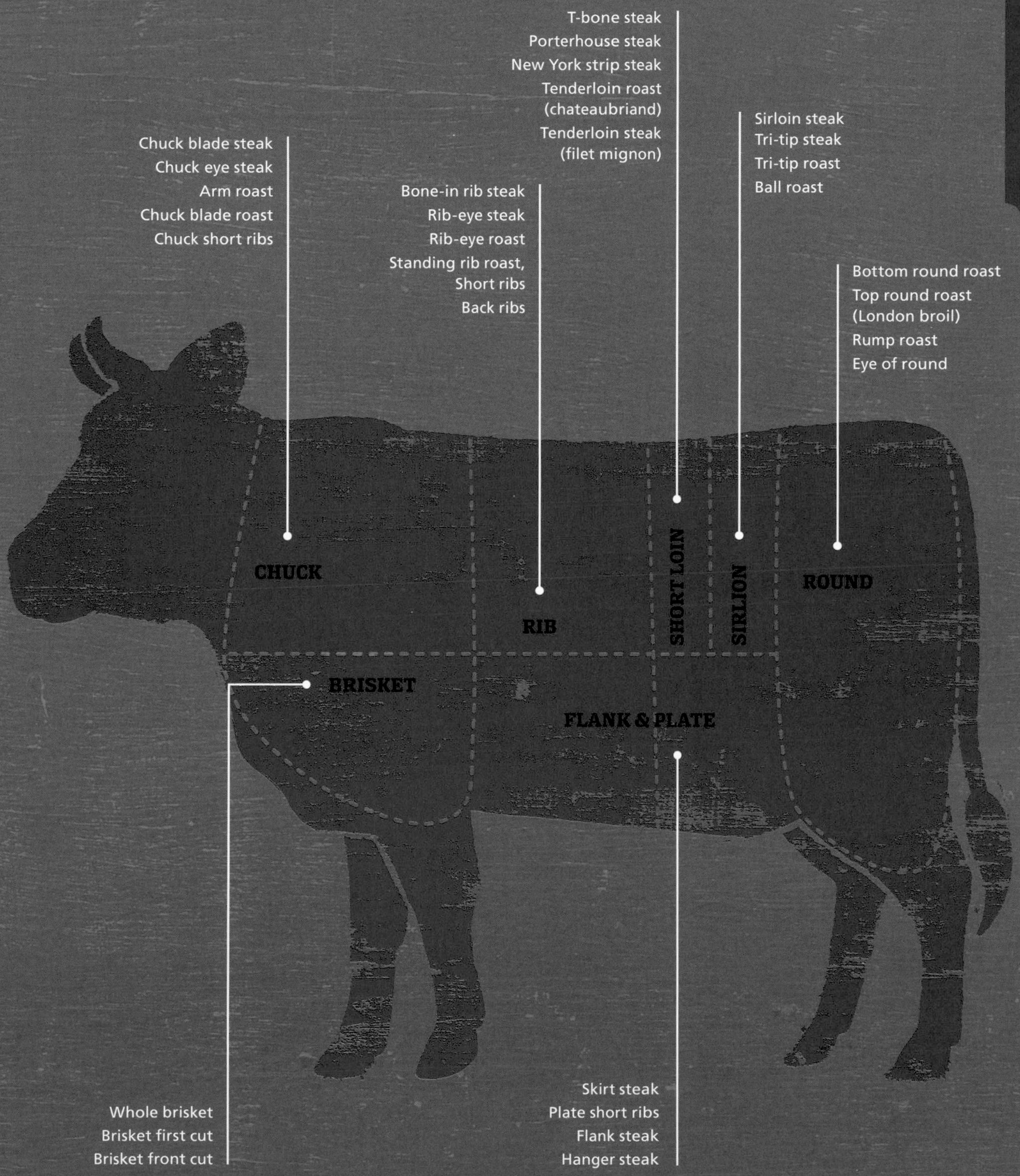

Chuck blade steak
Chuck eye steak
Arm roast
Chuck blade roast
Chuck short ribs

Bone-in rib steak
Rib-eye steak
Rib-eye roast
Standing rib roast,
Short ribs
Back ribs

T-bone steak
Porterhouse steak
New York strip steak
Tenderloin roast
(chateaubriand)
Tenderloin steak
(filet mignon)

Sirloin steak
Tri-tip steak
Tri-tip roast
Ball roast

Bottom round roast
Top round roast
(London broil)
Rump roast
Eye of round

CHUCK

RIB

SHORT LOIN

SIRLION

ROUND

BRISKET

FLANK & PLATE

Whole brisket
Brisket first cut
Brisket front cut

Skirt steak
Plate short ribs
Flank steak
Hanger steak

# 048 Go for Classic Combos

So you know you want steak for dinner, but you're stumped on how best to prepare it? Try sticking with these classic combinations, rounding out the menu with traditional sides and sauces. You'll be taking advantage of traditional flavor combinations that experienced chefs have been cultivating for years.

## AMERICAN STEAK HOUSE

**CUT** Chateaubriand
**TREATMENT** Salt and pepper
**TECHNIQUE** Direct heat
**SAUCE** Béarnaise sauce
**SIDE** Turned potatoes, steamed asparagus
**PAIRING** Cabernet sauvignon

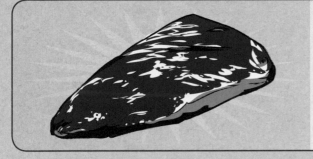

## AMERICAN RANCH

**CUT** Tri-tip
**TREATMENT** Spice rub
**TECHNIQUE** Indirect heat
**SAUCE** Bourbon steak sauce
**SIDE** Baked potato, baked beans
**PAIRING** Zinfandel or beer

## MEXICAN

**CUT** Skirt steak
**TREATMENT** Cilantro-lime marinade
**TECHNIQUE** Direct heat
**SAUCE** Fresh tomato salsa
**SIDE** Black beans and rice
**PAIRING** Margarita

## ITALIAN

**CUT** Porterhouse (*bistecca alla fiorentina*)
**TREATMENT** Chopped fresh rosemary, olive oil, salt
**TECHNIQUE** Direct heat over hardwood charcoal including hickory mix
**SAUCE** Lemon wedges and sea salt
**SIDE** Baked tomatoes with oregano, sautéed swiss chard
**PAIRING** Barolo, Barbaresco, or Brunello

BEEF

### FRENCH
**CUT** Hanger steak
**TREATMENT** Salt and pepper
**TECHNIQUE** Direct heat
**SAUCE** Red wine–shallot sauce
**SIDE** Pommes frites
**PAIRING** Red Burgundy or Bordeaux

### SOUTH AMERICAN
**CUT** Long, thin, crosswise cut of skirt steak
**TREATMENT** *Churrasco* marinade
**TECHNIQUE** Direct on hardwood fire or indirect
with oak smoking chips
**SAUCE** *Chimichurri*
**SIDE** Potato galette and simple green salad
**PAIRING** Chilean or Argentine red

### JAMAICAN
**CUT** Flank steak
**TREATMENT** Jerk seasoning
**TECHNIQUE** Direct heat on gas or charcoal grill
**SAUCE** Grilled pineapple salsa
**SIDE** Carribbean fried rice
**PAIRING** Red wines with low tannins:
Barbera, late-harvest Zinfandel

### SINGAPOREAN
**CUT** Rib-eye cut into cubes, threaded onto skewers
**TREATMENT** Marinade of brown sugar, coriander,
turmeric, cumin, pepper, Asian fish sauce
**TECHNIQUE** Indirect heat
**SAUCE** Peanut sauce
**SIDE** Cucumber relish
**PAIRING** Beer

### KOREAN
**CUT** Thinly sliced boneless rib-eye
**TREATMENT** Sweet-salty sesame-soy marinade
**TECHNIQUE** Charcoal tabletop grill
**SAUCE** Grilled garlic and chiles
**SIDE** Lettuce leaf wraps
**PAIRING** Robust Zinfandel or Malbec;
sparkling white wine; beer

# 049 Build a Better Burger

Exactly what makes a great burger is a hotly contested question around the barbecue. Some prefer little more than a soft bun and a perfectly cooked patty, others an artistic layering of meat, cheese, toppings, and sauces. Of course, the best choices to be made are subjective ones. With a reliable cooking technique and an array of top-notch toppings and sauces to choose from, any burger can become a masterpiece. Your choice of beef is the first and most important step in crafting a burger the way you want it. Classic burgers "like Mom used to make" might have started with ground chuck or non-descript "hamburger" meat, but chefs these days have plenty of excellent options.

**CHUCK** The well-marbled shoulder meat from a steer remains one of the best cuts to choose for burgers; when ground, it boasts the perfect ratio of 80% meat, 20% fat.

**ROUND** Meat from the hindquarters has little intramuscle fat, which makes it particularly lean and wonderfully accepting of rich accompaniments.

**GRASS-FED** Pasture-raised cattle produce lean meat with a clean, mineral flavor.

**GROUND HAMBURGER** The meat labeled as "ground hamburger" in stores is typically a blend of trimmings from various steaks and roasts. The percentage of fat to meat is usually listed on the label.

**SHORT RIB** Meaty and tender short ribs, also called chuck flap tail, make for a nice, juicy burger.

**BRISKET** One of the most flavorful cuts for burgers. "Flat cut" is the leanest grind of brisket, while "point cut" is from the fattier end and therefore best for burger making.

**SIRLOIN** Sirloin is nicely marbled with lots of beef flavor. Go for top sirloin, tri-tip, or knuckle for the most full-flavored patty.

**WAGYU** U.S. cattlemen have crossbred Japanese wagyu cattle with other breeds to produce beef of unsurpassed melt-in-your mouth flavor and tenderness.

# 050 Mix in Flavor

A sprinkle of salt and pepper can go a long way toward the tastiness of your basic burger—but that's just the beginning. Do you want to go spicy? Sophisticated? Tangy? All of the above? Flavors that are worked into the meat before grilling add a new dimension for those of us who might have thought of flavor as something you add after the burger comes off the grill (and you can do that, too!). Sample a few of these tried-and-true additions and then experiment with your own modifications. Start small and work your way to perfection—you want to enhance, not overwhelm, the meat's flavor.

| MIX IN | EFFECT | MIX IN | EFFECT |
|---|---|---|---|
| Sriracha | Subtle heat and sweetness | Capers | Concentrated brine and saltiness |
| Worcestershire | Sweet-tart tang and depth | Steak sauce | Enhanced beefiness |
| Dijon mustard | Mellow spiciness | Grated onion | Sweetness and juiciness |
| Anchovies (grind before adding) | Briny flavor | Herbed bread crumbs | Lighten the texture and add toasty flavor |
| Sesame oil | Nutty character | Onion soup mix | Saltiness and depth of flavor |
| Chopped thyme | Subtle, woodsy taste | Raw egg | Rich flavor and dense texture |

# 051 The Perfect Burger

Cooked up on a grill, burgers achieve a crusty exterior and smoky flavor not produced by any other cooking method. For best results in acquiring just the right amount of char, try using a smaller grill (such as a hibachi or Smokey Joe) whereby the rack sits closer to the heat, or utilize the "searing station" available on some grills during the first minute or so of cooking time.

- 2 lb (1 kg) ground beef (your choice of grind and cut)
- 4 hamburger buns (your choice of type)
- Flavor additions, toppings, and condiments (your choice)

**PREHEAT** Prepare a charcoal or gas grill for direct-heat grilling over medium-high heat. If using a gas grill, soak wood chips (such as hickory, mesquite, or a combination of the two) for at least 30 minutes. Drain, transfer chips to a smoker box or foil packet, and place on the fire at least 5 minutes before cooking.

**SHAPE** Add any additional flavoring agents (if using) to ground beef and mix in with hands. Divide meat into four ½-lb (225-g) portions. Shape each portion into

a patty a little wider than the buns you will be using. Press a wide, shallow dimple into each patty (so burgers will cook to even heights when centers expand with heat.) Season with salt and pepper, as well as any other seasonings you prefer.

**GRILL** Place burgers on grill rack and cook, without turning, until browned on the bottoms, about 4 minutes. Turn and cook the other side until browned and burgers are cooked to desired doneness, about 10 minutes total for medium-rare. (Place cheese, if using, on the burger just after the first flip.)

**REST** Let burgers rest away from the heat for 5 minutes. Transfer to buns, layer with desired toppings, and serve.

Makes 4 servings.

## QUICK TIP

There are those, even among the grilling crowd, who stubbornly maintain that a griddle is the best apparatus upon which to cook the perfect burger. The most enlightened of these naysayers have devised a cooking strategy that hits the strengths of each method in a triumph of collaboration—they place a cast-iron griddle right on the grill rack. The griddle sears the burger to crisp perfection and traps the juices otherwise lost on the grill, while the charcoal (or smoking chips) perfume the burger with smoky flavor.

# 052
## Add Fruits, Veggies, and More

Entire books have been written just on the multitude of various topping combinations to be had on a single patty. Whether you opt for bold, contrasting flavors or subtle nuances, the choice—as usual—is a personal one. Here are a few common favorites.

Pickles (sliced, relish, or cornichons), onions (raw sliced red or slow-cooked yellow), lettuce (iceberg, Bibb, or red leaf), sliced tomato, sliced avocado, sliced grilled pineapple, pepperoncini or pickled jalapeño slices, sprouts or microgreens, roasted bell peppers, coleslaw, pickled beets, fried egg, bacon, sautéed garlic, sautéed mushrooms

# 053
## Add Some Cheese

Some burger aficionados may prefer to give a pass to the melted creaminess of cheese in favor of more meaty flavor. But for those who couldn't imagine a perfect burger without the addition, there are plenty of great burger-pairing options to choose from.

**AMERICAN** American cheese is the choice of many a disciple of the "classic" burger. Presliced, brightly hued, and quick-melting, it was destined for burger stardom.

**BLUE** With bold, salty tartness and a creamy texture, blue cheese is a decadent option.

**MONTEREY JACK** Jack is a great melting cheese in a range of flavor options; garlic and pepper jack are favorites.

**BRIE** Ripe, French Brie, with its rind intact, melts to a silky smoothness with a rich aroma.

**SWISS** Swiss cheeses, such as Emmentaler and Gruyère, are known for their mild, nutty flavor and superior melting.

**CHEDDAR** Go for sharp, aged Cheddar for a pleasant hint of caramel when melted.

# 054
## Get Saucy

Sauces add the final, signature touch to the finished burger. Choose condiments that embellish the theme initiated by your choice of ingredients.

| CONDIMENT | HINTS |
|---|---|
| Ketchup | Spiked versions add pizzazz that classic varieties lack. Try those with chiles or roasted tomatoes. |
| Mustard | Classic yellow mustard adds bite that stands up well to grilled beef. Dijon provides a more refined, European flavor. |
| Mayonnaise | Try lemony, garlic-spiked aioli. |
| Relish | Whether sweet or dill, relish adds a hit of salty flavor and crunch to most classic combinations. Try those derived from zucchini pickles or sweet chiles. |
| Barbecue Sauce | BBQ sauce provides smoky flavor and spice to rugged, ranch-style preparations. |
| Thousand Island | This secret sauce usually consists of mayonnaise, pickle relish, and chile sauce, and it can complement many burger preparations. |
| Chili | With or without meat, generous gobs of bean-heavy chili offer a spicy, over-the-top finish. |
| Olive Tapenade | Olives are ideal for a briny, Mediterranean vibe. |

# 055 Smoke a Great Brisket

For most Texan pit masters, good beef brisket is close to nirvana, and an individual's preferred technique is akin to gospel. Every aspect (choice of smoking wood, grilling wood, charcoal, gas, seasonings, timing, and more) lends its own particular nuances to the finished dish. Every cook seems to have his or her own tried-and-true method, but most can agree that slow and steady wins the race.

Briskets are the pectoral muscles from the chest of a steer between the forelegs. As you can imagine, these muscles get quite a workout, making them rich in connective tissue—which can only be rendered to succulent tenderness with a long and slow cooking process. Many a brisket chef has been know to pull up a lawn chair, pop a cold one, and nurse the brisket through the day (and often into the night). So what does it take to cook up a perfect, swoonworthy brisket? Try these Texan tips.

**BUY THE RIGHT SIZE** Thin cuts of brisket cook very fast, so they don't have time to absorb the smoky flavor. Buy a whole brisket that is as evenly thick as possible, with the surrounding fat trimmed to about ¼ inch (6 mm) to keep the meat nice and moist over the long cooking time.

**SEASON WITH CARE** In a surprising departure from the usual state of mind in Texas, less is more when it comes to seasoning a brisket. Most Texan grill masters rarely use anything other than salt and pepper, perhaps adding a little granulated garlic or a hint of cayenne if they're feeling frisky. Let the wood and smoke do most of the seasoning.

**CHOOSE THE RIGHT WOOD** For wood choice, mesquite is traditional. It burns hotter than other common woods, like hickory and oak. Oak imparts a more mellow, woodsy flavor.

**GO LOW AND SLOW** A good smoked brisket—meltingly tender and full-flavored—is all about patience. You need to maintain a steady, low temperature of 200–250°F (95–120°C) in a covered grill or smoker, and you need time—at least 6 hours—but it's worth every minute. (If you run out of time, wood, or patience, finish the brisket in the oven. You're the only one who will know.)

**WRAP IT UP** If you're not going to be eating the brisket right away, wrap it in aluminum foil for a few hours to prevent it from drying out.

**REMEMBER THE SIDES** Brisket is at its best with great accompaniments. Keep it simple, if you like (potato rolls or slices of thick white bread for soaking up all the juices are a must). And if you want to get fancy, add some smoky baked beans or coleslaw (see items 098, 235).

# 056 Texas-Style BBQ Brisket

The best briskets don't require much more than time, practice, and a good cut of meat. A blend of kosher salt, cracked black pepper, and flakes of granulated garlic make a simple, classic rub in this classic Texan recipe, which cooks low and slow over a smoky fire for about 10 hours. A day spent nursing your brisket on the grill—replenishing smoldering coals and adding wood chips—is the secret to tender and succulent brisket.

- 1 beef brisket, about 10 lb (5 kg), fat trimmed to ¼ inch (6 mm)
- ½ cup (125 g) *each* kosher salt and coarsely ground pepper
- 1 tablespoon granulated garlic, optional
- About 6 cups (540 g) wood chips, preferably oak or mesquite (or a combination), soaked in water at least 30 minutes or overnight, plus 2 cups (180 g) dry wood chips
- Barbecue sauce for serving

**PREP** Remove brisket from refrigerator at least 1 hour before cooking. Season generously all over with salt and pepper, packing the coating on well. Sprinkle with garlic, if using, then gently rub over seasoning.

**PREHEAT** Prepare a smoker or a charcoal or gas grill for smoking over low heat. The grill temperature should be 225–250°F (107–120°C). If using charcoal, bank lit coals on either side of grill bed, leaving a strip in the center without heat. Place a drip pan in the center strip and fill with water. Add 1–2 cups soaked wood chips to the fire just before grilling. (Keep remaining chips in water until ready to use.) If using gas, fill smoker box with about ½ cup chips, then preheat grill. The wood chips should begin to smolder and release a steady stream of smoke. To get more smoke without increasing grill heat, add a few dry chips to soaked ones. Turn off one or more of the burners to create an indirect-heat zone. Brush and oil grill grate.

**SMOKE** Place brisket on grill, fatty side up, as far away from the fire as possible. Cover and cook 4–6 hours, or until an instant-read thermometer inserted into the thickest part of the meat registers 150–170°F (66–77°C). Check wood chips every 30–45 minutes, adding more chips by the half cup to keep smoke levels constant. If using charcoal, add lit coals every few hours to maintain heat level.

**COOK** Remove brisket from grill and wrap in aluminum foil. Return to smoker or grill, or place in 250°F (120°C) oven an additional 4–6 hours. The brisket is ready when fork tender and an instant-read thermometer registers 195–205°F (91–96°C), 8–12 hours total.

**SERVE** Transfer brisket to a cutting board and remove foil. Let rest at least 30 minutes. Thinly slice across the grain, arrange slices on a platter, and serve at once. Serve with BBQ sauce—reheated or at room temperature.

Serves 12–14.

**QUICK TIPS:**

Maintaining temperature and smoke levels can be a tricky bit of fire mastery. When smoking in a charcoal grill, have a chimney starter filled with glowing coals at the ready, so you can replenish your fire every 30 minutes or so.

If you like a nice crusty "bark" on a finished brisket, here's how to get it: After seasoning with salt and pepper, don't pop the brisket on the grill just yet. Place it on a rack in a sheet pan, cover loosely, and refrigerate for at least 8 hours (or up to 36 hours). The seasoned coating will dry slightly, leaving a nice crisp exterior on the brisket. If you're looking for a crisp exterior without the wait time, wrap the brisket in butcher paper before wrapping it in aluminum foil to finish cooking.

# 057 Spot the Difference

Most folks assume a T-bone and a porterhouse steak are pretty much the same thing. Well, not exactly. Both the T-bone and the porterhouse are made up of two different cuts of meat separated by a T-shaped bone (the steer's vertebrae) running through the middle. Hence the name T-bone. The two steaks on either side of the T-shaped bone are the larger sirloin (New York strip) and the smaller tenderloin (filet mignon). To be considered a true T-bone, the prized tenderloin section needs to be at least ½ inch (1.3 cm) wide from the edge of the bone to the edge of the meat. On a porterhouse steak, which comes from the back of the short loin, the tenderloin section is bigger—measuring in at 1½ inches (4 cm) or wider.

# 058 Bourbon Steak Sauce

- ½ cup (4 oz/125 g) Dijon mustard
- ¼ cup (2 oz/60 g) ketchup
- 3 tablespoons steak sauce, preferably A.1.
- 2 tablespoons bourbon
- 2 tablespoons well-drained prepared horseradish
- 1 tablespoon *each* Worcestershire sauce, pure maple syrup, dark corn syrup, and tamari or reduced-sodium soy sauce
- 4 anchovy fillets, mashed to a paste
- Kosher salt and freshly ground pepper

Cuts from around the T-bone need a classic sauce that's refined but has a bit of kick. This sauce includes mustard and horseradish for some bite, and bourbon and maple syrup for their telltale smoky sweetness. It's a great all-around sauce that's so much better than anything you can find in a store. In a bowl, mix all ingredients. Use at once, or store in an airtight container in the refrigerator for up to one week. Bring to room temperature before serving.

Makes 1 cup (8 fl oz/250 ml).

# 059 Classic Porterhouse with Garlic Marinade

Porterhouse steaks are like T-bones on steroids. Their hefty size and massive tenderloin make them a bit pricey at the meat counter but well worth it when you get them on the grill. Since they generally measure 1½–2 inches (4–5 cm) thick, bring them to room temperature before cooking, and make sure your rack is searing hot. A blazing fire is your best bet for cooking them just right.

**MARINATE** In a baking dish, mix garlic, oregano, thyme, oil, vinegar, and red pepper flakes. Add steaks and turn to coat. Cover with plastic wrap and refrigerate overnight.

**PREP** Remove steaks from refrigerator at least 30 minutes before grilling. Discard the marinade and pat steaks dry with paper towels. Season generously with salt and pepper.

**PREHEAT** Prepare a charcoal or gas grill for direct grilling over high heat. Brush and oil grill grate.

**GRILL** Brush steaks on both sides with oil. Place steaks on the grill and cook about 3 minutes. Using tongs, rotate each steak a quarter turn, and continue cooking another 3 minutes. Turn steaks over and continue to cook until well marked and done to your liking, about 6 minutes longer for medium-rare, or until an instant-read thermometer (inserted horizontally into the center, away from bone) registers 135°F (57°C).

**SERVE** Transfer the steaks to warmed plates and let rest 5–10 minutes. Sprinkle steaks evenly with oregano and thyme. Serve at once.

Serves 4.

- 4 cloves garlic, halved
- 4 fresh oregano sprigs
- 2 fresh thyme sprigs
- ¼ cup (2 fl oz/60 ml) extra-virgin olive oil
- 2 tablespoons red wine vinegar
- ⅛ teaspoon red pepper flakes
- 4 porterhouse steaks, each ¾–1 lb (375–500 g) and 1½ inches (4 cm) thick
- Kosher salt and freshly ground black pepper
- Olive oil for brushing
- 1 tablespoon fresh oregano leaves
- 1 tablespoon fresh thyme leaves

# 060 New York Strip Steak

New York strip, the meaty sirloin running along the back of a steer, is a cut both rugged and refined. Its light texture with definite grain means the meat is moderately tender but still has a bit of chew. The steaks have good marbling and flavor, but no large pockets of fat, making them perfect for the grill. They are best cooked up nice and quick over a hot fire. Take advantage of the residual heat to grill fresh vegetables for serving alongside. Halved tomatoes and thick-sliced onions are especially good choices.

- 4 bone-in New York strip steaks, each about 10 oz (315 g) and 1½ inches (4 cm) thick
- ½ cup (4 oz/125 g) unsalted butter, melted and cooled
- ¼ cup (2 fl oz/60 ml) canola oil
- Kosher salt and freshly ground black pepper

**MARINATE** Remove steaks from the fridge at least 30 minutes before grilling. In a shallow dish, mix butter and oil. Add steaks and turn to coat, then remove, allowing excess oil mixture to drip off, and transfer to a platter. Coat each steak with 1 teaspoon each salt and pepper.

**PREHEAT** Prepare a charcoal or gas grill for direct grilling over high heat. Brush and oil grill grate.

**GRILL** Place steaks on the grill directly over the fire, cover, and cook 3 minutes. Use tongs or a spatula to rotate each steak a quarter turn; continue cooking another 3 minutes. Flip steaks and continue to cook, covered, until well marked, about 5 minutes longer for medium-rare, or until an instant-read thermometer registers 135°F (57°C). (If medium doneness is preferred, move steaks to a cooler portion of the grill and cook for a few minutes longer.)

**SERVE** Transfer the steaks to warmed plates and let rest 5–10 minutes. Serve at once.

Makes 4 servings.

# 061 Debunk the Salt Myth

There's a nasty rumor going around about salt and steak—even some seasoned grill cooks believe that salt toughens the beef and shouldn't be added until after cooking is completed—and it couldn't be more wrong. A generous dusting of nubby salt (kosher or coarse sea salt) and cracked black peppercorns right before grilling can build the rich flavor and savory crust characteristic of a great steak house steak. (Think twice, however, before seasoning hours ahead of time, as the salt will draw out the juices and make the meat dry.)

In the Basque region of southern France, and in Spain and Argentina, cooks have been employing salt-grilling techniques for centuries. In these cattle-heavy regions, steaks are often cooked on a rack over an open fire, with a generous coating of rock salt (and often a rich layer of beef fat) on top. The meat is served rare, encased in a crisp, lightly browned crust, and accompanied by a nutty Romesco sauce (see item 208) in Spain or a ubiquitous chimichurri (see item 070) in Argentina. This preparation isn't ideal for a gas stovetop, although it would certainly work in a pinch; a medium-hot hardwood fire provides your best chance of reproducing the crisp exterior and smoky flavor of the best salt-grilled steaks.

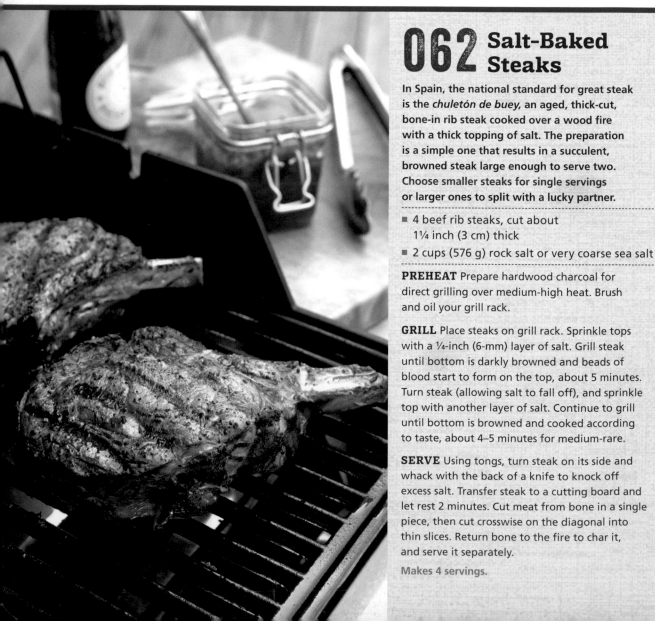

# 062 Salt-Baked Steaks

In Spain, the national standard for great steak is the *chuletón de buey,* an aged, thick-cut, bone-in rib steak cooked over a wood fire with a thick topping of salt. The preparation is a simple one that results in a succulent, browned steak large enough to serve two. Choose smaller steaks for single servings or larger ones to split with a lucky partner.

- 4 beef rib steaks, cut about 1¼ inch (3 cm) thick
- 2 cups (576 g) rock salt or very coarse sea salt

**PREHEAT** Prepare hardwood charcoal for direct grilling over medium-high heat. Brush and oil your grill rack.

**GRILL** Place steaks on grill rack. Sprinkle tops with a ¼-inch (6-mm) layer of salt. Grill steak until bottom is darkly browned and beads of blood start to form on the top, about 5 minutes. Turn steak (allowing salt to fall off), and sprinkle top with another layer of salt. Continue to grill until bottom is browned and cooked according to taste, about 4–5 minutes for medium-rare.

**SERVE** Using tongs, turn steak on its side and whack with the back of a knife to knock off excess salt. Transfer steak to a cutting board and let rest 2 minutes. Cut meat from bone in a single piece, then cut crosswise on the diagonal into thin slices. Return bone to the fire to char it, and serve it separately.

Makes 4 servings.

# 063 Slow-Smoked Beef Ribs

Beef ribs profit from long and slow cooking, so they rarely make it to the grill. It's an ironic blunder on the part of short-sighted chefs, since smoldering, indirect-heat cooking in a grill or traditional smoker can bring beef ribs to their absolute best. Smoking, in particular, offers the prolonged, low-heat cooking best for tougher rib cuts, while adding the complex, multilayered flavor of wood smoke to the meat.

- 2 racks beef ribs, 8 bones each
- 2 teaspoons (6 g) granulated garlic or garlic powder
- Salt and freshly ground pepper
- About 4 cups (0.36 kg) wood chips, soaked in water for 30 minutes
- 2 cups (16 fl oz/500 ml) barbecue sauce

**PREP** Remove thin membrane from back of each rib rack and trim off excess fat. Season all over with garlic, salt, and pepper.

**PREHEAT** Prepare a smoker or a charcoal or gas grill for smoking over low heat; the temperature inside the grill should be 200–250°F (95–120°C). If using charcoal, bank lit coals on either side of the grill bed, leaving a strip in the center without heat. Place a drip pan in the center strip and fill with water. Add about 1 cup (90 g) wood chips to the fire just before grilling. If using gas, fill the smoker box with about 1 cup (90 g) chips, then preheat grill. Turn off one or more burners to create an indirect-heat zone. Brush and oil grill grate.

**GRILL** Place ribs, bone side down, on grill rack over indirect heat area. Cover and cook until tender, about 2 hours, adding additional wood chips every 30 minutes or so; add more coals as needed if using charcoal.

**SERVE** Transfer racks to a cutting board and let rest for 10 minutes. Cut racks into individual ribs and pile on a platter. Serve at once with barbecue sauce.

Makes 4 servings.

# 065
## Chipotle Spice Paste

- ¼ cup (2 fl oz/60 ml) olive oil
- 1 cup (1 oz/30 g) loosely packed fresh cilantro sprigs
- 4 cloves garlic, coarsely chopped
- 3 chipotle chiles in adobo sauce, chopped
- 2 tablespoons *each* ground cumin and ground coriander
- 1 tablespoon dry mustard
- Salt and freshly ground pepper
- Fresh lime juice

Chipotle chiles are jalapeños that have been ripened, dried, and smoked. Popularly canned in adobo sauce—a smoky, spiced mixture of tomatoes and ancho chiles—chipotles offer rich and nuanced south-of-the-border zing to any meat with which they are paired. Try this spice paste as a rub—its rugged appeal is especially welcome on large, slow-cooked cuts of beef such as beef tri-tip and rib-eye.

In a blender or food processor, combine olive oil, cilantro, garlic, chipotle chiles, cumin, coriander, mustard, 1 tablespoon salt, and 2 tablespoons pepper. Pulse to chop roughly, then process until smooth. Season to taste with lime juice. Use at once, or cover and refrigerate for up to one week.

**Makes 1 cup (8 fl oz/250 ml).**

# 064 Cowboy Rib-Eye with Spice Paste

There are few cuts more macho to cook up on a grill than a super-thick, nice and juicy, bone-in rib-eye. Many of these supersize steaks can weigh in at nearly 2 lb (1 kg) and are cut with the rib bone left long and frenched, giving them the appearance and moniker of "tomahawk steaks." It's a manly cut that's well suited to grill cooking—when it's done right.

A "reverse sear" method works great: Smoke it first over indirect heat, then sear just the meat over high heat. A zesty chile rub cooks up the steaks just as wranglers might have made them out on the range—spicy and piping hot. These are rugged cuts meant for rustic suppers. Eat them like the cowboys do, using the bone like a drumstick, and leave the knife and fork at home.

- 4 bone-in rib-eye steaks, preferably long bone, each about 1½ inches (4 cm) thick
- Chipotle Spice Paste (see item 065), or similar spice rub or paste

**SEASON** Remove steaks from refrigerator at least 30 minutes before grilling. Rub spice paste or rub over both sides of steaks.

**PREHEAT** Prepare a charcoal or gas grill for direct grilling over two levels of heat, one high and one medium-high. Brush and oil grill grate.

**GRILL** Place steaks on hottest part of grill and cook 4 minutes. Using tongs, rotate each steak a quarter

turn, continue cooking another 3 minutes, then flip. Cook until well marked and done to your liking, about 5 more minutes for medium-rare. (If you prefer medium, move steaks to a cooler portion of grill and cook for a few minutes longer.)

**SERVE** Transfer steaks to warmed plates and let rest 5–10 minutes. Serve at once.

Serves 4.

# 066 Chile-Rubbed Smoked Tri-Tip

When it comes to popular beef cuts for the barbecue, tri-tip is the hands-down favorite in terms of flavor and value. It takes to marinade like a bee to honey and loves a long, slow, indirect-heat grill to bring out its full, rich flavor. A triangular muscle cut from the sirloin, tri-tip is wonderfully lean, tender, and boneless. Zesty chiles make for the perfect partner to its rustic character.

- 1 tri-tip roast, 3 lb (1½ kg)
- 1 tablespoon chile powder
- 1 teaspoon garlic salt
- Freshly ground black pepper
- About 4 cups (360 g) wood chips, soaked in water, beer, or apple cider for 30 minutes
- Fresh tomato salsa or *pico de gallo* for serving

**SEASON** Remove roast from refrigerator at least 30 minutes before grilling. Season with chile powder, garlic salt, and a generous amount of pepper.

**PREHEAT** Prepare a charcoal or gas grill for smoking over medium heat; the grill temperature should be 350–375°F (180–190°C). If using charcoal, bank lit coals on either side of the grill bed, leaving a strip in the center without heat. Place a drip pan in the center strip and fill pan with water. Add about 2 cups of the wood chips to the fire just before grilling. If using gas, fill smoker box with up to 2 cups wood chips, then preheat grill. Turn off one or more burners to create a cooler zone. Brush and oil grill grate.

**GRILL** Place roast on grill over direct heat and sear, turning as needed, until browned but not charred on all sides, 15–20 minutes total. Move roast to indirect-heat area, cover the grill, and cook about 45 minutes longer for medium-rare or 1 hour for medium, adding the remaining wood chips after about 30 minutes. (Time will vary according to the shape of the roast.) Remove the roast when an instant-read thermometer inserted into thickest part registers 135°F (57°C) for medium-rare or 140°F (60°C) for medium.

**SERVE** Transfer roast to a cutting board, tent with aluminum foil, and let rest 15 minutes. Slice very thinly against grain, capturing any released juices, and arrange on a platter. Serve with salsa or pico de gallo.

Makes 6–8 servings—with leftovers.

# 067 Bacon-Wrapped Filet Mignon

Filet mignon, dubbed "The King of Steak," is the center cut of a beef tenderloin, yielding arguably the leanest and most tender piece of meat from a steer or heifer. Here, the King is made all the more tasty and juicy with a "crown" of bacon. Because the fillets are cut from the center (like chateaubriand), they are usually of roughly the same size and cook up with precision over a hot fire. Blanching the bacon before wrapping the fillets keeps grease (and any related burner flare-ups) to a minimum. Béarnaise sauce is the classic—and ultimate—accompaniment.

- 8 slices thick-cut applewood-smoked bacon
- 4 filets mignons, each about 10 oz (315 g) and 1½ inches (4 cm) thick
- Kosher salt and freshly ground black pepper
- Canola oil for brushing

**PREP** Bring a saucepan half full of water to a boil over high heat. Add bacon, reduce heat to medium, and cook for 5 minutes. Transfer bacon to paper towels to drain. Discard water. Remove steaks from refrigerator at least 30 minutes before grilling. When bacon is cool enough to handle, wrap two slices around edge of each steak; secure with kitchen string. Season steaks on both sides with salt and pepper, then brush with oil.

**PREHEAT** Prepare charcoal or gas grill for direct grilling over high heat. Brush and oil grill grate.

**GRILL** Place steaks on grill and cook 4 minutes. Using tongs, rotate each steak a quarter turn, and cook another 2 minutes. Turn steaks over and continue to cook until done to your liking, about 6 minutes longer for medium-rare. (If medium doneness is preferred, move steaks to cooler portion of grill and cook for a few minutes longer.)

**SERVE** Plate steaks and let rest 5–10 minutes. Remove string. Serve with warm béarnaise sauce (see item 068).

Serves 4.

# 068 Buttery Béarnaise Sauce

If filet mignon is the king of steaks, then béarnaise sauce is the royal robe. The sumptuous tarragon-studded hollandaise is second-to-none as a classic accompaniment to beef fillet. Although traditionally paired with prime cuts, béarnaise sauce can glam up any type of beef with which it's served. The successful preparation of Sauce de Béarnaise is a prerequisite for any steak house chef and usually isn't easy, involving as it does a long, slow heating and emulsifying of eggs without curdling them. This method takes a simpler (and more foolproof) approach, skipping the lengthy reduction of vinegar and onion in favor of an easy tarragon-vinegar-water mixture, and relying on a blender (rather than a whisk) for easy emulsification.

- 6 large egg yolks
- 1 cup (8 oz/250 g) unsalted butter
- Juice of 1 lemon
- ⅛ teaspoon ground cayenne pepper
- ½ teaspoon salt
- 1 tablespoon chopped fresh tarragon
- ½ teaspoon tarragon vinegar or white wine vinegar

**BLEND** In a blender or food processor, blend eggs yolks until creamy and pale yellow. In a small saucepan, melt butter over low heat. (Watch closely and act quickly, as you don't want it to separate.) Add lemon juice and cayenne pepper, raise heat to medium, and bring to a boil. Remove and pour into a small pitcher. With blender running at medium speed, slowly pour hot mixture into egg yolks and process until smooth. Season with salt. In the same pitcher, mix tarragon, vinegar, and 3 tablespoons hot water. Add hot water mixture as needed to yield a good consistency.

**SERVE** Serve at once, or pour into a thermos and set aside at room temperature. Sauce will stay warm for up to 4 hours.

Makes 2 cups (16 fl oz/500 ml).

# 070
## Chimichurri Sauce

- ½ cup (4 fl oz/125 ml) *each* extra virgin olive oil and red wine vinegar
- ¼ cup (1½ oz/45 g) minced red onion
- 2 tablespoons minced bell pepper
- 2 tablespoons minced fresh flat-leaf parsley
- 2 teaspoons chopped fresh oregano
- 2 teaspoons minced garlic
- ¼ teaspoon red pepper flakes
- Kosher salt and freshly ground black pepper

This zesty herb, garlic, and chile-studded sauce is possibly Argentina's greatest contribution to 21st-century gastronomy. The piquant, fresh relish is a popular companion to all types of rugged preparations, from grilled vegetables to steak.

In a bowl, whisk together oil, vinegar, onion, bell pepper, parsley, oregano, garlic, red pepper flakes, a pinch of salt, and a few grinds of pepper. Let stand at room temperature for about 30 minutes to allow flavors to develop. Whisk again before serving. (The sauce can be made up to two days in advance and refrigerated. Bring to room temperature before serving.)

**Makes 1 cup (8 fl oz/250 ml).**

# 069
## Argentine Beef Tenderloin

**Argentine chefs know how to make a statement and grab your attention. Fires are big and open. Meat is large and cooked in massive slabs. Where elegant beef dishes of French origin might focus on a single fillet grilled to perfection, Argentine chefs cook up hunks of beef—in this case a whole 6- to 7-lb (2.7-kg to 3.15-kg) tenderloin—and ditch the refined butter emulsion sauce in favor of a zesty chile-and-herb chimichurri.**

- 1 whole beef tenderloin, about 6½ lb (3.26 kg), trimmed
- 6 cloves garlic, thinly sliced
- Salt and freshly ground pepper
- Chimichurri Sauce (see item 070)

**PREP** Remove meat from refrigerator at least 45 minutes before grilling. Make shallow, evenly spaced slits all over surface of tenderloin. Slide garlic slices into slits. Season tenderloin generously with salt and pepper. Make your chimichurri sauce (see item 070).

**PREHEAT** Prepare charcoal or gas grill for indirect grilling over medium heat; temperature inside the grill should be 350–375°F (180–190°C). If using charcoal, bank lit coals on one side of the grill bed, and place a drip pan in the area without coals. If using

gas, preheat burners, then turn off one or more burners to create a cooler zone. Brush and oil grill grate.

**GRILL** Place tenderloin on grill over direct heat. Sear, turning as needed, until nicely browned on all sides, 8–10 minutes total. Move tenderloin to indirect-heat area, cover grill, and cook for 1½ hours for medium-rare, or until an instant-read thermometer inserted in thickest part of the meat registers 135°F (57°C).

**SERVE** Transfer to a cutting board and let rest for 15 minutes. Thinly slice across grain and arrange on a platter. Spoon chimichurri over top. Serve warm or at room temperature.

**Serves 8–10.**

# 071 Age Your Beef

All fresh beef is aged for at least a few days and up to several weeks to allow natural enzymes a chance at breaking down the muscle tissue, resulting in improved texture and flavor. These days, most beef is aged in plastic wrap—a process known as wet-aging. Dry-aged beef, on the other hand, is exposed to air so dehydration can further concentrate the meat's flavor. Aging beef for a few days by either method makes for some richly flavored meat, but dry-aging results in a more mellow, succulent, and beefier flavor than a wet-aged roast (which can taste almost watery in comparison).

Aged beef can be purchased at well-stocked meat counters, but you can also age your own. It's not a process for chops and smaller cuts, but it can be a worthwhile extra step for large, special-occasion roasts. Here's how.

**STEP 1** Buy a prime or choice boneless beef rib or loin roast from your favorite butcher.

**STEP 2** Unwrap the beef, rinse it well, and pat it dry with paper towels. Don't trim away any of the fat. Wrap the roast loosely in a triple layer of cheesecloth and set it on a rack over a rimmed baking sheet or other tray.

**STEP 3** Refrigerate for three to seven days; the longer the beef ages, the tastier it gets. After the first day, carefully unwrap and then rewrap with the same cheesecloth to prevent the cloth fibers from sticking to the meat.

**STEP 4** When ready to roast, unwrap the meat and, with a sharp knife, shave off and discard the hard, dried outer layer of the meat. Shave away any dried areas of fat, too, but leave behind as much of the good fat as possible. Roast whole or cut into steaks.

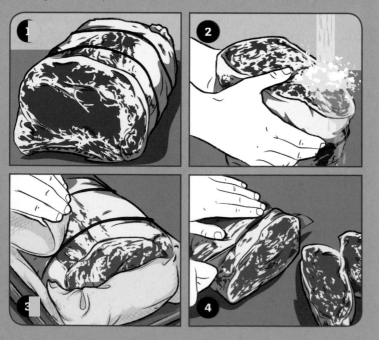

# 072 Horse(radish) Around!

Smoked prime rib and horseradish is a match made in heaven. The tart, slightly acidic character of the sauce heightens the smoky flavor of the beef. It's best made a day ahead so the flavors have a chance to meld. To make, mix ¼ cup (2 fl oz/60 ml) mayonnaise, ½ cup (4 oz/ 125 g) sour cream, 3 tablespoons freshly grated horseradish root, 2 tablespoons chopped fresh chives, and 1 teaspoon each English mustard and steak sauce in a small bowl. Use at once, or cover and refrigerate for up to three days. Let it come to room temperature before serving.

# 073 Slow-Smoked Prime Rib Roast

When a special occasion rolls around, few dishes will establish your authority in the realm of ultimate grill mastery better than a succulent, juicy, slow-smoked prime rib roast. This recipe relies on a nicely orchestrated trio of flavor basics and bonuses: first, the natural meatiness of a good-quality roast (use aged meat for an even greater depth of flavor); second, the addition of an herb-infused garlic-and-mustard rub; and third, the added enhancement of smoky flavor from smoldering wood chips added to the fire. Fresh horseradish sauce (see item 072) is a classic accompaniment and a good match for the roast's rugged, yet refined, appeal.

**SEASON** Remove roast from refrigerator at least 30 minutes before cooking. In a food processor, combine garlic, rosemary, basil, and 2 teaspoons each salt and pepper. Pulse to mince finely. Add mustard and pulse to combine. With motor running, slowly pour in oil and process to a paste. Smear paste evenly over roast.

**PREHEAT** Prepare a charcoal or gas grill for smoking over medium heat; the grill temperature should be 350–375°F (180–190°C). If using charcoal, bank lit coals on either side of the grill bed, leaving a strip in the center without heat. Place a drip pan in this center strip and fill pan with water. Add about 1 cup wood chips to the fire just before grilling. If using gas, fill smoker box with about 1 cup wood chips, then preheat grill. Turn off one or more of the burners to create a cooler zone. Brush and oil grill grate.

**SMOKE** Place roast, bone side down, on grill over indirect-heat area. Cover and cook for 1½–2 hours for medium-rare, adding more wood chips every 30 minutes or so and more coals as needed if using charcoal. The roast is ready when an instant-read thermometer inserted into the center of the meat away from bone registers 130–135°F (54–57°C).

**SERVE** Transfer roast to a cutting board, tent with aluminum foil, and let rest for 20–30 minutes. Using a sharp knife, remove bones from the roast. Carve meat into thin slices and arrange on a warmed platter. Serve at once.

*Makes 8–10 servings.*

- 1 bone-in standing rib roast, 5–6 lb (2½–3 kg), trimmed of excess fat
- 6 large cloves garlic
- ¼ cup (¼ oz/7 g) lightly packed fresh rosemary leaves
- ¼ cup (¼ oz/7 g) lightly packed fresh basil leaves
- Kosher salt and freshly ground black pepper
- 3 tablespoons Dijon mustard
- 3 tablespoons olive oil
- About 4 cups (360 g) wood chips, soaked in water for 30 minutes

# 074 Vietnamese Flank Steak Salad

Grilled steak salad is the ultimate perfect protein. Partnering lean yet hearty cuts of beef with greens and fresh vegetables makes for a fantastically healthy option and gastronomic treat. Asian-inspired compositions are among the most popular, marrying the rugged flavor of charred beef with fresh herbs and spices that nicely complement its intensity.

- Ginger-Soy Marinade (see item 088)
- 1 flank steak (1½–1¾ lb/750–875 g), trimmed
- 1 head Bibb (Boston) lettuce
- 1 head romaine lettuce
- 1 carrot
- 1 cucumber
- 1 small red onion
- 2 tablespoons *each* minced fresh basil, mint, and cilantro leaves, plus leaves for garnish
- 1 lb (500 g) dried Asian cellophane noodles
- Salt and ground pepper

**MARINATE** Mix marinade (see item 088). Pour half into small serving bowl and set aside. Using a sharp knife, score meat on both sides in a shallow crosshatch pattern. Place steak in a shallow dish, pour marinade over the top, and turn to coat. Cover and refrigerate 1 hour or overnight.

**PREHEAT** Prepare charcoal or gas grill for direct grilling over medium-high heat. Brush and oil grill grate.

**PREP** Rinse and dry lettuces. Tear Bibb lettuce into bite-size pieces and chop romaine lettuce into 1-inch (2.5-cm) chunks. Place in salad bowl. Peel carrot and cucumber. Using a mandoline, cut into julienne strips. Add to bowl. Thinly slice red onion and add to bowl along with minced herbs. Toss to mix. Reconstitute noodles according to package directions. Set aside.

**GRILL** Remove steak from marinade and pat dry with paper towels. Season with salt and pepper. (Discard used marinade.) Grill steak, turning once and brushing with some of the reserved marinade, until done to your liking, about 8–10 minutes for medium-rare.

**CUT** Transfer steak to cutting board and let rest 5 minutes. Cut across the grain into thin slices. Set aside.

**SERVE** Divide salad among four plates. Top equally with noodles and steak. Pour 1 tablespoon marinade over each salad, garnish with herb leaves, and serve any remaining dressing on the side.

Serves 4–6.

# 075

## Italian Steak Salad with Arugula, Parmesan & Lemon

Featuring lean, made for-the-grill cuts such as flank, flat-iron, and tri-tip, steak salads can easily morph from one flavor profile to another, depending on the trimmings. This Italian-influenced salad serves up a great balance by merging the robust character of grilled beef with the sharpness of fresh Parmesan and the peppery bite of arugula.

- 1 teaspoon chopped fresh thyme
- ¼ teaspoon salt
- ½ teaspoon freshly ground pepper
- 4 flat-iron or flank steaks (¼ lb/125 g)
- 2 lemons, halved
- 1 tablespoon snipped fresh chives
- 1 tablespoon *each* extra-virgin olive oil and fresh lemon juice
- ½ teaspoon Dijon mustard
- ⅛ teaspoon kosher salt
- 4 cups loosely packed baby arugula
- ¼ cup (1 oz/28 g) shaved fresh good-quality Parmesan cheese

**PREP & PREHEAT** Prepare charcoal or gas grill for direct grilling over medium-high heat. Brush and oil grill rack. Rub thyme, salt, and ¼ teaspoon pepper over steaks.

**GRILL** Place steaks on grill rack and sear, turning once, until nicely charred on the outside and medium-rare in the center, about 8 minutes. About halfway through cooking time, place lemons on grill rack, cut sides down, and sear until nicely charred, about 3 minutes.

**CUT** Transfer steaks to cutting board and let rest 5 minutes. Thinly slice across the grain.

**MIX** In a small bowl, whisk together remaining ¼ teaspoon pepper, chives, olive oil, lemon juice, mustard, and salt. Drizzle over arugula and toss to coat.

**SERVE** Divide salad among four serving plates. Top each serving with steak, a lemon half, and 1 tablespoon cheese.

Serves 4.

# 076 Thai Grilled Beef, Tomato & Mint Salad

While marinating the beef for this recipe, whip up a delicious vinaigrette: Mince 2 cloves garlic and 2 fresh small red or green chile peppers, then mix in 1½ tablespoons sugar, 3 tablespoons Thai fish sauce, and 5 tablespoons fresh lime juice. Set aside and continue the cooking process.

- 1 lb (500 g) beef tri-tip or flank steak
- 2 tablespoons finely chopped fresh cilantro, plus leaves for garnish
- 2 tablespoons soy sauce
- 1 tablespoon *each* Thai fish sauce and peanut or corn oil
- 1½ teaspoons sugar
- 1 teaspoon ground black pepper
- 2 cloves garlic, minced
- 6 large red lettuce leaves
- 3 small tomatoes
- 1 small red onion
- 1 small cucumber, peeled
- 8 mint leaves

**MARINATE** Place beef in a bowl. Add cilantro, soy sauce, fish sauce, oil, sugar, pepper, and garlic. Rub marinade onto beef. Let marinate at room temperature for 1 hour, or cover and refrigerate for up to 4 hours. Make your vinaigrette per previous instructions.

**PREHEAT** Prepare charcoal or gas grill for direct grilling over medium-high heat. Brush and oil grill grate.

**GRILL** Place beef on grill and cook, turning once, until medium rare, 8–10 minutes. Remove from heat and let cool. Cut across the grain into very thin slices. Place in large bowl. Add two-thirds of vinaigrette and toss to coat. Set aside.

**ASSEMBLE** Stack lettuce leaves and slice into thin shreds. Place in a large bowl. Cut tomatoes into wedges and add to bowl. Thinly slice onion, cucumber, and mint and add to bowl. Toss to mix. Drizzle remaining dressing over salad and toss gently to coat. Divide among six salad plates. Mound beef mixture evenly on top and garnish with cilantro.

Makes 6 servings.

## Hanger Steak Sliders

Adding sophisticated flavors to these bite-size wonders really elevates the recipe from snack time to party time. Hanger steak, blue cheese, caramelized onions—how could that combination not be sensational? Once known as the butcher's tenderloin, hanger steak has a deep, rich flavor that can readily hold up to this pairing of tart blue cheese and sweet onions.

**MARINATE** Prepare your favorite marinade (see item 084). Place the hanger steaks in a large zip-top plastic bag and pour in the marinade. Seal the bag closed, squish the marinade around the meat, and refrigerate overnight.

**PREP** At least 30 minutes before you are ready to begin grilling, remove the steaks from the refrigerator. Discard the marinade and pat the steaks dry with paper towels. Brush the steaks with oil. Prepare a charcoal or gas grill for direct grilling over high heat. Brush and oil grill grate.

**SAUTÉ** In a sauté pan over low heat, melt the butter. Add the onions and cook slowly, stirring often, until they are tender and caramelized, about 20 minutes. Remove from heat and keep warm. (If necessary, reheat just before serving.)

**GRILL** Place the steaks on the grill directly over the fire and cook, turning once, until nicely charred on both sides and barely firm to the touch, about 4 minutes per side for medium-rare or 6 minutes per side for medium.

**TOAST** Transfer the steaks to a cutting board and let rest about 5 minutes. Meanwhile, put the rolls, cut side down, on the edge of the grill to toast for about a minute.

**SERVE** Thinly slice the steaks against the grain, capturing any released juices. Toss the sliced meat and juices together in a bowl. Divide the meat and juices evenly among the roll bottoms. Top with blue cheese and onions, dividing evenly. Cap with the roll tops and serve at once.

Serves 6.

- 4 hanger steaks, each about 6 oz (185 g)
- Your favorite marinade (see item 084)
- Canola oil for brushing
- 1 tablespoon unsalted butter
- 2 sweet onions, thinly sliced
- 12 slider rolls, split
- ¼ lb (125 g) blue cheese, crumbled

**QUICK TIP**

This cut tastes best served medium-rare—definitely don't cook the meat past medium.

# 078 Carne Asada Tacos

If you live too far from a taco truck or border town to enjoy the real thing as often as you'd like, this recipe may just solve all your problems. It calls for authentic seasonings, the correct cut of meat, and, true to street-food tradition, doesn't overstuff the tacos with condiments—just a little smoky salsa and a slice of avocado. If you can find fresh, thick corn tortillas, you'll only need to use one per taco.

- 1 skirt steak, about 2 lb (1 kg)
- 2 tablespoons spice rub of your choosing
- 1 lime, halved, plus lime wedges for serving
- 4 cloves garlic, coarsely chopped
- 2 tablespoons chopped fresh cilantro
- Kosher salt and freshly ground black pepper
- Olive oil for brushing
- 24 corn tortillas, about 6 inches (15 cm) in diameter
- Smoky Tomato Salsa (see item 079) for serving
- 2 avocados, pitted, peeled, and sliced

**SEASON** Sprinkle the rub evenly over both sides of the steak, then squeeze 1 lime half over each side. Rub the garlic and cilantro into both sides, then season generously with salt and pepper. Place the steak in a large zip-top plastic bag, seal, and refrigerate overnight.

**PREP** At least 30 minutes before you are ready to begin grilling, remove the steak from the refrigerator. Brush the steak on both sides with the oil, and oil grill grate.

**GRILL** Place the steak on the grill directly over the fire and cook, turning once, until nicely charred on both sides and fairly firm to the touch, about 4 minutes per side for medium-rare or 6 minutes per side for medium. (Rare skirt steak can be a little tough. Medium-rare or medium works best.)

**REST** Transfer the steak to a cutting board and let rest for 5 minutes. Meanwhile, warm the tortillas on the grill, about 1 minute on each side, then stack and wrap in a kitchen towel.

**SERVE** Thinly slice the steak against the grain. To assemble each taco, overlap two tortillas, top with the meat, add a spoonful of the salsa, and add a slice or two of avocado. Add a lime wedge to each plate. Fold and enjoy!

Serves 6.

> **QUICK TIP**
> Slice the steak against the grain to enhance its tenderness: hold the knife at a 45-degree angle and cut thin slices.

# 079 Smoky Tomato Salsa

Grilled vegetables in a salsa add a layered, smoky flavor that can't be beat.

- 3 large, ripe tomatoes, thickly sliced
- 1 small red onion, thickly sliced
- 1 jalapeño chile, halved lengthwise and seeded
- Olive oil for drizzling
- Juice of 2 limes
- ¼ cup (⅓ oz/10 g) finely chopped fresh cilantro leaves
- Kosher salt and freshly ground black pepper

**PREP** Brush and oil grill grate. Drizzle the tomato, onion slices, and chile halves with oil.

**GRILL** Place on the grill and cook, turning once, until a nice char develops, about 2 minutes per side.

**MIX** Remove from the grill, chop coarsely, and place in a bowl. Stir in the lime juice and cilantro.

**SERVE** Divide the mixture in half, purée half of it in a food processor, then return to the bowl. Mix well and season with salt and pepper. The salsa tastes best if made a day in advance. Keep covered in the fridge for up to one week.

Makes about 1½ cups (9 oz/280 g).

# 080 Korean BBQ Short Ribs

Crispy, flavorful short ribs are at the heart of Korean barbecue. Known as *galbi*, or *bulgalbi* if they're cooked over an open fire, Korean-style ribs are cut across the ribs (flanken cut) rather than between the ribs (English cut). The resulting pieces of meat are about ½ inch (1.2 cm) thick and 8–10 inches (20–25 cm) long—the perfect size for a quick sear on a hot grill. Galbi is usually cut from the thicker chuck end of the short rib, making for some especially flavorful and meaty ribs.

- ½ cup (4 fl oz/125 ml) reduced-sodium soy sauce
- ¼ cup (2 fl oz/60 g) firmly packed light brown sugar
- 2 tablespoons *each* rice vinegar, Asian sesame oil, and minced garlic
- 1 tablespoon *each* ketchup and peeled and minced fresh ginger
- 1 teaspoon red pepper flakes
- 5 lb (2½ kg) flanken-cut beef short ribs, cut ½ inch (12 mm) thick by your butcher
- 1 cup (8 fl oz/250 ml) Asian-style barbecue sauce, store-bought or homemade (see item 086)

**MARINATE** In a large zip-top plastic bag, mix together soy sauce, brown sugar, vinegar, oil, garlic, ketchup, ginger, and red pepper flakes. Add ribs and turn bag to coat. Let stand for at least 2 hours at room temperature, or cover and refrigerate overnight, turning once or twice.

**PREHEAT** Prepare a charcoal or gas grill for direct-heat grilling over high heat. Brush and oil grill grate.

**GRILL** Remove ribs from marinade and discard marinade. Pat ribs dry with paper towels. Place ribs on grill directly over fire and cook, turning once, until medium, 6–8 minutes total. During the last 2 minutes of cooking, brush ribs with some of the sauce.

**SERVE** Transfer ribs to a platter and let rest 5–10 minutes. Serve at once with more barbecue sauce on the side.

Makes 6 servings.

# 081 Grilled Satay Skewers

When you serve up skewers of crispy, marinated grilled beef, what could have been just a simple supper feels like a party. Many believe satay to be a quintessential dish of Thailand, although the meaty skewers are actually of Indonesian origin. This preparation, with its hit of lemongrass and lime, could just have you fooled. The Southeast Asian marinade incorporates many of the region's signature flavors, adding just enough sweetness to assist in the perfect caramelization of the meat over a hot fire. Offer the skewers alongside a light ginger dipping sauce (see item 087) or a spicy peanut sauce (see item 251) for a bit of zing.

- ½ cup (4 fl oz/125 ml) soy sauce
- 3 tablespoons Asian sesame oil
- 2 stalks lemongrass, white parts only, finely diced
- Zest and juice of 1 lime
- 3 cloves garlic, minced
- 2 green (spring) onions, white parts only, finely diced, plus extra for garnish
- 2 tablespoons firmly packed light brown sugar
- 1 flank steak, about 1½ lb (750 g)
- 24 bamboo skewers

**MARINATE** In a blender or food processor, combine soy sauce, sesame oil, lemongrass, lime zest and juice, garlic, green onions, and brown sugar. Process until smooth. Pour into a large zip-top plastic bag, seal, and set aside. Using a sharp knife, slice meat across the grain on the diagonal into strips ½ inch (12 mm) thick. Place steak in bag, seal, and turn to coat. Let marinate in the refrigerator at least 2 hours or overnight.

**PREP & PREHEAT** Soak bamboo skewers in water for at least 30 minutes. Remove meat from refrigerator and bring to room temperature—this should take at least 30 minutes. Prepare a charcoal or gas grill for direct grilling over medium-high heat. Brush and oil grill grate. One at a time, thread steak strips lengthwise onto bamboo skewers.

**GRILL** Place skewers on grill directly over fire and cook, turning once, until nicely charred and done to your liking, 2–3 minutes per side.

**SERVE** Arrange skewers on a serving platter and sprinkle with remaining green onion. Serve at once.

Makes 6 servings.

# 082 Baste with Fat

Flank steak, skirt steak, and other lean, quick-cooking cuts may seem the logical choice for grill cooking over direct heat, but that doesn't mean that many longer-cooking cuts can't cook up nice and juicy over a medium-hot fire. Some enterprising cooks trim the fat from tri-tip, top sirloin cap steak, or rib-eye; dice it; then thread it onto skewers, alternating the fat with pieces of the diced meat. The fat self-bastes the meat while it cooks over the fire. Any extra fat is rendered in a hot pan, then mixed with the marinade—making a flavor-blaster basting sauce to use while the skewers are on the heat.

# 083 Construct a Heat Barrier

Giving bamboo skewers a good soaking is a great way to help prevent them from overbrowning on the grill, but it may not be enough to entirely arrest the charring effects of the heat. Solve the problem with metal skewers, or create a heat barrier to protect the thin wooden skewers from the flames. Triple-fold two pieces of heavy-duty aluminum foil into long rectangles about 6 inches (15 cm) wide and as long as the width of your foil. Run a lengthwise crease down the center of each one to make two peaked heat barriers. To use the barriers, place them on the grill, then set the wooden ends of your skewers over the foil, allowing the meat to rest on the grill grates. The meat will cook, but the skewers won't.

# 084 Mix Up a Marinade

Many cooks, especially the purists among us, believe that a truly great piece of meat needs no embellishment. Most also agree, somewhat ironically, that there's always room for just a little bit of adornment. In this chapter you'll find the ultimate accompaniments for great steak: buttery béarnaise (see item 068), bourbon steak sauce (see item 058), and horseradish sauce (see item 072) for steak house fillets, and chimichurri (see item 070) for traditional Argentine *asado*. With those in hand—along with the following marinades, pastes, and sauces—there's something to appeal to every palate and every cut.

# 085 Cilantro-Lime Marinade

- 8–10 limes
- 1 bunch fresh cilantro, leaves and tender stems only
- ¼ cup (2 fl oz/60 ml) vegetable oil, such as canola, safflower, or grapeseed

Grate enough zest from limes to measure 2 tablesp.oons; halve and juice enough limes to measure 1 cup (8 fl oz/250 ml) juice. In a blender or food processor, combine zest, juice, and cilantro. Pulse to desired consistency. Scrape down sides of bowl. Add oil and pulse to blend. Use at once, or cover and refrigerate for up to two days. Great with flank, skirt, or hanger steak.

Makes 2 cups (16 fl oz/500 ml).

# 086
## Asian-Style Barbecue Sauce

- ¼ cup (2 fl oz/60 ml) hoisin sauce
- ¼ cup (2 fl oz/60 ml) sweet-hot pepper sauce
- 2 tablespoons mirin
- 1 tablespoon Asian sesame oil

In a bowl, whisk together all ingredients plus ¼ cup (2 fl oz/60 ml) water. Taste and adjust with more sesame oil, if desired. Use at once, or store in an airtight container in the refrigerator for up to two months. Bring to room temperature before using. Great with beef short ribs, baby back ribs, and Korean BBQ Short Ribs (see item 080).

Makes about 1 cup (8 fl oz/250 ml).

# 087
## Ginger Dipping Sauce

- ½ cup (4 fl oz/125 ml) soy sauce
- ¼ cup (2 fl oz/60 ml) mirin
- 2 tablespoons sesame oil
- 2 tablespoons peeled and grated fresh ginger
- 2 cloves garlic, minced
- 1 green (spring) onion, thinly sliced
- 1 Thai chile, seeded and thinly sliced
- Juice of 1 lime

In a bowl, whisk together all ingredients. Transfer to small serving bowls for use as a dipping sauce. Serve at once. Great with flank, skirt, or hanger steak.

Makes about ¾ cup (6 fl oz/180 ml).

# 088
## Ginger-Soy Marinade

- ¼ cup (2 fl oz/60 ml) Worcestershire sauce
- 3 tablespoons soy sauce
- 2 tablespoons fresh lemon juice
- 1 tablespoon hoisin sauce
- 2 tablespoon chopped fresh cilantro
- 1 tablespoon peeled and minced fresh ginger

In a small bowl, mix together all ingredients with a few grinds of fresh pepper. Use at once, or cover and refrigerate for up to one day before using. Great with flank, skirt, and hanger steak.

Makes about ¾ cup (6 fl oz/180 ml).

# 089 Spicy Marinade

In a medium bowl, whisk together 2 tablespoons fresh ginger (peeled and grated), ½ cup (4 fl oz/125 ml) soy sauce, 2 tablespoons fish sauce, 2 tablespoons sesame oil, 3 minced garlic cloves, 2 thinly sliced green onions, a minced shallot, 1 seeded and thinly sliced Thai chile, and the zest and juice of one lime. Use as a marinade or transfer to a small serving bowl to use as a dipping sauce.

Makes ¾ cup (6 fl oz/180 ml).

# 090

## Beef Barbecue Sauce

- 2 tablespoons margarine (not butter!)
- ¼ cup (1½ oz/45 g) finely chopped yellow onion
- 1 clove garlic, pressed
- 1 cup ketchup (8 oz/250 g)
- ¼ cup (2 oz/60 g) firmly packed light brown sugar
- ¼ cup (2 oz/60 g) fresh lemon juice
- 1 tablespoon *each* Worcestershire sauce and yellow mustard

In a small saucepan over medium heat, melt margarine. Add onion and garlic and cook, stirring, until softened but not colored, about 3 minutes. Stir in ketchup, sugar, lemon juice, Worcestershire, and mustard. Bring to a boil. Reduce heat to low and simmer, stirring occasionally, until thickened, 15–20 minutes. Use at once, or cover and refrigerate for up to two weeks. Great with beef brisket, ribs, and tri-tip.

Makes about 2 cups (16 fl oz/500 ml).

# 091 Red Wine Shallot Sauce

- 4 shallots, thinly sliced
- 2 tablespoons olive oil
- 1 cup (8 fl oz/250 ml) red wine
- 1 cup (8 fl oz/250 ml) beef broth
- Salt and freshly ground pepper

In a saucepan over medium-high heat, sauté shallots in olive oil until lightly caramelized, 5–7 minutes. Raise heat to high, add red wine, and reduce by half, stirring frequently. Stir in broth and reduce by half again. Taste and adjust seasoning with salt and pepper. Great with flank, skirt, or hanger steak, and fillets or roasts.

Makes about ¾ cup (6 fl oz/180 ml) sauce.

# 092 Churrasco Marinade

- 1 large head garlic, about 15 cloves
- 1 teaspoon salt
- ½ teaspoon black peppercorns or cracked black pepper
- ½ cup (4 fl oz/125 ml) orange juice
- 2 tablespoons *each* fresh lime juice and fresh lemon juice
- ½ cup (6 oz/92 g) minced onion
- 1 teaspoon fresh oregano
- ½ cup (4 fl oz/125 ml) extra-virgin olive oil

In a mortar with a pestle, mash garlic, salt, and peppercorns. (Or, if using a garlic press, press garlic into bowl and add salt and cracked black pepper.) Stir in orange juice, lime juice, lemon juice, onion, and oregano. Let stand at room temperature 30 minutes for flavors to meld. Whisk in the olive oil until blended. Great with large cuts suitable for slow cooking.

Makes 1½ cups (12 fl oz/240 ml).

# PORK

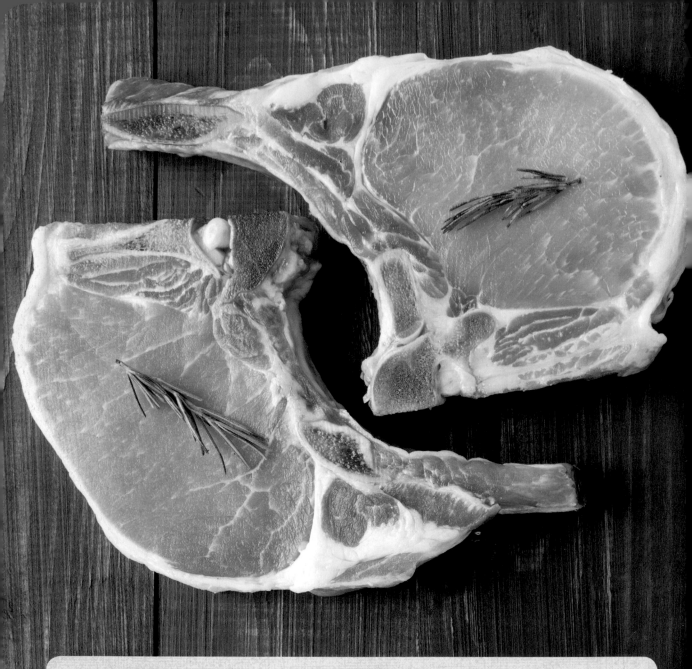

# 093 Shop for Pork

The 21st-century consumer is a bit squeamish about dietary fat. As a result, pork has been bred to become leaner and leaner in recent years—a move that reduces fat and calories, but also lessens flavor. As is the case with most meat, fat marbling is the most important consideration when it comes to flavor. For especially flavor-packed meat, look for heirloom breeds such as Berkshire, Duroc, and Yorkshire—these animals' varied diet yields rich-tasting, tender, and juicy meat. Let your butcher guide you to the most flavorful cuts and producers.

Once the cut is selected, only trim the excess fat surrounding the meat—avoid the inclination to trim any further. In addition to flavor, the fat acts as a natural basting agent to keep the meat moist, especially on leaner cuts such as the loin and tenderloin. Exterior fat on larger cuts, such as the shoulder, can be trimmed slightly but preferably to strips no less than ⅛–¼ inch (3–6 mm) wide.

# 094 Identify Fresh Cuts

Pork comes in a range of rosy hues. The general rule is: The more color, the better the flavor. Pale pork can signal blandness and a susceptibly to dry out when cooked.

Look for even marbling and exterior fat that is perfectly white (never yellow); in addition, the surface of the meat should be springy and moist, not slick or wet. When in doubt, let your nose be your guide—one good sniff should let you know if a particular cut is to be avoided.

# 095 Time It Right

Pork is not a meat to be cooked rare. Fear of trichinosis, caused by a parasite, once dictated that pork be cooked to a very high internal temperature. Food scientists have since ascertained that trichinosis is actually killed at 137°F (63°C), so the widely accepted temperature range for pork

doneness is now 140–150°F (60–65°C), depending on the size and cut. Well-marbled cuts will grill up nice and juicy when cooked slowly to a higher internal temperature, but leaner cuts such as the loin and tenderloin will dry out quickly when cooked over 145°F (63°C).

Still confused about how long to cook it? Here are some approximate cooking times for various cuts and sizes. Check for accuracy with a good meat thermometer.

| CUT | SIZE | GRILL TIME |
|---|---|---|
| CHOP, BONELESS OR BONE-IN | ½ inch (13 mm) thick | 5–7 minutes over direct high heat |
| | ¾ inch (2 cm) thick | 6–8 minutes over direct high heat |
| | 1 inch (2.5 cm) thick | 8–10 minutes over direct medium heat |
| | 1¼–1½ inches (3–4 cm) thick | 10–12 minutes: sear for 6 minutes over high heat, then grill 4–6 minutes over medium-high heat |
| TENDERLOIN | 1 lb (0.5 kg) | 15–20 minutes over direct medium heat |
| LOIN ROAST, BONELESS | 2–3 lb (1–1.4 kg) | 40–50 minutes over indirect medium heat |
| LOIN ROAST, BONE-IN | 3–5 lb (1.4–2.3 kg) | 1¼–1¾ hours over indirect medium heat |
| SHOULDER (BOSTON BUTT), BONELESS | 5–6 lb (2.3–2.7 kg) | 5–7 hours over indirect low heat |
| PATTY (GROUND) | ½ inch (13 mm) thick | 8–10 minutes over direct medium heat |
| HAM, STEAK | ½ inch (13 mm) thick | 8–11 minutes over direct medium heat |
| HAM, BONE-IN, SMOKED OR PRECOOKED | 8–10 lb (3.6–4.5 kg) | 1¼–2 hours over indirect low heat until internal temperature reaches 135°F |
| HAM, BONELESS, SMOKED OR PRECOOKED | 3–5 lb (1.4–2.3 kg) | 1¼–1½ hours (15–18 minutes per pound) over indirect low heat until internal temperature reaches 135°F |
| RIBS, BABY BACK | 1½–2 lb (0.7–1 kg) | 3–4 hours over indirect low heat |
| RIBS, SPARERIBS | 2½–3½ lb (1.1–1.6 kg) | 3–4 hours over indirect low heat |
| RIBS, COUNTRY-STYLE, BONELESS | 1½–2 lb (0.7–1 kg) | 12–15 minutes over direct medium heat |
| RIBS, COUNTRY-STYLE, BONE-IN | 3–4 lb (1.4–1.8 kg) | 1½–2 hours over indirect medium heat |
| BRATWURST, FRESH | Any | 20–25 minutes over direct medium heat |

# 096 Choose Your Cut

Pigs are usually butchered into four large sections, then into smaller cuts for cooking. Knowing your cuts is not too difficult a task, but understanding which are suitable for the grill can be something of a puzzle. As with other animals, the muscles of the pig that work the hardest—the shoulder and the rear legs (ham)—produce tougher meat, which benefits from low and slow cooking (such as smoking or indirect-heat grilling). The more sedentary parts of the animal, like the belly and loin, are more tender, highly marbled, and can be cooked over higher and more direct heat. Dense fat in some cuts means they'll need some careful tending on the grill; as always, move the meat to cooler parts of the rack when flare-ups occur.

## SHOULDER
**Blade steak, Boston butt roast, picnic shoulder roast**

The rich marbling in shoulder cuts give the meat a deep, rich flavor and makes it more forgiving when cooked. Shoulder cuts contain a relatively high proportion of collagen, or connective tissue. This has the potential to make the meat tough, but with long cooking over low heat, the collagen melts and the resulting meat is tasty and tender. On the grill, shoulder cuts require some patience—they're best when slow-smoked or grill-roasted over indirect heat for a period of hours.

## LOIN
**Rib chop, loin chop, sirloin chop, pork loin roast, crown roast, rack of pork, pork tenderloin, baby back rib, country-style rib**

The loin is where you'll find the best cuts for the grill. The many cuts from the rib section (see item 104) are tops when it comes to barbecue classics, and pork chops—especially leaner center-cut and loin end chops with their T-shaped bones—are other favorites. The lean meat can stand up well to the grill's direct heat. Blade chops cut from the shoulder end carry a bit more marbling and benefit from low, indirect-heat cooking, making them less ideal for the grill. And a loin roast can be spectacular with grill cooking: brine first, then smoke or cook over indirect heat.

## HAM/LEG
**Ham steak, whole ham, shank**

When cooking for a crowd, nothing beats a meaty ham, cured and then smoked. Smoking low and slow is the best option, though thick ham steaks can be grilled over direct heat (glaze them toward the end of cooking time for the finishing touch). Shanks contain lots of collagen and are most often cured and/or smoked.

## BELLY
**Spareribs, belly, bacon**

In the restaurant world, everybody's talking about pork belly. This once-underutilized cut now seems to be on every menu. Many people don't realize that they have long been eating cured pork belly in the form of bacon. With this cut, the fat and skin are as important as the meat. Boneless belly with skin on is tender and delicious when cooked over hybrid heat on the grill—first indirect to render the fat, then direct to crisp the skin. Bone-in belly (with or without the skin) needs slow cooking and is trickier to grill. Spareribs from the belly are both more boney and more fatty than back ribs, and they grill best wrapped in foil over low, indirect heat, or baked and then grilled for a delectable, smoky flavor.

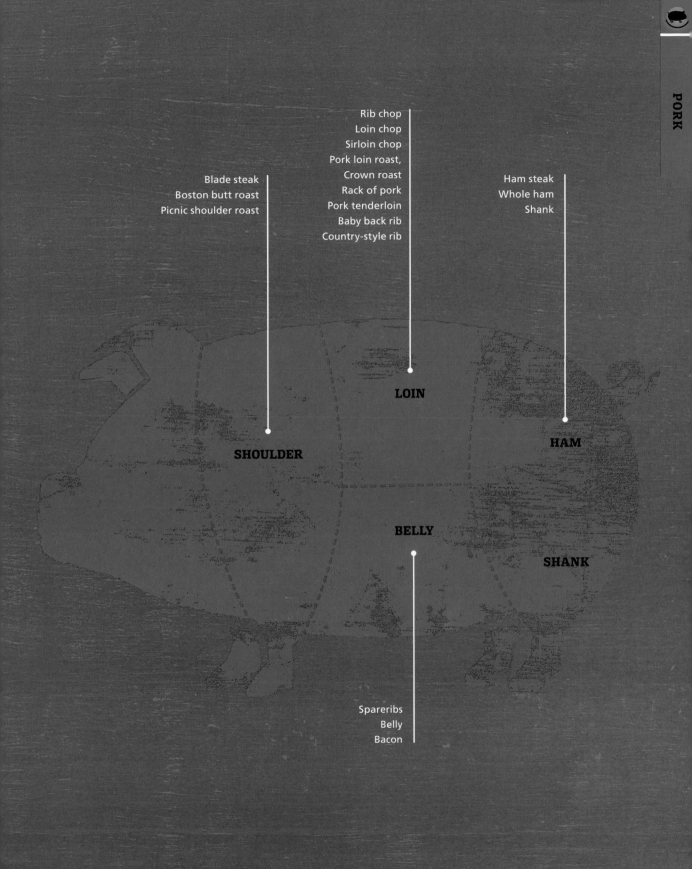

Blade steak
Boston butt roast
Picnic shoulder roast

Rib chop
Loin chop
Sirloin chop
Pork loin roast,
Crown roast
Rack of pork
Pork tenderloin
Baby back rib
Country-style rib

Ham steak
Whole ham
Shank

**LOIN**

**SHOULDER**

**HAM**

**BELLY**

**SHANK**

Spareribs
Belly
Bacon

# 097 Partner Up Pork

There's something quite sad about a plain old pork chop or a perfectly grilled piece of juicy pork tenderloin going solo on the plate. It's not that the meat isn't delicious on its own—but pork is better when it has a partner. And it's not choosy, either. Pork's mild, gamey taste has a natural affinity for cooked fruits and chutneys, and it's equally at home with the tang of pickles or as a mellow foil for a hefty spice. When contemplating the right partner (whether for chop or loin or sausage), stick with sides that mirror pork's unique brand of savory and sweet. It would be hard to go wrong with these tried-and-true companions to the porcine plate.

# 099 Grilled Apple Purée

- ¼ cup (4 oz/125 g) unsalted butter
- 1 cup (7 oz/220 g) firmly packed light brown sugar
- ½ teaspoon ground cinnamon
- ¼ teaspoon *each* ground nutmeg, allspice, cardamom, and cloves
- 2 lb (1 kg) tart apples, such as Granny Smith, Gala, or Gravenstein
- 2 tablespoons Calvados or other brandy

Melt butter in a large saucepan over medium-high heat. Stir in sugar and spices. Reduce heat to medium-low and stir until fragrant and sugar is melted, 5–7 minutes. Add apples and Calvados, toss to coat, then grill apples over direct heat, turning often, until caramelized and soft, 10–12 minutes. Let cool slightly, then place in bowl and mash with a fork (or purée in food processor) until the mixture is a chunky consistency. Serve.

# 098 Smoky Baked Beans with Bacon

- 1 lb (500 g) thick-sliced applewood-smoked bacon
- 2 large cans (each 32 oz/1 kg) Great Northern, navy, or cannellini beans
- 1 can (15 oz/470 g) *each* black beans and kidney beans
- 1 yellow onion, finely chopped
- ½ cup (4 fl oz/125 ml) barbecue sauce (see item 251)
- ½ cup (5½ oz/170 g) dark maple syrup
- ½ cup (5 oz/155 g) firmly packed dark brown sugar
- 3 tablespoons prepared yellow mustard
- 1 teaspoon dry mustard
- Kosher salt and freshly ground black pepper

Preheat oven to 350°F (180°C). In a large frying pan over medium heat, fry half the bacon until crisp, about 5 minutes. Transfer bacon to paper towels to drain and cool, then crumble. Reserve crumbled bacon and bacon drippings separately.

Drain and rinse beans. In a 9x13-inch (23x33-cm) baking dish with at least 3-inch (7.5-cm) sides, stir together beans, onion, barbecue sauce, maple syrup, brown sugar, both mustards, and crumbled bacon. Lay the uncooked bacon slices in a single layer over top of mixture and cover dish with aluminum foil.

Bake for 45 minutes. Uncover and continue to bake until thickened, about 1 hour more. Remove from oven, season with salt and pepper, and serve hot or at room temperature. The beans taste best when baked a day in advance, cooled, covered, refrigerated, and then reheated in the oven.

# 100 Pear Chutney

- 3 large, firm pears, such as Bartlett, Bosc, or Comice, peeled, quartered, cored, and coarsely chopped
- 1½ tablespoons white wine vinegar
- ⅔ cup (5 oz/155 g) firmly packed golden brown sugar
- 1¼ tablespoons peeled and minced fresh ginger

In a small saucepan over low heat, combine pears and vinegar. Cook, stirring frequently to prevent scorching, until pears begin to break down, about 15 minutes. Remove from heat and add brown sugar, stirring until dissolved. Add ginger and return to low heat. Cook, stirring almost constantly, until dark brown and very thick, about 10 minutes. Let cool, then cover and refrigerate. The chutney will keep for up to five days.

# 101 Spicy Tomato Jam

In a saucepan over medium heat, warm the oil. Add garlic and cook, stirring, for about a minute. Add tomatoes and cook, stirring, for 3 minutes. Stir in thyme, broth, Worcestershire sauce, and red pepper flakes. Simmer until the tomatoes have cooked down, about 15 minutes, then season with salt and pepper. Remove from heat and let cool (discard thyme sprig). Use at once, or cover and refrigerate for up to four days. Serve at room temperature.

- 1 tablespoon canola oil
- 1 clove garlic, finely chopped
- 2 large tomatoes, peeled, seeded, and coarsely chopped
- 1 fresh thyme sprig
- ½ cup (4 fl oz/125 ml) reduced-sodium chicken broth
- ½ teaspoon Worcestershire sauce
- ⅛ teaspoon red pepper flakes
- Kosher salt and freshly ground black pepper

# 102 Pickled Red Onions

- 1 cup (8 fl oz/250 ml) red wine vinegar
- 1 cup (8 fl oz/250 ml) dry red wine
- ½ cup (4 oz/125 g) sugar
- 1 tablespoon yellow mustard seeds
- 2 tablespoons black peppercorns
- 2 teaspoons red pepper flakes
- Kosher salt
- 2 small or 1 large red onion, cut crosswise into rings ¼ inch (2 cm) thick

In a saucepan over low heat, combine vinegar, wine, sugar, mustard seeds, peppercorns, red pepper flakes, and 2 tablespoons salt. Stir until sugar and salt have dissolved. Add onion rings and bring to a boil over high heat. Reduce heat to medium-low and simmer about 5 minutes. Let cool before serving.

# 103 Perfect Barbecued Ribs

Take into consideration that most of the flavor and tenderness in any meaty dish comes from the bone, and you know why truly great grilled ribs are a carnivore's dream come true. Learning to cook them with perfection, whether the ribs come from the belly or the loin, is a must for any meat-eating grill maestro.

- 8 lb (4 kg) baby back pork ribs or 4 lb (2 kg) St. Louis–style spareribs (see item 104)
- Spice rub of your choice
- 3 cups of your favorite BBQ sauce (see item 251)

**PREP** Preheat oven to 300°F (149°C). Peel off membrane that covers bony side of ribs.

**BAKE** Apply rub to all sides of racks. Lay each rack on a large piece of heavy-duty aluminum foil, shiny side out and meat side down. Crimp foil edges together to seal. Place racks in a single layer on rimmed baking sheets and bake 2–2½ hours for baby backs and about 3 hours for spareribs, or until meat is just barely starting to shrink away from bone ends. Remove from oven and let cool.

**GRILL** Prepare charcoal or gas grill for medium heat. Grill ribs, basting with sauce and turning frequently, until lacquered, charred in places, and heated through, 7–10 minutes.

**SERVE** Transfer to a cutting board and cut between the ribs to separate them. Mound ribs on a platter, drizzle with more sauce, and serve.

# 104
## Know Your Ribs

Pork ribs are virtually synonymous with barbecue, and grilling up a juicy, tasty slab starts with choosing the right cut. Here are the most popular.

**SPARERIBS** What's left over once the meat has been cut from the belly is known as spareribs. Look for large slabs with a thick layer of meat and a little bit of fat. A full, 11- to 14-rib slab should be in the 3-lb (1.4-kg) range and feed about three people. St. Louis–style spareribs are what you get when you trim the breastbones from the ribs; their squared-off size cooks better on the grill. A 2-lb (1-kg) rack feeds about two people.

**BABY BACK RIBS** This tender cut is trimmed from the rib section of the pork loin when the butcher cuts boneless pork loin roast or chops. Since they come from the loin, they're much more tender and dainty than spareribs and cook in about half the time—even less if you cook them quickly over direct heat. Look for lean racks of ribs with plenty of meat, the heavier the better.

**COUNTRY-STYLE RIBS** The meatiest cut, country-style ribs are butterflied or split chops from the shoulder end of the loin. Whether cut from the blade end of the pork loin or from the Boston butt, they're tender enough to marinate and cook over direct heat just like pork chops, or they can be cooked low and slow over indirect heat like spareribs. Bone-in or boneless, they're nice and meaty, inexpensive, and easy—in short, country-style ribs are the bomb.

# 105
## Smoke 'Em If You Want To

Babying your ribs to perfectly smoked perfection is the holy grail for some grill masters and just a lot of hot air for others. To smoke ribs, follow this simple strategy: First, coat your ribs with a spice rub as you would for direct-heat grilling. Set the spice-rubbed ribs aside while you soak a mixture of hickory and fruitwood chips in water for 30 minutes. Meanwhile, prepare a medium-low fire in a charcoal or gas grill.

**CHARCOAL GRILL** Push coals to sides and place a drip pan half full of water in the center of the fire bed. Sprinkle soaked wood chips over coals. Place ribs on the grill rack over a drip pan.

**GAS GRILL** Place a shallow pan half full of water at the edge of the grill rack. Add wood chips to the grill in a smoker box or perforated foil

packet. Place ribs on the grill rack away from heat elements.

Cover the grill and smoke ribs, turning them every 30 minutes or so and adding more wood chips, more coals (to charcoal grill), and more water to the drip pan as needed, until the ribs are fork-tender, 2½–3 hours.

# 106
## Judge When They're Done

Some misguided grill cooks believe that the ribs are done when the meat begins to pull a full inch (2.5 cm) or so away from the bones. Wrong! On the competitive grill circuit, ribs that look like that are called "shiners" because they are overcooked and dried out. It's okay if a little bone is showing, of course, but the best way to see if your rib rack is ready is to grab the long side of the rack with tongs—if it bends without resistance, they're done!

# 107 Learn Your Chop Strategy

Pork chops are right up there with baby back ribs and fat-rimmed rib-eye steaks on the list of tricky meats to cook up on a grill. The intact bone can make for something of a headache when it comes to grilling evenly, and the chop's super-lean meat and lack of fat means that it can get tough, rubbery, and flavorless unless it's done just right. Follow these simple steps to get killer pork chops, every time.

**CHOOSE THE RIGHT CHOPS** Cut selection is key to the success of a grilled pork chop. You'll have your choice of many cuts along the loin: the blade chops at the front shoulders, the rib chops, and the loin chops. The muscular blade chops can be tough and chewy with anything other than low and slow cooking. The loin chops contain both loin and tenderloin, which cook at different speeds and temperatures, creating their own set of culinary challenges. The rib chops, from the center of the loin, are your best bet. They're mainly loin meat, which has enough fat to stand up to the heat of the grill and is the most flavorful. Request the center-cut rib chops, as they will have the greatest portion of loin meat.

**SIZE WISELY** Deciding on cut is only half the battle, because in the world of pork chops, size matters. If your chops are too thin, the meat can become tough; too thick, and cooking evenly can be a challenge. Look for chops about 1½ inches (3.8 cm) thick. It's a good size for a two-zone hybrid cooking approach.

**BRINE WITH SALT & FLAVOR** A salt-and-sugar-infused brine works over the proteins in meat so that they retain moisture better when cooking. A good 1-hour soak will infuse chops with added flavor from salt and seasonings and prevent them from drying out if they're cooked a bit too long. Make sure to pat the brined chops dry with paper towels before setting them on the grill; a wet chop will steam instead of sear.

**SET UP A HYBRID GRILL** Make the most of a grill's unique capability to both sear and roast. Set up your grill for cooking over indirect heat (see items 006, 035). Sear the chops directly over high heat first, then move them to indirect heat for longer cooking. The sear will give you a flavorful, caramelized crust, and the long, low-heat cooking will deliver delicious, juicy meat.

**PAIR IT WELL** Even with two-zone cooking, pork chops cook in a flash—leaving the grill empty and perfectly primed for grilling up any range of flavorful accompaniments. Though delicious on its own, pork can be wonderfully accepting of flavor enhancers—fruit is the surprising and undeniable favorite. Wedges of fresh stone fruit, brushed with olive oil and grilled atop the caramelized meat juices left on the grate, provides an easy final touch that will make your finished chops all the more memorable. The pairing of fruit and meat not on your hit parade? Try any combination of our suggested sides (see items 231–246) or savor your brined, well-seasoned, and perfectly grilled chop on its own.

# 108

## Best Grilled Pork Chops

**BRINE** In a large nonreactive bowl or zip-top plastic bag, mix all brine ingredients with 6 cups (48 fl oz/ 1.5 l) water. Stir until sugar and salt dissolve. Add pork chops and turn to coat. Cover or seal bag and refrigerate at least 8 hours or up to one day.

**PREP** Remove chops from refrigerator at least 30 minutes before grilling. Discard brine, rinse chops briefly in cold water, and pat dry with paper towels.

**PREHEAT** Prepare a charcoal or gas grill for indirect grilling over medium heat; grill temperature should be 350–375°F (180–190°C). If using charcoal, bank lit coals on either side of the grill bed, leaving a strip down the center without heat, then place drip pan in center. If using gas, preheat burners, then turn off one or more burners to create a cooler zone. Brush and oil grill grate.

**GRILL** Place pork chops on the grill over direct heat and sear, turning once, until nicely charred on both sides, 2–3 minutes per side. Move chops to indirect-heat area, cover the grill, and cook until chops are somewhat firm to the touch, about 15 minutes for medium, or until an instant-read thermometer (inserted horizontally into the center of the chop and away from bone) registers 140°F (60°C). Transfer chops to a platter and let rest 10 minutes. Meanwhile, brush stone fruit with olive oil and place on the grill. Cook, turning as needed, until evenly browned and softened, 3–4 minutes.

**SERVE** Place chops on serving plates and serve fruit alongside.

Serves 6.

### FOR THE BRINE

- ¼ cup (2 fl oz/60 ml) *each* cider vinegar and firmly packed brown sugar
- 2 tablespoons kosher salt
- 1 tablespoon freshly ground black pepper
- 1 teaspoon *each* dried thyme and juniper berries
- ⅛ teaspoon red pepper flakes

### FOR THE CHOPS

- 6 bone-in pork chops, each about 1½ inch (3.8 cm) thick
- 2 apples, pears, or stone fruits (such as peaches, plums, nectarines), cored or pitted and cut into wedges
- 1 teaspoon olive oil

# 109 Maple-Brined Pork Chops

Searing heat makes the most of a heavy infusion of maple syrup in this brine, lending the chops a sweet and caramelized crust on the grill. Finish the chops over indirect heat to prevent overbrowning. Chops this good need just the right enhancement: A gingery pear chutney (see item 100) is about as good as it gets.

- ⅔ cup (5½ oz/170 g) kosher salt
- ½ cup (5½ oz/170 g) maple syrup
- 2 bay leaves, crumbled
- 2 tablespoons peppercorns
- 6 bone-in pork loin chops, each about ½ lb (250 g) and ¾ inch (2 cm) thick
- Freshly ground black pepper

**BRINE** In a tall, narrow, nonreactive container (that will fit in your refrigerator later), mix salt, maple syrup, bay leaves, and peppercorns with 2½ qt (2.5 l) cold water. Stir until salt dissolves. Submerge chops in brine. Refrigerate for at least 6 hours or up to one day.

**PREP** Remove chops from refrigerator at least 30 minutes before grilling. Discard brine, rinse chops briefly in cold water, and pat dry with paper towels. Let stand on a rack to dry further, about 10 minutes.

**PREHEAT** Prepare a charcoal or gas grill for indirect grilling over medium heat; grill temperature should be 350–375°F (180–190°C). If using charcoal, bank lit coals on either side of grill bed, leaving a strip down the center without heat, then place a drip pan in the center. If using gas, preheat burners, then turn off one or more burners to create a cooler zone. Brush and oil grill grate.

**GRILL** Place pork chops on the grill over direct heat and sear, turning once, until nicely charred on both sides, 2–3 minutes per side. Move chops to indirect-heat area, cover the grill, and cook until chops are somewhat firm to the touch, 10–15 minutes for medium (depending on size of chop), or until an instant-read thermometer registers 140°F (60°C). Transfer chops to a platter and let rest 10 minutes.

**SERVE** Arrange the chops on plates and serve at once.

Serves 6.

Thick-cut chops sport an ample and tasty tenderloin that's prime for stuffing. Nicely configured with a bone (or bones) along one side, you can pack in the stuffing with ease, adding loads of extra flavor during cooking. This recipe packs a double punch of smoky flavor with sweet *piquillo* peppers and chorizo sausage. Fat rendered from the sausage is incorporated into the mix, acting as an internal basting agent to keep the chops moist on the grill. Can't find piquillo peppers? No worries! Use a roasted and peeled red bell pepper and ¼ teaspoon smoked paprika instead.

- ¼ cup (2 oz/60 g) *each* kosher salt and firmly packed dark brown sugar
- 1 tablespoon molasses
- 6–8 ice cubes
- 4 thick-cut pork rib chops, each 10–12 oz (315–375 g) and 1½ inches (4 cm) thick
- ¼ lb (125 g) fresh chorizo sausage, casing removed
- 3 green (spring) onions, white and light green parts, finely chopped
- 3 roasted piquillo peppers, from a jar, drained, patted dry, and finely chopped
- 1 teaspoon minced fresh thyme or rosemary
- Olive oil for brushing
- Freshly ground black pepper

**BRINE** In a large nonreactive bowl or zip-top plastic bag, combine salt, sugar, and molasses with 3½ cups (28 fl oz/875 ml) water. Stir until salt and sugar dissolve, then add ice cubes. Add pork chops and turn to coat. Refrigerate 4–6 hours.

**PREP** Remove chops from refrigerator at least 30 minutes before grilling. Discard brine, rinse chops briefly in cold water, and pat dry with paper towels. In a frying pan over medium heat, cook chorizo until crumbly, about 6 minutes. Stir in green onions and cook for 1 minute more. Remove from heat and stir in peppers and thyme. Let cool. Finely chop chorizo mixture or pulse in a food processor.

**PREHEAT** Prepare a charcoal or gas grill for indirect grilling over medium heat; grill temperature should be 350–375°F (180–190°C). If using charcoal, bank lit coals on either side of grill bed, leaving a strip down the center without heat, then place a drip pan in the center. If using gas, preheat burners, then turn off one or more burners to create a cooler zone. Brush and oil grill grate.

**STUFF** Working with one chop at a time, make a horizontal cut along the meaty side, pointing toward the bone, to form a pocket. Loosely stuff with the chorizo mixture and secure the edges with two toothpicks. Brush chops lightly with oil, and season both sides generously with pepper.

**GRILL** Place pork chops on the grill over direct heat and sear, turning once, until nicely charred on both sides, 2–3 minutes per side. Move chops to indirect-heat area, cover the grill, and cook until chops are somewhat firm to the touch or until an instant-read thermometer registers 140°F (60°C). Transfer to a platter, tent loosely with aluminum foil, and let rest 3–4 minutes.

**SERVE** Remove toothpicks and serve at once.

Makes 4 servings.

# 111 Inject Flavor

Tool-obsessed grill masters swear by the oversize syringes used to inject liquids, filling them with extra brine or marinade to deliver added flavor and tenderness to pork on the grill. Low-salt brines work best—to keep cured flavor to a minimum—but you can also try fruit juices. To use, inject meat at 2-inch (5-cm) intervals before cooking, using about 1 oz (28 g) liquid per pound of meat. Let the meat stand for as long as you would marinate it, then grill as usual.

PORK

# 112 El Cubano Perfecto

If you're of the mind that it takes some time to truly perfect a dish, then the Cuban sandwich, popularly known as *el cubano*, should be flawless by now. The venerable pork and melted cheese sandwich has been a mealtime favorite in Cuba since the 1500s, traveling to Florida shores during the first part of the 19th century, when Cuban immigrants manned the many cigar factories in the area. Cuban sandwiches traditionally call for slow-roasted pork shoulder, but a smoked pork loin cooks more quickly and makes a sandwich that's especially tasty. For even more flavor, the loin in this recipe is injected with a citrus infusion that adds both a sweet tang and a certain amount of tenderness to the meat. This updated version ditches the classic *plancha*, or sandwich press, in favor of a heavy hand and a long spatula on *la parilla* (grill).

- ¼ cup (2 fl oz/60 ml) each fresh orange juice and fresh lime juice, combined
- 1 boneless pork loin roast, about 3 lb (1½ kg)
- 5 cloves garlic, finely chopped
- 1 teaspoon cumin, crushed
- 1 teaspoon dried oregano
- Kosher salt and freshly ground black pepper
- About 8 cups (720 g) wood chips (see item 114), soaked in water for 30 minutes
- 8 hoagie or soft French rolls, split
- Yellow mustard for spreading
- ½ lb (250 g) ham, thinly sliced
- Dill pickle chips for serving
- ½ lb (250 g) provolone or Swiss cheese, sliced

**MARINATE** Load a marinade injector with the orange and lime juice mixture, and inject into pork in several places. In a small bowl, stir together garlic, cumin, oregano, 1½ teaspoons salt, and ½ teaspoon pepper. Rub mixture evenly over pork. Place loin in a large zip-top plastic bag, seal the bag closed, and refrigerate for 24 hours.

**PREHEAT** Remove roast from refrigerator at least 30 minutes before grilling. Prepare a charcoal or gas grill for smoking over medium heat; the grill temperature should be 350–375°F (180–190°C). If using charcoal, bank lit coals on either side of the grill bed, leaving a strip in the center without heat. Place a drip pan in the center and fill pan with water. Add half of the wood chips to the fire just before grilling. If using gas, fill the smoker box with wood chips, then preheat grill. Turn off one or more burners to create a cooler zone. Brush and oil grill grate.

**GRILL** Place pork on the grill over direct heat and sear, turning as needed, until nicely browned on all sides, about 10 minutes. Move roast to indirect-heat area, cover, and cook for about 1 hour, or until a thermometer registers 145°F (63°C), adding remaining wood chips after about 30 minutes.

**TOAST** Transfer pork to a cutting board, tent with aluminum foil, and let rest about 10 minutes. If using a charcoal grill, spread coals evenly over the fire bed. If using a gas grill, turn the burners to high. Coat cut sides of rolls with mustard. Evenly divide ham among rolls and top with a few pickles. Thinly slice pork and place over pickles. (You will have leftover pork; it will keep in the refrigerator for a week.) Top with the cheese slices. Place sandwiches on the grill over direct heat. Using a long spatula, press down on each sandwich until cheese melts, 2–3 minutes.

Makes 8 servings.

# 113 Quick Pickles

This no-frills homemade refrigerator pickle is an easy process. In a large bowl, combine 2 cups (16 fl oz/50 ml) water, 1¾ cups (14 fl oz/415 ml) white vinegar, 1½ cups (12 oz/350 g) chopped fresh dill weed, ½ cup (4 oz/125 g) granulated sugar, 8 chopped garlic cloves, 1½ tablespoons coarse salt, 1 tablespoon pickling spice, and 1½ teaspoons dill seed. Stir, then let stand 2 hours. Transfer 12 pickling cucumbers to jars and cover with liquid, place a piece of dried chile pepper and a sprig of dill into each jar, and seal. Refrigerate for 10 days, then eat; they'll keep for a month.

# 114 Select a Smoking Wood

Pork is a favorite for the smoker because its mildness adapts well to even the most subtle flavor nuances. Fruit woods like cherry, apple, and peach can impart a delicate sweetness, while hickory and oak lend a slightly more intense smokiness and a rich mahogany color. The ultimate smoking wood mix for pork is a combination of the two, contributing both complex flavor and color to the meat.

# 115 Carolina-Style Pulled Pork Sandwich

Southerners love to brag about their pulled pork. And it's no wonder! Injected with doctored apple cider and smoked all day over a hardwood fire, the hard-working pork shoulder becomes meltingly tender and can boast out-of-this-world flavor. Charcoal smoking can make for an extra dose of smoky flavor, so some pork masters prefer finishing it in the oven when charcoal is the exclusive smoke source. Have plenty of wood chips on hand—applewood lends a mellow flavor, or throw in some hickory for an extra hit of smokiness and rich color.

- 1 bone-in pork shoulder, 4–5 lb (2–2½ kg)
- ¾ cup (6 fl oz/180 ml) apple cider
- ½ cup (4 oz/125 g) sugar
- ¼ cup (2 oz/60 g) kosher salt, plus salt as needed
- 2 tablespoons Worcestershire sauce
- 1 tablespoon hot-pepper sauce
- Freshly ground black pepper
- 5 lb (2½ kg) applewood or hickory chips, or a mixture, soaked in water for 30 minutes
- BBQ sauce (see item 251) for serving
- 12 soft hamburger buns

**MARINATE** Remove pork from the fridge an hour ahead of time. Combine apple cider, sugar, salt, Worcestershire, and pepper sauce with ½ cup (4 fl oz/125 ml) warm water in a jar. Cover and shake until dissolved. Inject into the pork in several places; season well.

**PREHEAT** Prepare a smoker or grill for smoking over low heat; the temperature should be 200–250°F (95–120°C). If using charcoal, bank lit coals on either side of the grill bed, leaving a strip without heat. Place a drip pan in the center and fill with water. Add half of the wood chips to the fire just before grilling. If using gas, fill the smoker box with wood chips, then preheat. Turn off one or more burners to create a cooler zone. Brush and oil grill grate.

**SMOKE** Place pork over indirect-heat area of grill, cover, and smoke about 4 hours, adding more wood chips and more coals as needed if using charcoal. After 4 hours, remove pork and double wrap in aluminum foil; return to the grill and smoke slowly for an additional 6 hours. If smoking over charcoal, transfer to roasting pan and finish cooking in a 250°F (120°C) oven for 6 hours. When you can slide out the bone with a pair of tongs, it's ready.

**SERVE** Transfer pork to a board and let cool 30 minutes. Remove any fat cap; use two forks to pull and shred meat. Add about ½ cup (4 fl oz/125 ml) BBQ sauce and toss to blend. Divide meat on buns and serve.

Makes 12 servings.

# 116 Put on a Pig Pickin'

In the South, you might say "barbecue," but what you mean is "party!" And no wonder. Historically, the traditional southern barbecue is at the very least a daylong affair. It begins in the morning with the digging of a large pit that is filled with hardwood. The wood is burned down to smoldering embers before whole hogs, skewered on poles, are hung over the fire. Pit masters sit up through the day and night, turning the hog on its spit. The carving takes place after the guests arrive. The crisp skin is removed and the cooked meat is pulled in lumps from the carcass before being slathered with a favorite finishing sauce. That's why, to this very day, a social affair centered around pork barbecue is affectionately called a Pig Pickin'.

# 117 Grilled Beer Brats

Though a cruise down the refrigerated meat section nowadays might turn up a half dozen artisanal sausages, there was a time when bratwurst was considered the gourmet option in place of a regular hot dog. The plump, handmade pork sausages were first popularized in America by German immigrants residing in Wisconsin during the 1920s. They originated the famed "beer brat" recipe, a regional favorite in which the sausages are poached in beer and onions before being grilled over charcoal.

- 6 cans (12 fl oz/375 ml each) lager-style beer
- 8 fresh bratwurst (about 2 lb/1 kg)
- 2 large yellow onions, coarsely chopped
- 3 green bell peppers, halved lengthwise and seeded
- 3 red onions, thickly sliced into rings
- Canola oil for drizzling
- 8 hoagie or sub rolls, split
- Whole-grain mustard for spreading
- Sauerkraut for serving (optional)

**POACH** In a large pot over high heat, combine beer, sausages, and yellow onions, and bring to a boil. Reduce heat to medium and simmer gently about 30 minutes. The brats can sit in this mixture, off the heat, for up to 2 hours.

**PREHEAT** Prepare a charcoal or gas grill for indirect-heat grilling over medium heat; the temperature inside the grill should be 350–375°F (180–190°C). If using charcoal, bank the lit coals on either side (or on one side) of the grill bed, and place a drip pan in the area without coals. If using gas, preheat burners, then turn off one or more burners to create a cooler zone. Brush and oil grill grate.

**GRILL** Remove brats from beer bath, and discard liquid. Drizzle peppers and red onions with a little oil. Place the brats, bell peppers, and red onions on the grill over direct heat and sear, turning occasionally, until nicely charred, about 2 minutes. Move brats, peppers, and onions to indirect-heat area and cook, turning frequently, until nicely browned, and when vegetables are tender but not wilted (about 15 minutes). During the last minute of cooking, place rolls, cut side down, along the edge of the grill and grill 1–2 minutes until toasted.

**SERVE** Transfer brats to a large platter and set rolls to one side. On a cutting board, coarsely chop red onions and peppers. Spread cut sides of the rolls with the mustard. Place a brat in each roll and cover with onion-pepper mixture. Spoon some sauerkraut on top, if desired. Serve at once.

Makes 8 servings.

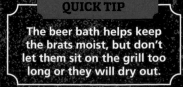

**QUICK TIP**

The beer bath helps keep the brats moist, but don't let them sit on the grill too long or they will dry out.

# 118 Spiral Cut a Dog

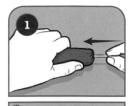

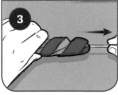

Plain grilled sausage a bit blasé? Wield your paring knife with ingenuity to devise a corkscrew cut that grills up nice and crispy. Here's how you do it:

**STEP 1** Poke a skewer down the center length of your sausage.

**STEP 2** Place the skewered sausage on a cutting board. Begin cutting on the diagonal at the end of the sausage while rolling the sausage away from you (and stopping at the skewer) so that the entire length of the sausage is cut.

**STEP 3** Remove skewer to reveal the spiral.

# 119 Choose Your Toppings

Once you've mastered the ultimate sausage grilling technique, toppings and add-ins become the crowning glory to your consummate creation. Here are a few you might try:

Sauerkraut (of course), grilled peppers and onions (second best), relish, chiles, cheese, avocado, tomato, grilled stone fruit, grilled pineapple, grilled apples and pears, corn chips and potato chips, chili, barbecue, vinaigrette, thousand island dressing, ranch dressing, sriracha, French onion dip, chipotle mayonnaise, cilantro, basil, mint, parsley

# 120 Cook Sausages Just Right

Sausages are king among many grilling favorites. Quick to cook, a snap to purchase, easy on the pocketbook—they have lots of attributes that make them universally popular. Problem is, not everyone knows how to cook them just right.

**HIGH HEAT** Grill them over too high a heat and you get a "burster." The sausage casing contracts too quickly over the intense heat, cracking and bursting open to unleash a torrent of fat and juices that cause flare-ups—and lend the sausage a sooty, burned, and dry character with an undercooked center.

**LOW HEAT** Grill them over too low a heat and you get a "wrinkler." The sausage interior plumps up over low and slow cooking but contracts once it's removed from the fire. Since the skin hasn't become firm and brown with heat, it shrivels with the contraction and is sadly lacking in any of the wonderful caramelized flavor we all look for in nicely browned sausages.

**JUST RIGHT** The solution is an educated blend of the dual-heat technique. Cook sausages over medium heat until the interior is plump and cooked through, then sear over higher heat to firm up the skin and caramelize the exterior. The interior temperature of a perfectly cooked sausage should be about 150°F. Just don't check the temperature too much; each time you pierce the skin with a meat thermometer, precious juices will leak out, causing flare-ups and increased dryness in the meat.

# 121 Coffee-Rubbed Pork Roast

Ground coffee is an unexpected, but not unheard of, ingredient to spark up the flavor of smoked meat. The coffee flavor is subtle, but the ground beans add an earthy quality to an already complex mix of flavors. Here, coffee does double duty: as a rub (which has an added hit from cocoa powder and raw sugar) and in a spice-spiked sauce.

- 1 tablespoon freshly ground dark-roast coffee
- 1 teaspoon each instant espresso powder, unsweetened cocoa powder, and demerara or turbinado sugar
- Kosher salt and freshly ground black pepper
- 1 boneless pork loin roast, about 2½ lb (1¼ kg)
- Coffee BBQ Sauce (see item 122) for serving

**SEASON** In a lidded jar or container, mix coffee, espresso powder, cocoa powder, sugar, 1 teaspoon salt, and 1 teaspoon pepper. Cover tightly and shake. Rub pork all over with seasoning mix and let stand at room temperature at least 30 minutes.

**PREHEAT** Prepare a charcoal or gas grill for indirect grilling over medium heat; the temperature inside the grill should be 350–375°F (180–190°C). If using charcoal, bank lit coals on either side of the grill bed, leaving a strip in the center without heat, and place a drip pan in the center strip. If using gas, preheat burners, then turn off one or more to create a cooler zone. Brush and oil grill grate.

**GRILL** Place pork loin on grill over indirect-heat area and cook 1–1¼ hours for medium, or until an instant-read thermometer inserted into the thickest part of the roast registers 145°F (63°C).

**REST** Transfer pork to a cutting board, tent with aluminum foil, and let rest 15 minutes. Meanwhile, warm sauce on stove.

**SERVE** Slice pork, arrange on a platter, and serve with sauce on the side.

Serves 6–8.

> **QUICK TIP**
> Always let pork loin rest for a solid 15 minutes before slicing it.

# 122 Coffee BBQ Sauce

- ¼ cup (2 fl oz/60 ml) canola oil
- 1 yellow onion, chopped
- 10 cloves garlic, coarsely chopped
- ¾ cup (3 oz/90 g) dark-roast whole coffee beans
- ¼ cup (⅓ oz/10 g) chopped fresh cilantro
- 1 jalapeño chile, seeded and chopped
- 1 teaspoon *each* ground cumin and red pepper flakes
- 1 cup (8 oz/250 g) ketchup
- ¾ cup (6 fl oz/180 ml) red wine vinegar
- ¼ cup (2 oz/60 g) firmly packed dark brown sugar
- 3 cans (each 6 oz/185 g) tomato paste
- 1 tablespoon each kosher salt and freshly ground black pepper

In a saucepan over medium heat, warm oil. Add onion, garlic, coffee, cilantro, chile, cumin, and red pepper flakes, and cook, stirring, 2 minutes. Add ketchup, vinegar, and sugar, and continue to cook, stirring occasionally, until liquid has reduced by one-fourth, about 15 minutes. Add tomato paste, salt, and pepper, and stir. Cover, reduce heat to low, and simmer gently for 1 hour to blend flavors. Remove from heat and strain through a sieve into a bowl. Let cool. Use, or store in an airtight container in the fridge for up to a month.

Makes about 2 cups (16 fl oz/500 ml).

# 123 Garlic-Lime Dipping Sauce

In a bowl, combine sugar and hot water, stirring to dissolve sugar. Add chile, garlic, lime juice, and fish sauce.

**Makes about ¾ cup (6 fl oz/180 ml).**

- ¼ cup each (2 oz/60 g) sugar and hot water
- 1 red Serrano chile, seeded and finely chopped
- 2 cloves garlic, chopped
- ⅓ cup (3 fl oz/80 ml) lime juice
- ¼ cup (2 oz/60 ml) fish sauce

# 124 Rice Stick Noodles with Grilled Pork

The Vietnamese are ace when it comes to creating flavorful and satisfying grilled dishes that are also light and refreshing. This noodle bowl is a case in point. Extra-thin slices of lean pork loin are richly glazed, then grilled to crisply caramelize the cut edges. Served atop a bowl of rice noodles, fresh herbs, and julienned carrot and cucumber, the dish is a study of contrasting flavors and textures.

- 1 lb (500 g) boneless pork loin
- ¼ cup (2 oz/60 g) sugar
- 1 teaspoon lemon juice
- ½ teaspoon freshly ground black pepper
- 2 shallots, finely minced
- 2 tablespoons peanut or corn oil
- 1½ teaspoons *each* soy sauce and fish sauce
- 1 lb (500 g) dried rice stick noodles
- Garlic-Lime Dipping Sauce (see item 123)
- ¼ cup (⅓ oz/10 g) *each* coarsely chopped fresh mint and fresh cilantro
- 1 cup (5 oz/155 g) finely julienned peeled cucumber
- 1 carrot, peeled and finely julienned
- 1 fresh red serrano chile, seeded and finely sliced
- 1 cup (3 oz/90 g) finely shredded red cabbage
- ¼ cup (1 oz/30 g) coarsely chopped roasted peanuts

**FREEZE** Wrap pork in plastic wrap and place in a freezer until partially frozen, about 1 hour.

**MAKE GLAZE** In a small, heavy saucepan over medium heat, mix sugar with ⅓ cup (3 fl oz/80 ml) cold water. Bring to a boil, and boil just until large, deep brown bubbles form, 5–8 minutes. Remove from heat and stir in ¼ cup (2 fl oz/60 ml) hot water. Place over medium-high heat and cook, stirring constantly, until a light syrup forms that coats the back of a spoon, about 3 minutes. Remove from heat, add lemon juice and pepper, and pour into a large bowl. Let cool, then stir in shallots, oil, soy sauce, and fish sauce.

**GLAZE MEAT** Cut partially frozen pork across grain into thick slices, then into strips 1 inch (2.5 cm) wide. Place strips between two sheets of plastic wrap, and use a mallet to pound until flattened. Add to sugar mixture, cover, and refrigerate 20 minutes.

**PREHEAT & PREP** Prepare a medium-hot fire for direct-heat cooking on a grill. Cook rice noodles according to package directions. Drain, rinse with cold running water, and drain again. Set aside. Make dipping sauce and set aside.

**PLATE** Divide 2 tablespoons each of the mint and cilantro among six bowls. Drizzle each with 1 tablespoon dipping sauce. Divide noodles among bowls and top with equal amounts of cucumber, carrot, chile, cabbage, and remaining mint and cilantro. Cover and refrigerate.

**GRILL** Brush and oil the grill rack. Lay pork strips flat on rack, and grill, turning once, until well marked, about 2 minutes per side.

**SERVE** Divide pork strips among bowls. Sprinkle with peanuts, drizzle with remaining dipping sauce, and serve.

Serves 6.

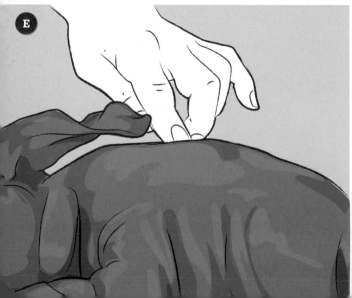

# 125 Roast a Pig on a Spit

Nothing quite establishes your prowess as a pit master more significantly than the successful roasting of a whole pig on a spit. Pit roasting is actually not as difficult as you might imagine and, with the right tools and techniques, can become almost second nature within the space of a few hours. Here's how it's done.

**CHOOSE YOUR PIG (A)** Purchase a quality pig that has been naturally raised with access to pasture. A young pig, 90 pounds (40 kg) or less, will yield the most tender meat. Count on about 1 pound (0.5 kg) dead weight per person, providing about 6 ounces (185 g) meat per serving after all the fat and bones are discarded.

**SET UP YOUR PIT (B)** Other than the pig, the most essential consideration in pig roasting is the spit. You can set up a traditional rotisserie over a backyard pit, but it's much easier to rent a spit with a two-bar electric rotisserie from your butcher. Fuel the spit with plenty of hardwood charcoal briquettes—plan on 1 pound of coals for every 1 pound of pig. Have an extra 25 pounds (11 kg) of the briquettes on hand, and keep the chimney starter consistently fired with extra coals at the ready.

**SKEWER THE PIG (C)** Remove any hair on the pig skin with a razor. (Any of the disposable varieties will do.) Rub kosher salt over the pig, inside and out. Run the skewer through the hole between the pig's butt cheeks (you know the one), along the spine, and out through the mouth. Poke two holes on either side of the spine in the middle of the pig's back. Using heavy-duty wire, poke the wire in one side, around the skewer inside the pig, and out the other side to secure the skewer to the spine. Twist the wire closed. Wire the pig's trotters to the secondary skewer for extra support.

**READY THE FIRE (D)** Using long tongs, spread the coals into an oblong circle, leaving the middle open so that juices seeping from the open belly won't flare on the fire. The coals should be ashy white. Add more lit coals to the fire from the chimney starter every 30 minutes or so to maintain a consistent temperature. Plan on 1¼ hours for every 10 pounds (4.5 kg) of pig. It's definitely a process: Pull up a few lawn chairs, grab some beer, and gather some friends for good conversation. The goal is cooking it low and slow.

**CHECK FOR DONENESS (E)** The pig is done when the skin is golden brown and the meat is tender and separating from the skin. A thermometer inserted into the shoulder, hindquarters, or belly cavity should read 155–160°F (70–90°C). Crispy pig skin is one of the perks of a pit-roasted pig. For the best crunch, fire up the coals to high heat during the last half hour or so of cooking, and move the pig and coals to expose as much of the pig skin to the heat as possible. If all goes well, the skin should bubble and blister, creating a self-fried skin that dissolves in your mouth when you eat it.

**CARVE IT UP (F)** Line a work table with plastic or aluminum foil. Enlist the services of a barbecue buddy to hoist the pig from the spit framework onto the table. Remove the spit rods from the pig, including all the wire used to secure it. Tent the pig with aluminum foil and let sit for 20 minutes to cool and let the juices redistribute. Carve the pig in sections, starting at the cheeks and shoulder and working your way through the ribs and tenderloin to the hindquarters. Serve with the barbecue sauce of your choice!

# 126 Follow the 7-6-5 Formula

When a simply marinated grilled tenderloin is on the evening's menu, the cooking approach is an easy one. Grill masters have devised the ultimate formula for perfectly grilled tenderloin every time: the 7-6-5 method. These numbers refer to the amount of time each side gets on a grill set at high heat: 7 minutes on the first side, 6 minutes on the second side, and then 5 minutes with the grill turned off and the lid closed. The method is so reliable that you can set a timer and go about your business. Even flare-ups aren't a worry; pork tenderloins are lean enough that there's no threat of dripping fat. Check the tenderloin with a thermometer toward the end of cooking time, and remove it from the fire when it clocks in at 140–150°F (60–65°C). It will continue to cook for a few minutes after being removed from the flames, so keep that in mind when you're reading temperature.

# 127 Glazed Pork Tenderloin

Tenderloin, like most cuts of pork, likes a nice mix of savory and sweet. The quick and unexpected combo of mustard and jelly in this recipe makes for a glaze that's sweet with a kick. Moderate heat on the grill is enough to caramelize the finish, making the tenderloin crispy on the outside and tender in the center.

- ½ cup (4 fl oz/125 ml) tamari or reduced-sodium soy sauce
- ¼ cup (2 oz/60 g) firmly packed light brown sugar
- 2 tablespoons dry sherry
- ½ teaspoon *each* granulated garlic and ground cinnamon
- 2 pork tenderloins, each 1½–2 lb (750 g–1 kg), silverskin removed
- 1 jar (10 oz/315 g) red currant jelly
- 2 tablespoons Dijon, English, or other spicy mustard

**MARINATE** In a large zip-top plastic bag, mix tamari, sugar, sherry, garlic, and cinnamon. Add pork, seal bag closed, and squish the marinade around. Refrigerate at least 4 hours—overnight is better.

**PREP** Remove pork from refrigerator at least 30 minutes before grilling. Discard marinade and pat tenderloins dry with paper towels. To make the glaze, heat jelly and mustard in a saucepan over low heat until jelly melts. Do not stir until just before jelly has melted. Set aside at room temperature.

**PREHEAT** Prepare charcoal or gas grill for direct grilling over medium heat. Brush and oil grill grate.

**GRILL** Place tenderloins on the grill directly over the fire and cook until nicely grill-marked, 3–4 minutes. Roll them about one-quarter turn, brush the cooked side with glaze, and cook another 3–4 minutes. Roll and brush again, then continue in this manner for a total of about 15 minutes for medium. If the glaze begins to burn, move the tenderloins to the edge of the charcoal grill, or lower the heat if using a gas grill. Pork is ready when it feels fairly firm to the touch or an instant-read thermometer registers 145°F (63°C). The internal temperature of the tenderloins will rise a few degrees as they rest.

**SERVE** Transfer tenderloins to a cutting board, brush one more time with glaze, and let rest about 5 minutes. Slice on the diagonal across the grain, and arrange slices on a platter. Brush with any remaining glaze and serve at once.

Makes 4–6 servings.

# 128 Thread a Kebab for Self-Basting

Ah, bacon! The crispy, fatty, salty strips from the belly and sides of a pig have a way of making everything taste better. Employed with a bit of ingenuity, bacon also lends a delicious brand of smoky fat that can elevate a dish from tasty to transcendent. These skewers have it all: bacon, which bastes the tender, lean pork; bread cubes, which turn into crisp, brown croutons; and sage leaves, which season the bread and meat as they cook on the grill. Serve the kebabs on their own or over a simply dressed green salad—romaine or iceberg is sturdy enough to stand up to the heat of the skewers. A frothy mug of nutty amber ale is the ultimate accompaniment.

- 1 pork tenderloin, about 1 lb (500 g), silverskin removed (see tip) and trimmed of excess fat
- 20 cubes coarse country bread, each about ¾ inch (2 cm)
- 3 slices bacon, cut into 20 squares, each about ¾ inch (2 cm)
- 3 tablespoons olive oil, plus extra for grill
- Kosher salt and freshly ground black pepper
- ½ teaspoon smoked paprika
- 20 large fresh sage leaves
- Lemon wedges for serving

**PREP** Cut tenderloin into 1-inch (2-cm) cubes. You will need about 20 cubes. Reserve any remaining pork for another use. If using bamboo skewers, soak four long skewers in water for at least 1 hour. In a bowl, combine pork, bread, bacon, and oil. Season with ¾ teaspoon salt and ¼ teaspoon pepper. Add paprika and sage, and toss gently but thoroughly. Let stand 15 minutes. The bread should be well coated with the oil; if it isn't, toss again.

**SKEWER** Thread the ingredients onto the skewers, alternating in the following order: pork, sage leaves, bread, and bacon. Wrap about 2 inches (5 cm) of the blunt end of each bamboo skewer with aluminum foil to make a handle.

**PREHEAT** Prepare a charcoal or gas grill for direct-heat grilling over medium-high heat. Brush and oil grill grate.

**GRILL** Place skewers on the grill rack over the hottest part of the fire and cook until pork is firm and lightly golden and bread is golden brown and crisp, about 4 minutes per side. Move skewers aside if fire begins to flare.

**SERVE** Remove foil from skewers and arrange on plates. Serve at once with lemon wedges.

Makes 4 servings.

## QUICK TIP

When removing the silverskin, insert your knife near the tapered end of the silverskin and cut toward the thick end. Keep the knife edge tilted up against the silverskin slightly, and the knife will glide between the skin and the meat. If you cut the other direction, you are fighting the grain and the knife can dig into the loin, causing choppy cuts.

# 129 Round Up the Favorites

Pork belly, shoulder, and ham are some of the most popular cuts of pork across many cuisines—and for good reason. Pork belly is just that, the belly of the pig. It's tasty and super-rich, so a few slices are all you'll need for each serving. When cured and smoked, pork belly is known as another favorite: bacon. Pork shoulder and ham are crowd-pleasing, big-plate favorites, great for hearty meals and a table full of elbows jostling for seconds.

# 130 Sizzle Bacon on a Grill

Keeping your stovetop free of greasy spatter is only one of the perks associated with cooking bacon on a grill. The strips grill up nice and crispy, the fumes remain out-of-doors, and cleanup is a snap. Here's how to do it like a pro.

**STEP 1** Prepare a charcoal or gas grill for direct grilling over medium-high heat.

**STEP 2** Fashion an edged griddle by placing a piece of heavy-duty aluminum foil on the grill rack and turning up the sides. (Or use a disposable aluminum roasting pan or an old cookie sheet with sides.)

**STEP 3** Lay bacon on the griddle and cook, turning as needed, until crispy and browned, about 10 minutes.

**STEP 4** When bacon is done, lay it on a double thickness of paper towel to drain.

**STEP 5** To clean up, slide makeshift griddle or cookie sheet to cooler part of grill, or remove roasting pan from heat, and let grease cool until thickened. Discard foil or disposable pan, or scoop fat from sheet into grease container and discard.

Enjoy the bacon while it's hot and crisp!

# 131 Smoked Hickory Ham

A fresh ham (or leg of pork) is large and popular enough to feed a good-size crowd, and it's especially great at holiday feasts. Have your butcher trim the ham of excess fat and tie it for roasting to get some of the prep work out of the way.

- 3 handfuls (about 5 oz/155 g) hickory chips
- 2 tablespoons coarse or kosher salt
- 2 teaspoons freshly ground black pepper
- 2 teaspoons dried thyme
- 2 teaspoons dried sage
- 3 cloves garlic, minced
- ½ teaspoon ground allspice or cloves
- 1 shank-end partial leg of pork, about 10½ lb (5¼ kg), trimmed of excess fat and tied for roasting
- 2 tablespoons vegetable oil or olive oil

**SOAK** Soak hickory chips in water for about 1 hour.

**PREHEAT** Prepare a fire for indirect-heat cooking in a covered grill. Position the grill rack 4–6 inches (10–15 cm) above the fire.

**PREP** In a small bowl, stir together the salt, pepper, thyme, sage, garlic, and allspice or cloves. Pat the meat dry with paper towels, and rub the entire surface of the meat with the oil, then with the spice mixture. Work it well into the meat and be sure to get full coverage.

**GRILL** Drop half of the soaked wood chips onto the fire, place the pork on the center of the rack, cover the grill, and open the vents halfway. Cook for about 1 hour. Turn over the roast and add a few more coals to the fire if needed to maintain a constant temperature. After an hour, add the remaining wood chips to the fire. Continue to cook until the pork is well browned all over and the herb rub has formed a dry, crispy crust, or until an instant-read thermometer inserted into the thickest part of the pork registers 160°F (71°C), about 2 hours longer. Add a few more coals to the fire as necessary to maintain a consistent temperature.

**SERVE** Remove the ham from the grill and transfer to a cutting board. Cover loosely with aluminum foil and let rest 15 minutes. To serve, snip the strings and carve the meat across the grain into slices about ¼ inch (6 mm) thick. Arrange on a warmed platter and serve with scalloped or mashed potatoes and cornbread.

Makes 10–14 servings.

# 132 Fire-Roasted Pork Belly

Pork belly has been the darling of restaurant chefs for several years, but many cooks have yet to prepare it at home. When purchasing pork belly, look for a nice balance of half meat and half fat. The cut is often braised, during which the generous amount of fat becomes deliciously jelly-like. But this recipe calls for a dry-heat method, which takes care of much of the fat by rendering it away. The result is tender and juicy meat—and if you manage your fire carefully, you'll get another bonus: blisteringly crispy skin.

- 15 large cloves garlic
- ½ cup (¾ oz/20 g) fresh rosemary leaves, coarsely chopped
- Grated zest of 4 lemons
- Juice of 1 lemon
- 1 tablespoon coarsely ground pepper
- Kosher salt
- 6 anchovy fillets, soaked in water for 5 minutes, drained, and patted dry
- Olive oil, as needed
- 2½–3 lb (1¼–1½ kg) skin-on pork belly, in a single piece, halved lengthwise

**PREP** The day before serving, begin preparing the pork belly. Place the garlic in a food processor and pulse until minced. Add the rosemary, lemon zest and juice, pepper, 1 tablespoon salt, and anchovies. Pulse to chop. Add just enough oil to form a thick paste and pulse to combine. With a sharp, heavy knife, slash just through the skin of each piece of pork belly at ½-inch (12-mm) intervals, cutting across the width, then make a long lengthwise slash. This will take a fair amount of pressure, but don't cut into the meat. With a small, sharp knife, poke ½-inch holes in the edges and underside of each piece, spacing them about every 2 inches (5 cm). Rub the garlic paste into the slashes in the skin and in all the holes. Set the belly pieces on a rack over a roasting pan, skin side up, and refrigerate, uncovered, overnight.

**CURE** Remove the pork from the refrigerator and let stand at room temperature, covered with paper towels, to cure for about 8 hours.

**PREHEAT** Prepare a charcoal or gas grill for indirect-heat grilling over low heat. Place a drip pan underneath the position on the grill where you will place the meat. Ideally, you want to maintain a temperature of about 300°F (150°C). Place the pork belly, skin side down, over the drip pan, cover the grill, and cook until an instant-read thermometer inserted into the pork belly registers 150°F (65°C), 1½–2 hours. If using a charcoal grill, about 15 minutes before the pork reaches 150°F, light a chimney full of coals, add the coals to the grill, and spread them out slightly; the grilling surface should be very hot. If using a gas grill, set one burner to high heat when the pork reaches 150°F.

**GRILL** Grill the pork belly pieces skin side down over direct heat 3–5 minutes, moving them frequently to avoid flare-ups. When the skin begins to blister at the edges, keep moving the pieces so that the skin blisters evenly but does not char or burn. Transfer to a cutting board and let rest 15–20 minutes.

**SERVE** Cut each piece down the long slash line, then cut crosswise between the slash lines into small rectangles, each with its own strip of crispy skin. Place several pieces on each plate, paired with a favorite salad or side. Serve at once.

Makes 6–8 servings.

# 133 Grill-Smoked Pork Shoulder with Spice Rub

Pork shoulder can be incorporated into recipes in a myriad of ways, and it's practically indestructible—suitable for long, slow cooking over the grill or even in a slow-cooker. In this recipe, you can even leave on a little more fat than you might otherwise—it will render off during cooking and help season the meat.

- ⅓ cup (1 oz/30 g) sweet paprika
- 2 tablespoons freshly ground black pepper
- 2 tablespoons firmly packed dark brown sugar
- 1½ tablespoons kosher salt
- 2 teaspoons celery salt
- 2 teaspoons garlic powder
- 2 teaspoons dry mustard
- 2 teaspoons ground cumin
- ¾ teaspoon cayenne pepper
- 4½–6 lb (2¼–3 kg) bone-in pork shoulder, fat trimmed to about ⅛ inch (3 mm)
- 2 tablespoons canola oil

**RUB** To make the spice rub, stir together the paprika, black pepper, sugar, kosher salt, celery salt, garlic powder, mustard, cumin, and cayenne.

**PREP** Rinse the pork under cold running water. Pat dry thoroughly, including all the nooks and crannies. Rub the oil all over the pork, then rub in the spices, working them in well. Let stand at room temperature for 1½–2 hours.

**PREHEAT** Prepare a charcoal grill for indirect-heat grilling over medium heat, using hardwood charcoal, or prepare a gas grill for indirect grilling at about 300°F (150°C). Place a drip pan underneath the spot on the grill rack where you will place the meat. Add about 2 cups (16 fl oz/500 ml) hot water to the drip pan, and, if you have room, put a small pan of hot water on the grill rack, as well. Be sure to leave room to add more coals as you cook.

**GRILL** Scatter a handful of oak, hickory, or fruit-wood chips over the hot coals, or, if using a gas grill, add the chips in a smoker box or foil packet, and place the pork on the grill rack over the drip pan. If you have a probe thermometer, insert it through the grill vents and into the center of the meat, without touching the bone. Cover the grill and maintain the temperature at 250–300°F (120–150°C). Cook the pork for 2½–5 hours. Your timing will depend on the diameter of the meat, the ambient temperature, how many times you check the temperature, and whether you add hot or cold charcoal to replenish the spent coals. (You will need to replenish about once every hour, when the temperature starts to drop. Add one handful of wood chips the second time you add more charcoal, or after about 2 hours in a gas grill. Don't worry if the temperature spikes higher, especially right after adding fresh charcoal.)

**TEST** The pork is done when it is fork-tender and the internal temperature registers 160–165°F (71–74°C). If you don't have a probe thermometer, use an instant-read thermometer—but remember that every time you lift the lid, the loss of heat will extend your cooking time.

**SERVE** Transfer the pork to a platter, tent with aluminum foil, and let rest 20 minutes. Carve into thick slices and serve at once. Try a hearty slaw (see item 234) alongside.

Makes 8 servings.

# LAMB

# 134

## Know Your Source

Lamb is a very adaptable and individual meat. Its flavor characteristics and physical attributes vary according to the diversity of the breed, their diets, and the climates where the animals were raised—more so than other meats you'll find on the market. Lamb raised in the United States is primarily grain-fed and therefore tends to be larger and more fatty. In Australia and New Zealand, the animals feed on grass or other forage, so their cuts are smaller but with fuller flavor. Lamb raised in Brittany feeds on another kind of forage—the grass and reeds from local salt marshes—and is prized for its subtle saltiness.

# 135 Shop Your Favorite Cuts of Lamb

If you compare butcher-shop lamb selections today with those of decades past, it's hard to believe the cuts could come from the same animal. The quality on the market today is vastly superior, so finding a good cut shouldn't be too much of a challenge for the home cook. Unlike beef, lamb's tenderness is a function of the age of the animal, the breed, and how it was raised—rather than the extent of the fat marbling. So when shopping for lamb, choose meat that is light red and finely textured. Bones, when present, should be reddish and moist, and exterior fat should be smooth and creamy white. The term "lamb" refers to any sheep within its first year of life, but there are also a few subcategories to be aware of. Here are a few identifiers.

**BABY LAMB** Also known as young lamb, baby lamb is slaughtered before 10 weeks of age and weighs less than 20 pounds (9 kg). The meat from young lamb is pale pink, very tender, and mild. As the lamb ages, the meat gains character and flavor, and darkens slightly in color.

**SPRING LAMB** Also called early or summer lamb, spring lamb refers to an animal weighing 20–40 pounds (9–18 kg) that is slaughtered between March and October.

**YEARLING** Meat from yearlings is commonly available, but it can be difficult to find more mature cuts (such as those from 1- to 2-year-old hogget, or even older mutton). These older cuts have more flavor but also tougher flesh that needs slow cooking to tenderize it; most are better suited to braising and roasting than to a grill's dry heat.

**PRIME** The highest grade of lamb, prime reflects a high amount of marbling and is usually reserved for specialty butchers and restaurants.

**CHOICE** The grade you'll most often find at the supermarket, choice lamb doesn't quite have the marbling of prime, but it's still great-quality meat.

# 136 Understand When It's Ready

Treat lamb as you would beef, cooking it to no more than medium for the best flavor. Like beef, the meat will continue to cook for a few minutes once removed from the heat, so keep that in mind when negotiating cooking time. Here's a quick reference to make it easy.

| DONENESS | COLOR | TEMPERATURE |
|---|---|---|
| Rare | Red | 125–130°F/49–54°C |
| Medium-rare | Pinkish-red | 130°F/54°C |
| Medium | Trace of pink | 140°F/60° |
| Medium-well | No trace of pink | 150°F/65°C |
| Well | Grayish-brown | 160+°F/74+°C |

# 137 Know Your Lamb Cuts

Lamb is commonly divided into five sections (known as primal cuts) for butchering, then into smaller retail cuts for sale. Though the meat comes from a young animal, not all cuts are lean or tender enough to make the most of a grill's dry heat. Leaner tenderloin and rib cuts, as well as butterflied legs, grill to perfection over direct heat. Tougher and more hardworking cuts, such as those from the shoulder, require longer cooking over indirect heat.

## SHOULDER

**Blade chop, shoulder roast**

Cuts from the shoulder have more marbling than any other section. Since these tough cuts only become tender with long, slow, moist cooking, they aren't great choices for the grill. An exception is the blade chop, which is tender enough for grill cooking— especially when cut closer to the rib.

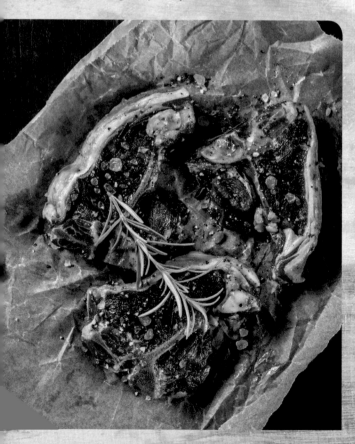

## RIB

**Rib chop, rack of lamb, crown roast**

Rib chops, with their diminutive size and delicate nugget of tenderloin, cook up quickly and effortlessly over direct heat on a grill. The chops, available individually or in a rack, are often sold "frenched," with the fat and sinew removed from the bones above the eye of the meat. Meat from this section is enrobed in a layer of fat that keeps it nice and juicy throughout any type of cooking method.

## LOIN

**Loin chop, loin roast, lamb tenderloin**

Loin cuts are excellent grilled and are usually more affordable than rib cuts. They contain less marbling and are generally leaner than lamb from the shoulder and rib. Because of their generous size, loin roasts are trickiest on the grill: low and slow cooking over indirect heat is the best method.

## LEG

**Sirloin roast, sirloin chop, whole leg, half leg, leg steak, shank**

The leg, with its lean and flavorful meat, is among the most satisfying cuts for grilling. To promote even cooking over direct heat, purchase a butterflied leg (one that is cut so that it lays flat) or have the butcher butterfly a leg for you. Bone-in legs require more time to cook, making them a better choice for oven roasting or slow, indirect heat. Lamb leg steaks, with their uniform thickness, are another good option for the grill.

## BREAST & FORELEG

**Foreshank, hindshank, breast**

The shanks are lean and tough cuts of meat that require slow, moist cooking for tenderness, so you don't often see them on the grill. Roasting and braising make the most of their high collagen content, yielding rich, falling-apart meat. The breast is a good-value cut, sold either bone-in or boneless, that is also best cooked over long periods with moist heat.

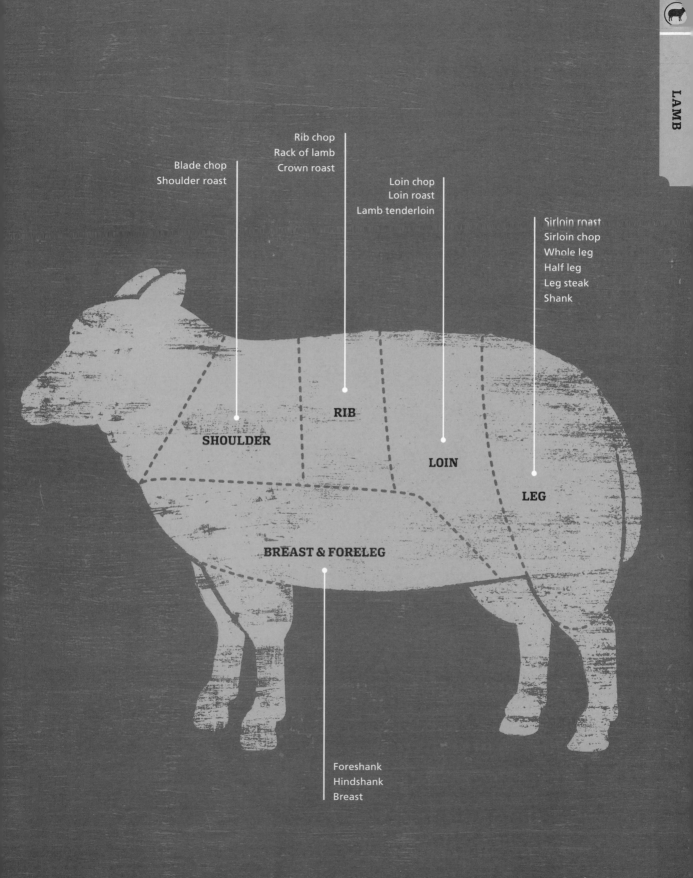

Blade chop
Shoulder roast

Rib chop
Rack of lamb
Crown roast

Loin chop
Loin roast
Lamb tenderloin

Sirloin roast
Sirloin chop
Whole leg
Half leg
Leg steak
Shank

RIB

SHOULDER

LOIN

LEG

BREAST & FORELEG

Foreshank
Hindshank
Breast

# 138 Middle-Eastern Lamb Shoulder Kebabs

Lamb shoulder wouldn't show up on a list of best cuts to cook on a grill. Muscular and hard working, it needs lots of slow, moist cooking in order to become tender. Grind it up and mix in lots of herbs and spices, however, and skewers of the ground shoulder are a grill's best friend. These have a decidedly Middle Eastern bent, adding that region's classic partner to lamb—the minty yogurt sauce known as *raita*—and toasted naan or *lavosh* for serving.

**MIX** Using the flat side of a chef's knife, crush and smear garlic into a paste with 1 teaspoon coarse salt. In a large bowl, stir together garlic paste, onion, bread crumbs, mint, parsley, cumin, coriander, and cayenne. Add ground lamb and generously season with salt and pepper. Using wet hands, mix well. Divide mixture into eight portions.

**SHAPE** Coat the bottom of a shallow dish with oil. Using wet hands, shape each meat portion into a sausage 3–3½ inches (7.5–9 cm) long and 1 inch (2.5 cm) in diameter. Carefully thread each sausage onto a skewer and set aside. Roll kebabs in oil to coat. Arrange in dish, cover with plastic wrap, and refrigerate at least 1 hour or up to 4 hours. Remove skewers from refrigerator 10 minutes before grilling.

**PREHEAT & PREP** Prepare a charcoal or gas grill for direct grilling over high heat. Brush and oil grill grate. Prepare mint raita. Set aside.

**GRILL** Place kebabs directly over heat and cook, turning often, until nicely charred on all sides and cooked through, 8–10 minutes total. During the last 2 minutes of cooking, warm bread on the edge of the grill, turning as needed to toast lightly.

**SERVE** Transfer kebabs and grilled flatbread to a platter. Serve with raita, tomatoes, cucumbers, and grilled onions. Stuff flatbreads with your choice of ingredients.

Makes 8 servings.

- 4 cloves garlic
- Coarse salt and ground pepper
- 1 yellow onion, minced
- ¼ cup (½ oz/15 g) each fresh bread crumbs and finely chopped fresh mint
- 3 tablespoons finely chopped fresh flat-leaf (Italian) parsley
- 2 teaspoons ground cumin
- 1 teaspoon ground coriander
- ½ teaspoon ground cayenne
- 2 lb (32 oz/1 kg) ground lamb shoulder
- 1 tablespoon olive oil
- 8 long, flat metal skewers
- Mint raita (see item 140)
- 8 pieces naan or lavosh bread
- Finely chopped tomatoes, cucumber, and grilled onions for serving

# 139 Greek Pesto Lamb Burgers

Lamb's distinctive flavor is mellowed when teamed up with ground chuck in these Greek-inspired burgers. For nice and juicy results, avoid compacting the meat when shaping patties—simply add a thumb depression to ensure they cook evenly. Serve the burgers in toasty pita pockets stuffed with lettuce and a spoonful of minty pesto.

- Mint-Feta Pesto (see item 140)
- 2 tablespoons *each* finely chopped shallot and fresh flat leaf (Italian) parsley
- 1 tablespoon *each* finely chopped fresh mint and Dijon mustard
- 2 teaspoons dried rosemary, crushed
- 1 clove garlic, minced
- 1½ lb (750 g) ground lamb (leg or shoulder)
- ½ lb (250 g) ground beef chuck
- Kosher salt and freshly ground black pepper
- 6 pita rounds

**PREHEAT & PREP** Prepare charcoal or gas grill for direct grilling over high heat. Brush and oil grill grate.

**MIX** In a bowl, mix shallot, parsley, mint, mustard, rosemary, and garlic. Using wet hands, mix in lamb and beef. Loosely shape into six patties about 1 inch (2.5 cm) thick. Season with salt and pepper. Make a depression in the center of each patty with your thumb.

**GRILL** Place patties indent side up directly over the fire and cook, turning once, until nicely charred on both sides, about 10 minutes total for medium. During last 2 minutes of cooking, warm pitas on edge of grill, turning once and toasting lightly.

**SERVE** Transfer burgers to a platter. Cut off and discard a third of each pita round and open up pocket. Place a dab of pesto in each pita, add a burger, and top with shredded lettuce and more pesto.

Serves 6.

# 140 Partner with Mint

Lamb and mint are one of those sine qua non partnerships. Of course, the pairing is a classic one, but the union goes beyond simple tradition. There's something inherently compatible about the two. One rich and flavorful, the other light and tasty. It just works. Raita is a typical Middle Eastern topping, and this riff on pesto is an Adriatic mix of ingredients from Italy and Greece. Either will offer fresh-tasting enhancement to any grilled lamb preparation.

## MINT RAITA

- 2 cups (16 oz/500 g) whole-milk Greek yogurt
- 3 tablespoons finely chopped mint
- 2 tablespoons chopped fresh cilantro
- ½ teaspoon ground cumin
- Zest and juice of 1 lime
- ½ teaspoon *each* coarse salt and garam masala

Place yogurt in a damp cheesecloth-lined sieve over a bowl. Cover and let drain for at least 1 hour or up to 4 hours; discard liquid. In a nonaluminum bowl, mix yogurt, mint, cilantro, cumin, lime zest, and salt. Stir in lime juice, 1 tablespoon at a time, until sauce is creamy. Taste and adjust seasoning with more lime juice and salt. Spoon into serving bowl and sprinkle with garam masala. Cover and refrigerate for at least 1 hour before serving, or up to three days.

## MINT-FETA PESTO

- 1 cup (1 oz/30 g) loosely packed fresh mint leaves
- 2 tablespoons pine nuts
- ⅛ teaspoon red pepper flakes
- 6 oz (185 g) crumbled feta cheese
- Salt and freshly ground black pepper

In a blender or food processor, pulse mint, pine nuts and red pepper flakes until chopped. With machine running, slowly add oil until a thin paste forms. Add feta and pulse to mix. Season with salt and pepper. Serve at once or cover and refrigerate for up to three days.

# 141 Reference the Classic Marinades

Other than a top-notch marinade, most lamb needs little embellishment on the grill. Lamb profits from many of the same accoutrements one might pair with beef, but, because of its unique and mellow pungency, lamb can also take on a heck of a lot more flavor prior to cooking. Garlic is a classic partner; so are rosemary and oregano. Lamb is awesomely accepting of a wide variety of flavors. Mix together the following sets of ingredients to whip up a few of your best bets.

## FIVE-SPICE MARINADE

- ¼ cup soy sauce or tamari
- 3 tablespoon hoisin sauce
- 2 tablespoons firmly packed light brown sugar
- 1 tablespoon *each* rice wine vinegar and dry sherry
- 2 teaspoons Chinese five-spice powder
- 3 cloves garlic, minced
- 2 star anise

## CRANBERRY-ROSEMARY MARINADE

- 1 clove garlic, finely chopped
- 1 shallot, finely chopped
- 1 tablespoon finely chopped fresh rosemary
- ½ cup *each* cranberry juice cocktail and full-bodied red wine
- 2 tablespoons olive oil
- ¼ teaspoon salt
- ⅛ teaspoon freshly ground pepper

## GREEK MARINADE

- Juice of 2 lemons
- ¼ cup (2 fl oz/60 ml) olive oil
- 2 cloves garlic, minced
- 2 teaspoons coarsely chopped fresh oregano
- 1 teaspoon chopped fresh thyme
- 1 teaspoon sea salt
- 1 teaspoon coarsely ground black pepper
- 1 bay leaf

## INDIAN MARINADE

- ¾ cup whole-fat plain Greek yogurt
- 2-inch piece ginger, peeled and grated
- 2 cloves garlic, pressed
- 2 tablespoons *each* garam masala and olive oil
- 2 teaspoons salt
- 1 teaspoon *each* ground cayenne, cumin, coriander, and cardamom

## JULIA CHILD'S MUSTARD MARINADE

- 2 cloves garlic, pressed
- 2 tablespoons *each* lemon juice and Dijon mustard
- 1 tablespoon low-sodium soy sauce
- 1 teaspoon fresh thyme, finely chopped

# 142 Butterfly a Leg of Lamb

Lamb cooks better on the grill if it's boned and cut to a uniform thickness—a technique known as butterflying. Most butchers are happy to butterfly a piece of meat for you, but you can easily master the procedure yourself in a few basic steps. Here's how.

**STEP 1** For all boning, use a very sharp, rigid knife with a narrow, thin blade. Boning knives are best, but paring knives will do in a pinch. Most legs are sold with the pelvic bone or aitchbone already removed by the butcher. To remove it yourself, you'll need to cut lengthwise along the leg and hip bones, making small cuts down to and around the bone, while pulling the meat away to free and remove the bone.

**STEP 2** Place the leg, meaty side down, on a cutting board. Find the knee joint, which is a knobby joint toward the narrow end of the cut. Cut from the hip toward the knee, carefully cutting around the bone with the tip of the knife to separate it from the meat.

**STEP 3** When you get to the knee joint, cut around it. The shank is attached to the knee—and it's a tough cut, best suited for stewing and braising, so leave the leg bone and knee joint attached to the shank and reserve for another use.

**STEP 4** At this point, you should be left with the main part of the leg, completely free of the bone. Place the leg, cut side up, on the cutting board. Cut away any large gobs of fat, but leave smaller pieces to flavor the meat.

**STEP 5** Examine the varying thicknesses of the meat as it lays open. If there are large lumps, slice into the middle of the lump, working parallel to the cutting board and without cutting all the way through, then open the meat up like a book so it lays flat and has semiuniform thickness. Repeat to cut any other large lumps of meat to a uniform thickness.

**STEP 6** Slash smaller lumps of meat from top to bottom, bringing them to a more uniform thickness and allowing more surface area for the marinade to penetrate.

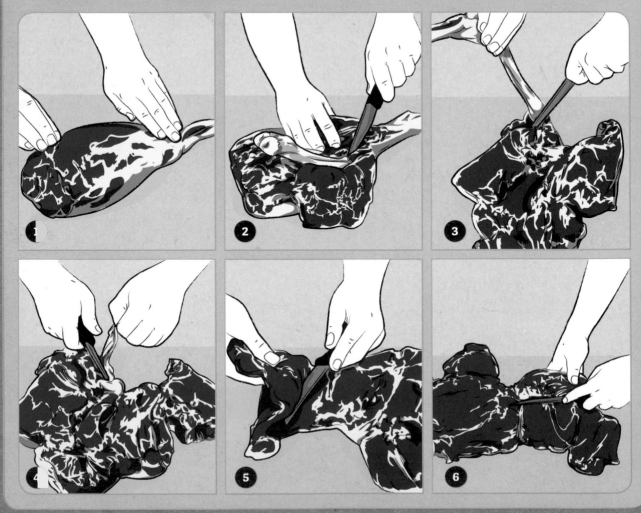

## 143 Fire Roast *al Asador*

The Argentines are enviably macho when it comes to their brand of outdoor cookery. There, meat is roasted *al asador*, meaning a whole carcass that has been splayed open and secured to a wrought-iron cross (*al asador*) to slow-cook near the low-flame heat of an open fire. Calves are often the most popular choice for an Argentine *asado*—the daylong social event—but lamb is a close second.

## 144 Fresh Mint Sauce

Sprightly mint sauce was once served as the fresh-tasting antidote to tough and gristly portions of stewed mutton. Now that mutton has given way to a new breed of tender lamb cuts, the crisp herb sauce remains the classic partner to all types of modern preparations for the mild and gamey meat (see item 140).

In a blender or mini food processor, combine ½ cup chopped fresh mint, 2 tablespoons confectioners' sugar, and ⅓ cup cider vinegar or rice wine vinegar. Process until mint is minced. Serve on the side.

## 145 Marinated & Grilled Leg of Lamb

Dense and meaty leg of lamb is one of the best cuts of meat to cook on a barbecue. The dry heat chars and caramelizes the exterior, making the yin to lamb's mild and gamey yang. Butterflied with lots of crevices for ultimate marinade penetration, lamb becomes wonderfully flavorful and juicy on the grill.

- ½ cup (4 fl oz/120 ml) extra-virgin olive oil
- ¼ cup (2 fl oz/60 ml) fresh lemon juice
- 4 cloves garlic, pressed
- 1 tablespoon dried oregano
- 2 teaspoons salt
- 1 teaspoon freshly ground black pepper
- 1 leg of lamb, about 5 lb (2½ kg), boned, butterflied, and trimmed of excess fat

**MARINATE** In a large zip-top plastic bag, mix olive oil, lemon juice, garlic, oregano, salt, and pepper. Add lamb, seal bag, and turn to coat evenly. Let marinate in refrigerator at least 2 hours or up to one day.

**PREHEAT** Remove lamb from refrigerator at least 1 hour before grilling. Prepare charcoal or gas grill for direct grilling over medium-high heat. Brush and oil grill rack.

**GRILL** Place lamb on grill rack, fat side up. Cook lamb, turning as needed and moving around grill rack to avoid flare-ups, until meat registers 125–128°F (52–53°C) for medium-rare.

**SERVE** Transfer lamb to cutting board, cover loosely with aluminum foil, and let stand for 20 minutes. (Internal temperature should rise to 135°F/57°C while standing.) Cut across the grain into slices. Serve at once.

# 146 Know Your Chops

Take a moment to consider chop placement on a lamb, and you'll understand what to look for in each cut. First along the backbone are the shoulder chops, also known as the blade chops (A), which are a tougher, fattier, and more economical cut that need long, slow cooking to render them tender. Bite-size rib chops (B), cut from the rack, are the most diminutive of the chop options and are characterized by a single portion of tenderloin attached to a delicate rib bone. At the waist of the lamb are the palm-size loin chops (C), meatier T-bone steaks that contain a portion of both the loin and tenderloin (and the two loin chops attached by the backbone are called an English chop). Of the chop cuts, those from the rib and loin chops are the best choice for direct heat on a grill. Next down the backbone, toward the leg, are the sirloin chops (D), which are nearly as tender as the loin chop, but less expensive.

# 147 Moroccan Lamb "Pops"

Individually cut and frenched rib lamb chops are the ultimate luxury finger food. Each one features a tender eye of lean meat encased in a thick layer of flavorful fat, and it's the ideal size for a generous bite. Infused with the fragrant spices of North Africa and served with a citrusy, yogurt sauce, these bite-size "pops" are a decadent treat. Grill individual rib chops on the grill rack or on a cast-iron griddle set over direct heat.

## FOR THE MARINADE
- ⅓ cup extra-virgin olive oil
- 2 tablespoons freshly squeezed lemon juice, plus lemon wedges for serving
- 2 teaspoons lemon zest
- 1 teaspoon *each* minced garlic, ground cumin, ground coriander, smoked paprika, and salt
- ½ teaspoon *each* ground cinnamon, cardamom, and freshly ground black pepper
- 1 rack of lamb (about 1½ lb/750 g), cut into individual chops

## FOR THE DIP
- 2 tablespoons hot water
- 1 teaspoon saffron threads
- ½ cup (4 oz/250 g) plain Greek yogurt
- 1 teaspoon *each* freshly squeezed lemon juice and chopped fresh mint
- ¼ teaspoon salt

**MARINATE** In a large zip-top plastic bag, mix olive oil, lemon juice and zest, garlic, cumin, coriander, paprika, salt, cinnamon, cardamom, and pepper. Add lamb, seal bag, and squish to coat. Refrigerate at least 6 hours or overnight.

**WHIP UP A DIP** Pour water into small bowl. Add saffron and let stand 10 minutes. Remove saffron and discard. Add yogurt, lemon juice, mint, and salt. Mix and refrigerate.

**PREHEAT** Prepare charcoal or gas grill for direct cooking over medium-high heat. Brush and oil grill grate.

**GRILL** Place lamb chops on grill directly over heat and cook, turning once, until medium-rare, 4–6 minutes total.

**SERVE** Arrange lamb on a platter and garnish with lemon wedges. Serve with dip on side.

Makes 4 servings.

# 148

## Rosemary-Garlic Lamb Loin Chops

Meaty T-bone steaks contain a portion of both loin and tenderloin and are among the leanest, tenderest, and priciest cuts. Cooked quickly on the grill, the juicy rounds of meat on either side of the bone develop a caramelized crust with a pink, juicy center. They have a smooth flavor similar to rib chops but are significantly meatier. Ask for chops that are at least an inch (2.5 cm) thick if you're going for medium-rare.

- 2 tablespoons finely chopped fresh rosemary
- 4 cloves garlic, finely chopped
- Kosher salt and freshly ground pepper
- 8 lamb T-bone chops, each about 1 inch (2.5 cm) thick
- 2 tablespoons olive oil

**RUB** On a cutting board, finely chop rosemary with garlic, salt, and pepper. Rub mixture onto chops, then brush with oil. Place on a plate, cover with plastic wrap, and refrigerate for at least an hour or up to one day.

**PREHEAT** Remove chops from refrigerator at least 30 minutes before grilling. Prepare charcoal or gas grill for direct grilling over high heat. Brush and oil grill grate.

**GRILL** Place chops on grill directly over the fire and cook, turning once, until nicely charred and medium-rare, about 8 minutes total grilling time.

**SERVE** Transfer to a platter and let rest for 5 minutes. Serve hot.

Makes 4 servings.

### QUICK TIP

Bone-in loin chops can be a bit tricky on the grill. The meaty part can wind up perfectly cooked while the pocket of meat next to the bone remains raw. To avoid uneven cooking, place the flat part of the bone on the grill rack first, allowing the bone to heat up first, which helps the meat near it to cook more evenly. You can also try reverse searing as for pork chops.

# 149 Maharajah-Spiced Lamb Kebabs

*Garam masala* is your shortcut to exotic. The fragrant North Indian spice blend—usually consisting of cinnamon, nutmeg, cloves, cardamom, mace, peppercorns, coriander, and cumin—lends a dynamic flavor profile to any dish. There are plenty of variations to the mix, and each spice plays its part: providing sweetness (cinnamon), heat (pepper), complexity (nutmeg), and texture (coriander)—plus a citrusy note, via the latter. The grill's direct heat brings out the smoky-sweet qualities of the spice blend, making it an ideal lamb partner.

- 2 lb (1 kg) boneless leg of lamb, trimmed of excess fat
- 2 tablespoons garam masala
- 6–12 bamboo or metal skewers
- 2 green bell peppers
- 2 Asian eggplants
- 6 green (spring) onions
- 6 cherry tomatoes

**SEASON** Cut lamb into 1-inch (2.5-cm) chunks. Place in a large zip-top plastic bag and season on all sides with garam masala. Refrigerate for at least 6 hours or overnight.

**PREHEAT** Remove lamb from refrigerator at least 1 hour before grilling. If using bamboo skewers, soak in water for at least 30 minutes. Prepare a charcoal or gas grill for direct grilling over high heat.

**PREP** Core and seed peppers, then cut crosswise into 1-inch- (2.5-cm-) thick slices; set aside. Cut eggplant in the same manner and set aside, then cut bottom 3 inches (7 cm) of green onions into 1-inch (2.5-cm) chunks. Thread lamb, bell pepper, eggplant, green onions, and tomatoes onto skewers, dividing them evenly, and starting and ending each skewer with a chunk of lamb.

**GRILL** Place skewers on grill directly over fire and cook, turning frequently, until nicely browned, 12–15 minutes total for medium rare.

**SERVE** Transfer skewers to platter and let rest 5 minutes, then serve.

# 150 Lamb Souvlaki

To say that souvlaki has long been a trademark of Greek cuisine is putting it mildly—the skewered kebablike recipe is referenced in the pages of Homer. A few centuries later, Aristotle and Aristophanes were still talking about the spit-roasted specialty, calling it by the name *obeliskos* (from *obelos*, which means spit). In ancient times, as today, souvlaki was the progeny of roadside vendors, who served it daily on the streets of Athens and in the busy market squares of island villages. In the States, lamb is the meat most often selected for souvlaki, although pork is the top choice of vendors in Greece and Cyprus. Take a world tour of city markets and you'll find souvlaki made with beef, chicken, and fish, as well.

- 1 cup (8 oz/250 g) whole-milk or low-fat plain Greek yogurt
- ½ cup (2½ oz/75 g) peeled, seeded, and finely chopped English (hothouse) cucumber
- 1 tablespoon chopped fresh dill or oregano leaves
- 2 teaspoons *each* olive oil, lemon juice, and red wine vinegar
- 1 clove garlic, pressed
- Salt and freshly ground black pepper
- ⅓ cup (3 fl oz/80 ml) fresh lemon juice
- 3 tablespoons olive oil
- 1½ tablespoons chopped fresh oregano
- 3 cloves garlic, pressed
- ½ teaspoon *each* salt and freshly ground pepper
- 1½ lb (750 g) boneless lamb from leg
- 16–20 long bamboo or metal skewers
- 4 pita breads
- 1 large tomato, chopped
- 2 cups (4 oz/125 g) chopped romaine lettuce

**MAKE TZATZIKI** Mix yogurt, cucumber, dill, olive oil, lemon juice, red wine vinegar, and garlic. Season to taste with lots of salt and a few grinds of pepper. Cover and refrigerate for at least an hour (or overnight).

**MARINATE** In a zip-top plastic bag, combine lemon juice, olive oil, oregano, garlic, salt, and pepper. Cut lamb into roughly 1-inch (2.5-cm) chunks. Add lamb to marinade and squish bag to coat the meat. Close bag and refrigerate for at least 1 hour or up to 4 hours.

**PREHEAT & PREP** Prepare a charcoal or gas grill for direct grilling over high heat. If using bamboo skewers, soak in water for at least 30 minutes. Remove lamb from marinade and thread chunks onto skewers.

**GRILL** Place skewers on grill directly over heat. Cook, turning to char all sides, until done to your liking (or, for medium rare, 5–7 minutes total). About 1 minute before lamb is done, gently warm pita breads at edges of grill, where the heat is less intense.

**SERVE** Place meat on platter and surround with separate bowls of tomato, onion, lettuce, and tzatziki. Have guests make their own, adding lamb and toppings to their liking.

Makes 4 servings.

## 151 Get to Know Your Chickens

Young chickens such as broilers, fryers, and roasters are the best choice for the grill. These youngsters are raised only for their meat and are perfectly suited to any type of grill cooking. Older birds (such as stewing chickens) and male chickens (capons and cocks) are best left for the stewpot. Choose your chicken according to how many people you would like to feed, rather than its age at the time of slaughter. A 2½-pound broiler chicken will likely serve three people, whereas a 5- to 6-pound roaster will serve eight. Here's a handy reference to aid in your selection.

| BROILERS | STEWING CHICKENS |
|---|---|
| **AGE:** 6–8 weeks old | **AGE:** usually hens more than 10 months old |
| **APPROX WEIGHT:** 2½ lb (1.1 kg) | **APPROX WEIGHT:** 5–7 lb (2.25–3.2 kg) |
| **FRYERS** | **CAPONS** |
| **AGE:** 6–8 weeks old | **AGE:** castrated males |
| **APPROX WEIGHT:** 2½–3½ lb (1.1-1.6 kg) | **APPROX WEIGHT:** 6–8 lb (2.7–3.6 kg) |
| **ROASTERS** | **ROOSTERS** |
| **AGE:** less than 8 months old | **AGE:** male chickens more than 10 months old |
| **APPROX WEIGHT:** 3½–5 lb (1.6–2.25 kg) | **APPROX WEIGHT:** 6–8 lb (2.7–3.6 kg) |

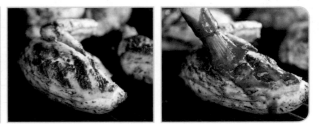

# 152 Set Up for Poultry Success

There are many choices to make and steps to take in order to grill poultry to perfection—there's a lot more to it than a well-bred bird and a good sauce. These should be among your primary considerations for the ultimate barbecued chicken dish.

**BRINE THE BIRD** Brining adds flavor, to be sure; more important, it ensures moist results. It also gives you a little wiggle room if you leave the bird over the heat a few minutes too long, keeping it nice and moist. It alone will make the difference between ordinary and supreme.

**KEEP IT DRY** Patting the chicken pieces dry with a paper towel before grilling helps them to properly caramelize over the grill's dry heat, becoming crisp and browned.

**GO HYBRID** Bone-in chicken is best cooked over two levels. The chicken meat gets a quick sear over direct heat but is finished over indirect heat to develop flavor and prevent overcooking.

**GET SAUCY** Cooking with indirect heat means that you won't risk flare-ups or burning if you brush on your sauces toward the end of cooking, when the meat's still on the grill. This way, you give the sauce a bit of extra time on the meat, which makes for a more flavorful final result.

# 153 Perfect BBQ Chicken

**Quality bird? Yes. Brine? Check. Awesome sauce? Yup. Once you have all the important elements, it's time to cook your chicken to perfection. Begin with a trusty brine and finish with a good hybrid cooking technique, and your crispy, saucy morsels of chicken will be ones to remember.**

- 1 chicken, 4 lb (2 kg), neck and giblets removed, cut into three pieces
- Basic poultry brine (See item 156)
- Freshly ground pepper and granulated garlic for sprinkling
- 2 cups (16 fl oz/500 ml) classic BBQ sauce (see item 251), or your favorite purchased barbecue sauce

**BRINE** Put chicken pieces in a large zip-top plastic bag and pour in brine. Seal bag, squish brine around chicken, and refrigerate overnight.

**PREP** Remove chicken from brine at least 30 minutes before grilling; discard brine. Rinse the chicken pieces briefly and pat dry with paper towels. Lightly sprinkle on all sides with pepper and granulated garlic.

**PREHEAT** Prepare a charcoal or gas grill for indirect grilling over medium heat; temperature inside grill should be about 350°F (180°C). If using charcoal, bank lit coals on either side of grill bed, leaving a strip in the center without heat, then place a drip pan in the center. If using gas, preheat burners, then turn off one or more burners to create a cooler zone. Brush and oil grill grate.

**GRILL** Place chicken pieces on the grill over direct-heat area and sear, turning once, 2 minutes on each side. Move chicken pieces to indirect-heat area, cover grill, and cook 30 minutes. Now, start brushing chicken with BBQ sauce, turning and brushing pieces every 5 minutes, for about 15 minutes longer. Chicken is ready when firm to the touch and juices run clear when a thigh or breast is pierced with a knife tip.

**SERVE** Transfer chicken to a platter and serve. Pass remaining sauce at table.

Serves 4.

# 154 Know When the Bird Is Done

There's only one foolproof way to make sure your poultry is ready for the carving board: Test it with a good instant-read thermometer. Take the temperature in the thigh (which takes longest to cook), away from the bone (where it can read hotter).

Here are the temperature targets:

| | |
|---|---|
| Chicken, turkey (whole) | 180°F/82°C |
| Poultry breasts | 180°F/82°C |
| Poultry thighs | 170°F/77°C |
| Game (duck, quail, pheasant) | 180°F/82°C |

If your thermometer is on the fritz, or if you need further proof of your chicken's table readiness, there are a few (less scientific) methods for doneness determination:

**CUT** Cut into the meat (try the meaty part of the thigh). The juices released should be nice and clear, not bloody or cloudy. The meat should look opaque, not pink and translucent.

**WIGGLE** On a whole chicken, the leg should wiggle at the joint rather than remain rigid.

# 155 Truss a Chicken

Trussing whole poultry for cooking secures the legs and wings close to the body, keeping wing tips and ends from burning and helping the bird cook more evenly. On a rotisserie, the compact shape keeps birds steady on the spit.

**STEP 1** Tuck wing tips over shoulders to rest behind back.

**STEP 2** Cut a piece of kitchen string about three times the length of your bird. Lay string on a work surface and place chicken tail over string.

**STEP 3** Lift string up and around legs, reversing twine to make a cross.

**STEP 4** Pull tightly on both ends so legs come together.

**STEP 5** Keeping string taut, pull it away from you, moving it along the sides of the body to loop it around the front of the chicken and over the wings. Then, flip the chicken upside down so that the neck is now facing you, keeping the string pulled tight.

**STEP 6** Tie a knot underneath the neck bone to secure the string.

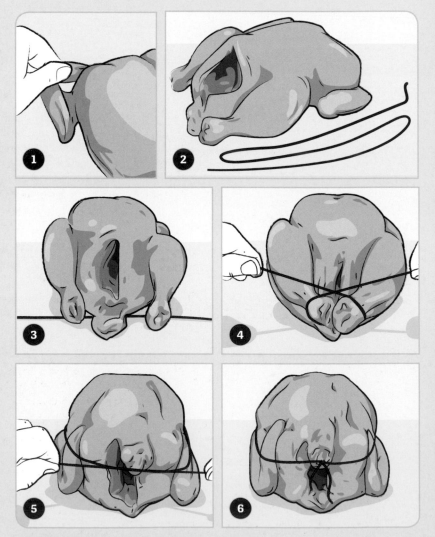

# Reference Poultry Basics

Most poultry is pretty darn good on its own, but there's always room for improvement. Spice rubs and brines are ideal when you're looking for a little extra flavor, some additional tenderness, or both. It's good to have an easy rub on hand for any part of the bird and any type of cooking, to add a subtle mix of sweet and spice and a rich brown finish. A good brine also takes flavor up a notch, helps keep meat juicy, and renders skin thin and crispy. For game birds, buttermilk brine is the perfect antidote, helping to mellow stronger flavors. The calcium in the buttermilk also triggers enzymes that break down proteins holding muscle fibers together, making meat significantly more tender. The rub or each of the brines is enough to season about 4 pounds (2 kg) of poultry pieces.

## BASIC POULTRY BRINE

- 8 cups (64 fl oz/2 l) water
- 5 tablespoons (2½ oz/75 g) kosher salt
- 2 tablespoons *each* dried basil and coriander seeds
- 1 tablespoon *each* peppercorns and yellow mustard seeds
- 1 teaspoon granulated garlic
- 2 bay leaves

Stir ingredients until salt dissolves. Add poultry and chill at least 12 hours. Remove from refrigerator at least 30 minutes before grilling. Rinse poultry and pat dry with paper towels. Continue to season and cook as directed in recipe.

## ALL-PURPOSE BARBECUE RUB

- ¼ cup (2 oz/60 g) granulated sugar
- 1 tablespoon firmly packed light brown sugar
- 1 teaspoon *each* kosher salt, cayenne pepper, and smoked paprika
- Freshly ground black pepper

Coat poultry with rub. Cover and refrigerate at least 8 hours or overnight. Remove from refrigerator at least 30 minutes before grilling. Cook as directed for type of cut.

## BUTTERMILK BRINE

- 1 quart (1 l) buttermilk
- 4 teaspoons kosher salt
- 1 teaspoon freshly ground black pepper

Add poultry and chill at least 4 hours or overnight. Remove from refrigerator at least 30 minutes before grilling. Rinse poultry briefly and pat dry with paper towels. Continue to season and cook as directed in recipe.

# Spicy Caramelized Chicken Wings

These cousins of the original buffalo wings differ from the American classic on one important count: They are grilled instead of fried. The variation makes for wings that are a bit crispier and boast a nice caramelized char.

- 3 lb (1½ kg) chicken wings, tips removed
- 3 tablespoons canola oil
- 2 tablespoons BBQ rub (see item 156)
- ½ cup (4 oz/125 g) unsalted butter
- 6 cloves garlic, minced
- ½ cup (4 fl oz/125 ml) hot-pepper sauce
- 1 tablespoon distilled white vinegar
- Blue Cheese Dip (see item 158) for serving
- 4 stalks celery, cut into sticks for serving

**MARINATE** In a large bowl, combine wings and oil. Toss to coat. Sprinkle BBQ rub over wings and toss again. Cover and refrigerate overnight.

**MAKE HEAT** Remove wings from refrigerator 30 minutes before grilling. In a large frying pan over medium heat, melt butter. Add garlic and cook, stirring, until fragrant and tender, about 2 minutes. Stir in hot sauce and vinegar. Remove from heat and set aside.

**PREHEAT** Prepare charcoal or gas grill for direct grilling over high heat. Brush and oil grill grate.

**GRILL** Place chicken wings on the grill directly over the fire and cook, turning frequently, until tender, slightly charred, and nicely browned on all sides, 15–20 minutes.

**COAT** Transfer wings to hot sauce in frying pan. Place pan over low heat and toss wings to coat evenly. Let wings marinate in the sauce for about 5 minutes.

**SERVE** Transfer wings to a platter. Pour any remaining sauce on top. Serve with blue cheese dip and celery sticks.

Serves 6–8 as an appetizer.

## QUICK TIP

You want to get a nice char on the wings, but if they are burning too quickly, move them to a cooler area of the grill. Also remember that celery stalks are sweeter and more tender if the ribs have been removed. Use a potato peeler to remove the outside ribs before you cut them into stalks.

## 158 Blue Cheese Dip

- 1 cup (8 oz/250 g) sour cream
- ¼ cup (2 fl oz/60 ml) mayonnaise
- 1 tablespoon fresh lemon juice
- 1 tablespoon Worcestershire sauce
- 1 teaspoon steak sauce
- 2 cloves garlic, finely minced, then crushed to a paste
- 2 tablespoons chopped fresh chives
- ⅛ teaspoon cayenne pepper
- 1 cup (5 oz/155 g) crumbled blue cheese
- Kosher salt and freshly ground black pepper

In a bowl, combine sour cream, mayonnaise, lemon juice, Worcestershire sauce, steak sauce, garlic, chives, and cayenne pepper, and mix well. Fold in cheese, then season with salt and pepper. Cover and refrigerate until serving. The dip tastes best if made a day ahead and will keep for up to two weeks. To use as a salad dressing, thin it a bit with milk.

Makes about 3 cups (24 fl oz/875 ml).

## 159 Master the Wing

Like any bone-in cut of meat, chicken wings can be tricky to cook in a way that ensures even doneness throughout. Here are a few tips to help you cook them up just right.

**GO INDIRECT** If the sauce begins to burn before the meat is cooked through, move the wings to indirect heat to finish cooking.

**WATCH CAREFULLY** Stand by the grill and move wings on the rack if flare-ups occur.

**GET INTO POSITION** Place wings on the grill rack with the tips pointed away from the heat to prevent burning.

**CUT THE JOINTS** Cut wings at the joints to separate them into three easy-to-grill sections: tip, middle, and drumette. Place thicker portions over hotter parts of the grill and smaller ones over more moderate heat.

**GO LUXE** Napkins are a necessity, damp hand towels drizzled with lemon juice a luxury. Prepare them in advance, wrap in aluminum foil, and place in a low-heat oven when you sit down to eat. Guests will appreciate the upgrade.

## 160 Honey-Sesame Bites

When it comes to chicken wings, a flavorful sauce makes the difference between brilliant and blasé. In this Japanese-inspired recipe, the wings are glazed with a mix of teriyaki, sesame oil, and *shichimi togarashi*, a popular seven-spice blend that gets its flavor from Sichuan pepper, ground chiles, roasted orange peel, seaweed, and sesame seeds. It's a heady blend of flavors, and the wings char up beautifully when grilled, staying super moist and intensely flavored.

- 3 lb (1½ kg) chicken wings, tips removed
- ¼ cup (2 fl oz/60 ml) canola oil
- 2 tablespoons shichimi togarashi spice blend or lemon pepper seasoning
- ¾ cup (6 fl oz/180 ml) sweet hot-chile sauce
- ¼ cup (2 fl oz/60 ml) teriyaki sauce
- 2 tablespoons honey
- 2 tablespoons Asian sesame oil
- Juice of 1 lime

**MARINATE** In a large bowl, combine wings and oil. Toss to coat. Sprinkle shichimi togarashi spice blend over wings and toss again to coat lightly and evenly. Cover and let stand at room temperature for about 30 minutes.

**PREHEAT** Prepare a charcoal or gas grill for direct grilling over high heat. Brush and oil grill grate.

**GLAZE** In a small saucepan, stir together chile sauce, teriyaki sauce, honey, and sesame oil. Place over low heat and bring to a gentle simmer, stirring. Remove from heat and let cool slightly. Stir in lime juice. Set aside.

**GRILL** Place chicken wings on grill and cook, turning frequently, until they are tender and nicely browned on all sides, with a little char, about 15–20 minutes.

**SERVE** Transfer wings to a large bowl, pour in the glaze, and toss to coat evenly. Let sit for about 5 minutes to allow the flavors to meld, then transfer to a platter, and serve. As a final touch, sprinkle with sesame seeds.

Serves 6–8 as an appetizer.

# 161 Spatchcock a Chicken

Tell your pal you've just spatchcocked a chicken and you might inspire a look that expresses something akin to absolute befuddlement. Spatchcocking—though it sounds quite technical and laborious—is really nothing more than butterflying a whole bird so it cooks more evenly. Here's how it's done in four easy steps.

**STEP 1** Place the whole chicken, breast side down, on a work surface.

**STEP 2** Starting at the leg end and moving toward the neck, cut along one side of the backbone using a pair of sharp kitchen shears.

**STEP 3** Turn the bird around; then, starting at the neck end and moving toward the leg, cut along the other side of the backbone to remove it. Discard backbone or set aside for your next chicken stock.

**STEP 4** Flip the chicken over and open it like a book. Flatten the chicken by pressing on the breastbone with the palm of your hand. It's okay if you hear some crunching— you want to get that bird good and flat.

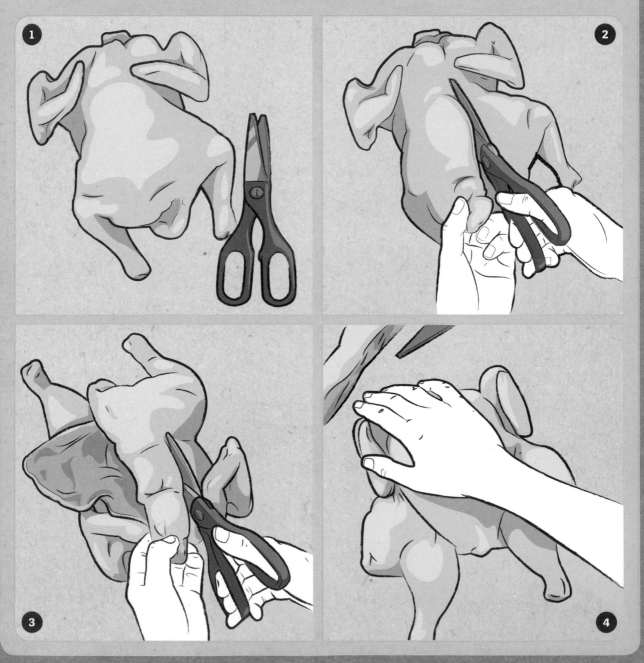

# 162 Chicken Under a Brick

Think of all the things you want a chicken to be when you cook it: crispy on the outside, moist on the inside, nice and juicy. This traditional Italian method achieves all those attributes in half the time it takes to grill whole birds. Known as *pollo al matone*, the dish is said to have originated in Impruneta, a town near Florence that's famous for its beautifully made terra cotta tiles. Cooks there reportedly used heavy terra cotta pots to weigh down the butterflied bird on the grill—and bricks or a heavy cast iron skillet work just as well.

- 1 large fryer chicken, about 3½ lb (1¾ kg), spatchcocked
- Salt and freshly ground pepper
- 6 tablespoons (3 fl oz/90 ml) fresh lemon juice
- 3 tablespoons olive oil
- 2 teaspoons grated lemon zest
- ¼ teaspoon red pepper flakes
- 3 cloves garlic, finely chopped
- 1 heavy cast iron skillet, or 1–2 bricks wrapped in aluminum foil

**PREP** Rinse chicken and pat dry with paper towels. Season all over with salt and pepper.

**MARINATE** In a large bowl, mix lemon juice, olive oil, lemon zest, red pepper flakes, and garlic. Add chicken and turn to coat. Cover and refrigerate, turning occasionally, for 30 minutes or up to 3 hours. (Bring to room temperature before cooking.)

**GRILL** Prepare charcoal or gas grill for direct grilling over medium heat. Brush and oil grill rack. Place chicken, skin side down, over the hottest part of the grill, then place a skillet or brick(s) on top of the chicken. Cook for 15 minutes. Turn chicken over, replace pan or brick(s), and cook until juices run clear when the thigh joint is pierced with a knife tip, about 15–20 minutes longer.

**SERVE** Transfer chicken to a cutting board and let rest for 5 minutes before carving. This allows the juices to distribute and keeps the meat nice and moist. Dig in and enjoy!

# 163 Beer Can Chicken

The Nascar crowd was on to something when they first starting smoking whole chickens stuck upright atop steaming cans of Pabst Blue Ribbon. In those early days, the dish was known as Redneck Chicken, Beer Butt Chicken, or quite simply as Beer Can Chicken. The latter, least-offensive moniker is the one most popularly used today, especially as fervor for the "steam-grilled" chicken has grown among even the fanciest of grilling enthusiasts. This rendition of the modern classic benefits from an especially perky spice blend and ample sprays of cider vinegar, which keeps the chicken moist and adds a nice hint of acidity.

- 1 tablespoon sugar
- 1 teaspoon *each* dry mustard, onion powder, garlic powder, and smoked paprika
- ½ teaspoon *each* ground coriander and ground cumin
- 1 teaspoon kosher salt
- ½ teaspoon freshly ground black pepper
- 1 chicken, 4 lb (2 kg), neck and giblets removed
- 1 tablespoon canola oil
- 1 large can (16 fl oz/500 ml) of your favorite beer
- About ⅓ cup (3 fl oz/80 ml) cider vinegar, in a spray bottle

**RUB** In a small container with a tight-fitting lid, combine sugar, mustard, onion powder, garlic powder, paprika, coriander, cumin, salt, and pepper. Cover tightly and shake vigorously to mix.

**PREP** Remove chicken from refrigerator 30 minutes before grilling. Brush oil evenly over surface of chicken. Season chicken inside and out with spice mixture.

**PREHEAT** Prepare charcoal or gas grill for indirect grilling over medium heat; the temperature inside the grill should be 350–375°F (180–190°C). If using charcoal, bank lit coals on either side of the grill bed, leaving a strip in the center without heat, and place a drip pan in the center. If using gas, preheat the burners, then turn off one or more of the burners to create a cooler zone. Brush and oil grill grate.

**GRILL** Open the beer and drink half of it (spoils to the chef). Set the half-full can on your countertop, and slide chicken onto it, so that the ends of the legs are even with the base of the can. Place chicken, keeping can upright, on grill over indirect-heat area. The legs will need to touch the grill grate for extra stability. (Beer can chicken racks are available, and they are worth the investment for the security they bring to this method.) Cook the bird for about 15 minutes, then spray with vinegar. Continue cooking, spraying bird every 15 minutes, until an instant-read thermometer inserted into the thickest part of a thigh away from bone registers 170°F (77°C) or the juices run clear when a thigh joint is pierced with a knife tip, about 1½ hours total.

**SERVE** Transfer chicken to a cutting board, taking care with the beer can, which will be very hot. Let chicken rest upright, still impaled on the can, about 10 minutes. Slide chicken off and cut into serving pieces. Serve at once.

Serves 4–6.

# 164 Keep It Upright

The type of cook who likes a good beer can chicken is the same kind who can appreciate a good set of tools. There are plenty of grill frames on the market made to help support an upright chicken atop a can: Ceramic stands are best at heating the beer to a steamy temperature; racks provide skewers for roasting corn or potatoes alongside your chicken; and single-chicken racks offer a good basic framework. Most important, they'll all help keep your bird (and your beer) upright on the grill rack, instead of dousing your coals.

# 165 Whole Rotisserie Chicken

Whole roast chicken is especially succulent when basted with its own juices, and a rotisserie spit makes the job easy by doing the basting for you. Rub these herbs on the bird's skin and stuff them into the cavity to infuse the juices with flavor.

- 10–12 sprigs fresh rosemary
- 10–12 sprigs fresh thyme
- Coarse salt and cracked black pepper
- 1 chicken, about 3½ lb (1¾ kg), neck and giblets removed
- 2 lb (1 kg) wood chips, soaked in water at least 30 minutes

**SEASON** Strip leaves from half of the rosemary and thyme sprigs and roughly chop. Stir chopped herbs together with 1 teaspoon salt and ½ teaspoon pepper. Generously season chicken inside and out with salt and pepper, then carefully loosen skin from breast and legs with your fingers and massage herb mixture under the skin. Finally, stuff the remaining herbs into the cavity.

**PREHEAT** Prepare charcoal or gas grill for rotisserie roasting over indirect grilling on medium heat; the temperature inside the grill should be 350–375°F (180–190°C). If using charcoal, bank lit coals on either side of the grill bed, leaving a strip in the center without heat, and place a drip pan in the center filled with ½ inch (12 mm) of water. Sprinkle half the wood chips over coals, then replenish chips and coals every 20 minutes to maintain heat and smoke. If using gas, raise a burner to high. Fill half of smoker box with wood chips and heat until smoking; reduce heat to medium-low and replenish chips every 20 minutes to maintain smoke.

**GRILL** Thread chicken onto spit and secure it over the grill. Turn on rotisserie motor, cover, and spit-roast or grill until skin is browned and juices run clear when thigh is pierced, 45–75 minutes, or until an instant-read thermometer inserted into the thickest part of thigh away from bone registers 170°F (77°C).

**SERVE** Transfer chicken to carving board and let rest 10 minutes. Carve at the table and serve.

# 166 Secure Your Bird to the Spit

Keeping your bird riveted to the spit is the trickiest part of the rotisserie process, but it's the one that will ensure your roast cooks evenly. You don't want one side sitting in the flames while the other is left out in the cold. It may seem tricky, but it can be accomplished quickly with just a few simple steps—especially if you've already mastered trussing (see item 155), since this is a similar, simplified version of the process.

**STEP 1** Tuck the wing tips around the back of the chicken. (Or remove them with kitchen shears.)

**STEP 2** Cross the drumsticks and tie together with kitchen string.

**STEP 3** Run spit skewer through the chicken, from the neck and through the open cavity.

**STEP 4** Secure rotisserie forks tightly over chicken and mount over the grill.

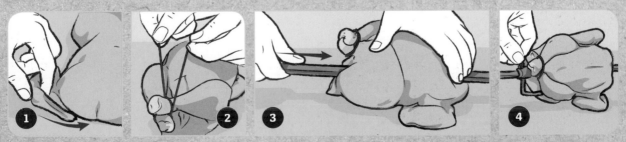

# 167 Chicken Yakitori with Honey Sauce

Japanese culinary tradition is filled with delicious grilled meats, and chicken yakitori is Japanese grilling simplicity at its best: small amounts of skewered thigh meat cooked quickly over very hot coals and served with dipping sauce.

- ½ cup (4 fl oz/125 ml) soy sauce
- ¼ cup (2 fl oz/60 ml) mirin or other rice wine
- ¼ cup (2 fl oz/60 ml) sake
- 3 tablespoons honey
- 2 cloves garlic, minced
- 2 tablespoons peeled and grated fresh ginger
- ½ head iceberg lettuce, cored and shredded (optional)
- 2½ lb (1¼ kg) boneless, skinless chicken thighs
- Salt for seasoning
- Sesame oil for brushing
- 24 bamboo skewers

**SOAK** Soak bamboo skewers in water for 30 minutes.

**MAKE SAUCE** In a small saucepan over high heat, combine soy sauce, mirin, sake, honey, garlic, and ginger, and bring to a boil. Reduce heat to medium and simmer until slightly thickened and glossy, about 10 minutes. Strain into a bowl, cover, and refrigerate until ready to use.

**PREP** Mound lettuce, if using, in center of a serving platter; set aside. Rinse chicken under cold running water and pat dry with paper towels. Using a sharp knife, cut each thigh into three strips, each about 2 inches (5 cm) long and ½ inch (12 mm) thick. Thread three or four chicken pieces onto each soaked skewer without crowding. Lightly season the skewers with salt and brush lightly with oil.

**PREHEAT** Prepare a charcoal or gas grill for direct grilling over high heat. Brush and oil grill grate.

**GRILL** Place skewers on grill directly over heat. Grill, turning once, until well marked and cooked through, 3–4 minutes per side.

**SERVE** Arrange skewers atop lettuce on the platter. Drizzle some honey sauce on top. Serve at once with remaining sauce on the side.

Makes 6 servings.

# 168 Discover Yakitori vs. Teriyaki

Take a look at the lineup of ingredients in traditional teriyaki and yakitori and you might not think there's much difference between the two—but the difference is in the details. Yakitori features skewers of bite-size chicken cooked on a hibachi close to charcoal flames, whereas teriyaki focuses on larger pieces of meat cooked on a grill, then sliced. Also, the sauce for yakitori tends to be lighter in flavor and texture than that of teriyaki, which often includes ingredients like pineapple and garlic, neither of which is Japanese. In fact, yakitori is most commonly served with its own separate sauce for dipping. Finally, yakitori is street food or bar food—a skewer for a quick bite—and teriyaki is commonly a sit-down dish, often served with rice and vegetables.

# 169   Asian Chicken Salad

Varieties of this refreshing salad show up in markets all over Southeast Asia—especially in Vietnam and Thailand, where fish sauce is a pantry staple. Hit with a fresh marinade, the chicken grills up crisp and flavorful. It's the star of the salad and pairs perfectly with mellow Asian noodles and grilled peppers. Boil the noodles while the chicken is grilling or even afterward, since the salad is as good at room temperature as it is warm.

- 4 boneless, skinless chicken breast halves, about 1½ lb (185 g) total
- ⅔ cup (2 oz/60 g) thinly sliced green (spring) onions
- ½ cup (4 fl oz/125 ml) canola oil
- ¼ cup (2 fl oz/60 ml) fresh lime juice
- ¼ cup *each* (⅓ oz/ 10 g) slivered fresh mint and slivered fresh thai basil or regular sweet basil
- 2 tablespoons Asian fish sauce
- 2 teaspoons peeled and chopped fresh ginger
- ¼ teaspoon red pepper flakes
- 2 cloves garlic, finely chopped
- 1 small green bell pepper, seeded and quartered lengthwise
- 1 small yellow bell pepper, seeded and quartered lengthwise
- ¾ lb (375 g) soba or *somen* noodles or Italian vermicelli
- ¼ cup (1 oz/30 g) sliced radishes

**PREP** Use the palm of your hand to flatten each chicken breast to an even thickness of about ¾ inch (2 cm). Set aside.

**MARINATE** In a bowl, mix ⅓ cup (1 oz/30 g) of green onions, plus the oil, lime juice, mint, basil, fish sauce, ginger, red pepper flakes, and garlic. Pour about one-third of marinade into a shallow, nonreactive dish just large enough to hold chicken; reserve remaining marinade to use as salad dressing. Add chicken to dish and turn to coat. Cover and refrigerate, turning once or twice, for at least 30 minutes or for up to 3 hours. (Remove chicken from refrigerator at least 30 minutes before grilling.) Add green and yellow bell peppers to marinade during last 15 minutes of refrigerator time.

**PREHEAT** Prepare charcoal or gas grill for direct grilling over medium-high heat. Brush and oil grill rack.

**GRILL** Place chicken on the grill directly over heat and cook, turning once or twice, until firm to the touch and opaque throughout, 8–10 minutes total. About halfway through the grilling time, place the bell peppers along the edges of the grill where the heat is less intense (or over medium-low heat on a gas grill). Grill, turning once or twice, until softened and lightly charred, 4–6 minutes.

**BOIL** Meanwhile, bring a large saucepan three-quarters full of salted water to a boil. Add noodles and boil until al dente, about 8 minutes or according to package directions. Drain well. Transfer to bowl, add reserved marinade, and toss well.

**MIX & SERVE** Cut bell peppers lengthwise into narrow strips. Cut chicken across grain into thin strips. Just before serving, add chicken, bell peppers, remaining ⅓ cup (1 oz/ 30 g) green onion, and radishes to the noodles, toss well, and serve.

Serves 4.

## 170 Cumin Crust Rub

- ¼ cup (1 oz/30 g) ground cumin
- 1 teaspoon *each* smoked paprika and firmly packed light brown sugar
- ¼ teaspoon *each* ground coriander and cayenne pepper
- Freshly ground black pepper

In a small, dry frying pan over low heat, toast cumin, stirring often, until aromatic, about 30 seconds. Pour onto a plate and let cool. In a small container with a tight-fitting lid, combine cumin, paprika, sugar, coriander, cayenne pepper, and ½ teaspoon black pepper. Cover and shake vigorously to mix. Use right away, or store in a cool, dark place for up to 1 month.

Makes about ⅓ cup (3 oz/85 g).

## 171 Cumin-Crusted Chicken Thighs with Grilled Salsa

Tomatillos are pretty good when they're eaten raw, but they really sing when they're on the grill—getting sweet and smoky with the dry, charring heat. Mixed with grilled jalapeño, lime juice, and cilantro, tomatillos make a savory salsa with a cool and refreshing character—the perfect complement to a spice-crusted chicken thigh. Cumin gets sweeter on the grill, too, mellowing its distinctive earthy and nutty flavor.

- ¼ cup (1 oz/30 g) Cumin Crust Rub (see item 170)
- 8 bone-in, skin-on chicken thighs
- ¼ cup (2 fl oz/60 ml) canola oil
- 7 large tomatillos, papery husks removed and cut in half
- 1 jalapeño chile, halved lengthwise and seeded
- ¼ cup (2 fl oz/60 ml) fresh lime juice
- 1 tablespoon olive oil
- ½ cup (¾ oz/20 g) chopped fresh cilantro
- Kosher salt

**MARINATE** In a large bowl, combine chicken thighs and oil. Toss to coat. Transfer thighs to a platter and sprinkle evenly on all sides with cumin rub (see item 170). Set aside.

**PREHEAT** Prepare charcoal or gas grill for indirect grilling over medium heat; temperature inside grill should be 350–375°F (180–190°C). If using charcoal, bank lit coals on either side of the grill bed, leaving a strip in the center without heat, and place drip pan in the center. If using gas, preheat burners, then turn off one or more burners to create cooler zone. Brush and oil grill grate.

**MAKE SALSA** Place tomatillos and chile over direct-heat area of grill. (You'll probably need a grill screen for the chile or you'll lose it through the grate.) Cook, turning as needed, until well charred on all sides, about 3 minutes. Transfer tomatillos and chile to a blender, add lime juice and oil, and pulse until combined but still chunky. Transfer to a bowl, fold in cilantro, and season with salt. You should

have about 2 cups (16 fl oz/500 ml). (The salsa can be made up to a week in advance and refrigerated. Bring to room temperature before serving.)

**GRILL** Place chicken thighs, meaty side down, over indirect-heat area of grill. Cook, turning once, until thighs are nicely grill-marked on both sides and firm to the touch and an instant-read thermometer inserted into the thickest part of the thigh away from the bone registers 170°F (77°C), 10–15 minutes per side. Try to turn the thighs only once so they develop nice grill marks.

**SERVE** Transfer thighs to a platter and let rest for 10 minutes. Serve at once with tomatillo salsa.

Serves 4–8.

## 172 Grilled Chicken Fajitas

In the two or three decades since skirt steak was a method of payment to Mexican vaqueros (cowboys), fajitas have become mainstream, and chicken has become a popular star of the Tex-Mex classic. It makes for perfect party food: Put together all the toppings in advance, grill up the chicken, and let the guests serve themselves.

- 1 bunch fresh cilantro, stems removed
- ¾ cup olive oil
- 5 tablespoons fresh lime juice
- 2 teaspoons ground cumin
- 1 teaspoons ancho chile powder
- Salt and freshly ground pepper to taste
- 6 skinless, boneless chicken breast halves
- 3 large poblano chiles, stemmed, seeded, and cut into strips
- 3 large yellow peppers, stemmed, seeded, and cut into strips
- 2 red onions
- Twelve 8-inch (20-cm) flour tortillas
- Toppings as desired: salsa, guacamole, sour cream, chopped fresh cilantro, sliced green (spring) onions, chopped jalapeño chiles

**BLEND** Place cilantro in a food processor or blender and pulse until chopped. Add olive oil, lime juice, cumin, and chile powder, and pulse. Season with salt and pepper.

**MARINATE** Place chicken in a large, zip-top plastic bag. Add ⅓ cup of the cilantro mixture; seal bag and squish to coat chicken. Place chiles, peppers, and onions in another zip-top bag. Add ½ cup of the cilantro mixture; seal bag and squeeze to coat vegetables. Reserve remaining marinade.

**PREHEAT** Prepare charcoal or gas grill for direct grilling over high heat.

**GRILL** Brush and oil grill grate. Grill chicken, turning once, until opaque throughout, about 7 minutes per side. Grill vegetables until tender, turning frequently, about 12 minutes for peppers and 15 minutes for onions. Grill tortillas, turning once, until charred, about 1 minute per side.

**SERVE** Transfer chicken to a cutting board. Slice crosswise into strips. Arrange peppers and onions on a platter. Place tortillas in a basket and offer reserved marinade for drizzling on top.

Serves 6.

## 173 Sear with la Plancha

Fajitas were already big news in Texas when a chef at the Hyatt Regency in Austin came up with the idea for "Sizzling Fajitas"—a steaming-hot meat platter served tableside with all the expected fixin's. Many have since come to prefer the sizzling griddle approach to the grilled one. If you fall in that camp, you'll likely want to invest in a cast iron griddle that heats up nice and hot over a gas flame or a charcoal grill. Used with an an outdoor grill, la plancha delivers cooked foods with the char marks and moisture retention of a griddle but the smoky flavor of a grill.

# 174 Learn a Foolproof Formula for Chicken Skewers

Some might call chicken fickle, others say it's simply adaptable. Truth is, chicken likes a lot of different treatments, and loves to take on the character of any marinade with which it's partnered. Skewers of the capricious poultry are the perfect receptors for highly seasoned marinades, with all those cut surfaces providing the ideal exterior for marinade penetration. Here's a foolproof formula:

**2 POUNDS CHICKEN + CHOICE OF MARINADE + 6–12 SKEWERS + GRILL (DIRECT HEAT OVER MEDIUM-HOT FIRE, TURNING AS NEEDED, 9–10 MINUTES) = TASTY CHICKEN SKEWERS**

**MARINATE** In a large zip-top plastic bag, mix marinade ingredients. Set aside. Holding the knife parallel to the cutting board, cut each chicken breast into two thin halves, then into bite-size pieces. Place chicken in marinade, seal bag, and squish to coat. Refrigerate for at least 1 hour or up to 4 hours.

**PREHEAT & PREP** Prepare a charcoal or gas grill for direct grilling over medium-high heat. If using wooden skewers, soak in water at least 1 hour before grilling. Remove chicken from marinade and thread pieces on skewers.

**GRILL** Place skewers on grill directly over heat. Cook, turning to char all sides, until chicken is opaque and fully cooked, 8–10 minutes total cooking time.

**SERVE** Serve immediately.

Makes 6–12 servings.

## 175 Tandoori-Style Marinade

- 2 cups (1 lb/500 g) plain whole-milk yogurt
- 2 tablespoons *each* fresh lemon juice and grated fresh ginger
- 4 cloves garlic, minced
- 1 teaspoon *each* ground coriander, ground turmeric, and salt
- ½ teaspoon *each* saffron threads, ground cumin, cayenne pepper, and freshly ground black pepper

India's tandoor is a clay oven stoked by intensely hot hardwood charcoal. The heat is controlled by the amount of oxygen that is let in or out, usually via a small door or window at the bottom. The ceramic walls of the tandoor reflect the heat of the fire, creating a cooking environment that easily reaches 600°F (315°C). Marinated meats are lowered into the oven on metal skewers and cooked in this smoky pit until they are grilled to perfection. To make the classic tandoori marinade, always begin with yogurt, which has the acidity to penetrate the meat and the thickness to coat it, nicely adhering the marinade's many spices. Mix all ingredients in a bowl and try the marinade with boneless, skinless chicken thighs and a hot fire.

## 176 Chicken Satay Marinade

- 1 cup (8 fl oz/250 ml) coconut milk
- ¼ cup (2 fl oz/60 ml) Asian fish sauce
- 4 cloves garlic, finely chopped
- ¼ cup (⅓ oz/10 g) chopped fresh cilantro
- 1 teaspoon curry powder
- 1 teaspoon freshly ground black pepper

Throughout Malaysia and Southeast Asia, satay refers to a skewer of grilled meats served with dipping sauce. Indonesians were the first to popularize peanut sauce (see item 251) as the preferred accompaniment. To make the marinade, mix all ingredients together and soak your skewers. If you're a real stickler for details, you'll skewer the meat onto the midrib of a coconut palm frond. (Bamboo skewers also work.) Coconut milk is a go-to ingredient of Southeast Asian cuisine for its sweetness and tenderness, and it doesn't disappoint in either regard.

## 177 Shawarma-Style Marinade

- 3 tablespoons safflower or canola oil
- 1 tablespoon white wine vinegar
- ½ lemon, juiced
- 6 cloves garlic, minced or pressed
- 1 teaspoon *each* kosher salt and ground cardamom
- ⅛ teaspoon ground nutmeg
- 2 bay leaves
- 1 cinnamon stick
- 1 star anise

It's hard to pass by a shawarma vendor on the street without a sudden hankering for the Middle Eastern fast food. It stars layers of richly marinated meat (chicken breast, lamb, beef, or goat), stacked on the single skewer of a vertical spit and slow-roasted alongside an open flame, then carved fresh with every order and popped into a warmed pita with hummus, tahini, tomatoes, cucumbers, and onions for a quick sandwich to go. Mix these marinade ingredients together, use on some home-grilled chicken, and serve single skewers the same way; no one would ever guess they weren't carved from the spit.

# 178 Caribbean Jerk Chicken

Caribbean jerk isn't just a seasoning, it's a license to party. Full of spicy heat, it needs something smooth (grilled plantains!), something sweet (pineapple salsa!), and something cold (rum punch!) to balance its intensity. Pull up some chairs around the barbecue—every item of this party menu cooks up on the grill. Chicken legs are the best part of the bird to pair with jerk spices since they stay on the grill long enough to develop a depth of flavor well matched to the chile's smoldering character.

- 3 green (spring) onions, including tender green parts, chopped
- 4 large cloves garlic, chopped
- 3 habanero chiles, seeded and chopped
- ¼ cup (2 fl oz/60 ml) fresh lime juice
- 3 tablespoons extra-virgin olive oil
- 2 tablespoons tamari or reduced-sodium soy sauce
- 1 tablespoon *each* firmly packed light brown sugar and chopped fresh thyme
- 2 teaspoons ground allspice
- 1 teaspoon ground nutmeg
- ½ teaspoon ground cinnamon
- Kosher salt and freshly ground pepper to taste
- 6 whole chicken legs

**MARINATE** In a blender or food processor, combine green onions, garlic, chiles, lime juice, oil, tamari, sugar, thyme, allspice, nutmeg, cinnamon, salt, and pepper. Process until smooth. Place chicken legs on a platter and coat evenly on all sides with jerk seasoning. Cover and refrigerate for at least 8 hours or overnight.

**PREHEAT** Remove chicken from refrigerator 30 minutes before grilling. Prepare charcoal or gas grill for indirect grilling over medium heat; grill temperature should be 350–375°F (180–190°C). If using charcoal, bank lit coals on either side of the grill bed, leaving a strip in the center without heat, and place a drip pan in the center. If using gas, preheat burners, then turn off one or more burners to create a cooler zone. Brush and oil grill grate.

**GRILL** Place chicken legs on the grill over direct heat and sear, turning once, until nicely browned on both sides, about 2 minutes per side. Move them to indirect-heat area and cook until firm to the touch and an instant-read thermometer inserted into the thickest part of the thigh away from bone registers 170°F (77°C), about 30 minutes.

**SERVE** Transfer chicken to a serving platter and let rest for 10 minutes, then serve.

Serves 6.

# 179 Grilled Pineapple Salsa

Pineapples are among the fruits that adapt best to the grill's searing heat, the natural sugars on their cut edges caramelizing to sweet perfection over a hot fire. Mixed with mild avocados, acidic onion, and bracing mint, this sweet-and-savory salsa makes a refreshing condiment complex enough to stand up to spicy jerk seasoning.

- ½ fresh pineapple, peeled, cored, and cut into slices, rings, or wedges
- 1 red onion, thickly sliced
- Olive oil for drizzling
- 1 jalapeño chile
- ½ avocado, peeled and diced
- 1 tablespoon finely chopped fresh mint
- Juice of 1 lime
- Kosher salt

**PREHEAT** Prepare a charcoal or gas grill for direct grilling over high heat. Brush and oil grill grate.

**GRILL** Drizzle pineapple and onion slices with oil, then place on the grill with the jalapeño. Grill pineapple and onion slices, turning once, until grill marked and heated through, about 8 minutes total. Grill chile, turning, until charred on all sides.

**MIX** Transfer pineapple, onion, and chile to a cutting board. Chop pineapple and onion into chunks and place in a bowl. When chile is cool enough to handle, peel, stem, seed, and dice it, then add to bowl. Add avocado and mint and stir to mix. Mix in lime juice and season with salt.

**SERVE** Use at once, or cover and refrigerate for up to two days. Bring to room temperature before serving.

Makes 1 cup (8 oz/250 g).

# 180 Grilled Plantains

Plantains (well-known cousins of the banana family) need to be cooked before their starchy flesh will become sweet. Cultivated in many tropical areas, they are a frequent accompaniment to Caribbean preparations. Like bananas, they range in color from green to yellow to brown to black. But unlike bananas, they are better when darker. Brown and even black plantains are best for the grill, cooking up sweet and tender.

- 3 tablespoons unsalted butter
- ¾ cup (6 oz/185 g) packed brown sugar
- 2 tablespoons apple cider vinegar or sherry vinegar
- 4 very ripe plantains

**GLAZE** In a small saucepan over medium heat, melt butter and sugar until sugar is dissolved. Stir in vinegar. Set aside.

**PREHEAT** Prepare charcoal or gas grill for direct-heat grilling over high heat. Reduce heat to medium-high. Brush and oil grill grate.

**GRILL** Slice unpeeled plantains in half lengthwise. Place, cut side down, on grill. Close lid and cook for 15 minutes. Turn plantains and brush cut sides with butter glaze. Close lid and continue cooking for another 15 minutes. Brush a bit more glaze on plantains before removing from grill.

**SERVE** Serve plantains in their skins while hot from the grill.

Serves 4–8.

# 181 Perfect Grilled Turkey

Pilgrims were certainly not the first to prepare turkey for a celebration, as its large size has always been suited to feeding a crowd, especially when the wild bird is rendered juicy and flavorful. Lucky for us, we not only have centuries of turkey-roasting technique to draw from, but a multitude of great-quality birds as well. Grill-roasted turkey is easy to master and benefits from the mellow smokiness of the smoldering woods.

- Apple-Bourbon Brine (See item 182)
- Spice-Herb Butter (See item 183)
- Country-Style Gravy (See item 184)
- 1 fresh whole turkey, 12–14 lb (6–7 kg), or 1 fresh wild turkey, neck, giblets, and wing tips removed, and turkey dressed
- Salt and ground white pepper
- 3 large carrots, peeled and halved lengthwise
- 4 ribs celery
- 2 yellow onions, peeled and quartered
- 1–2 lb wood chips or chunks, soaked for 30 minutes

**BRINE** Brine turkey (see item 182).

**SEASON** Prepare the Spice-Herb Butter (see item 183.) Season turkey, inside and out, with salt and white pepper. Starting at neck end, carefully loosen skin from breast with your fingers. Then, working from cavity end, loosen skin from breast and legs. Massage Spice-Herb Butter under skin and massage any remaining butter into outside of skin. Truss turkey (see item 155 for the basics).

**PREP & PREHEAT** Prepare a charcoal or gas grill for indirect grilling over medium-low heat. Arrange vegetables and reserved herb sprigs in a large aluminum roasting pan. Place turkey on top of vegetables. If using charcoal, sprinkle half of wood chips over coals. If using gas, raise a burner to high and place a smoker box half full of wood chips over it until smoking, then reduce heat to medium-low.

**GRILL** Place pan with turkey and vegetables over indirect-heat part of grill, cover, and cook until the skin is nicely browned and the juices run clear when the thigh is pierced, 2½–3½ hours or 12–15 minutes per pound. Replenish coals (if using) and wood chips, and baste the turkey with its own juices every 30 minutes. Turkey is done when an instant-read thermometer in the thickest part of the thigh away from bone registers 170°F (77°C) and when the breast registers at least 155°F (68°C).

**SERVE** Transfer turkey to a carving board, tent with aluminum foil, and let rest 20–30 minutes. Meanwhile, prepare Country-Style Turkey Gravy (see item 184). Carve and serve gravy alongside.

Makes 8–10 servings.

# 182 Apple-Bourbon Brine

Brine not only adds flavor, it also enhances the juiciness in your grilled food. To make this overnight brine for turkey, chicken, and game birds, combine 4 cups (32 fl oz/1 l) apple cider and 2 cups (16 fl oz/500 ml) bourbon or other whiskey in a large container. Whisk in ½ cup (4 oz/125 g) *each* of salt and sugar until dissolved. Add a quartered yellow onion and 3–4 whole bay leaves.

Place turkey or other poultry in another large container, stockpot, or clean plastic bucket. Pour brine over turkey, add enough water to cover, and weigh down with a plate to submerge bird in brine. Place in refrigerator (or in a cooler packed with ice) overnight (or 45–60 minutes per pound), then remove from brine, rinse with cold water, and pat dry with paper towels.

# 183 Spice-Herb Butter

Next to a good brine, a suped-up compound butter is key for adding savory flavor to roast turkey. This one calls for toasting the spices before mixing them into the butter—a great way to enhance their flavor, making it more earthy and sweet.

- 2 tablespoons *each* white peppercorns, fennel seeds, and coriander seeds, toasted
- 1 tablespoon *each* fresh chopped rosemary, sage, and thyme
- 1 cup (8 oz/250 g) unsalted butter, at room temperature
- 1 tablespoon granulated garlic
- 1 teaspoon coarse salt
- Zest and juice of 1 lemon

In a spice grinder or blender, combine peppercorns, fennel, and coriander seeds. Process into a coarse powder. In a small bowl, mix spice powder, chopped herbs, butter, granulated garlic, salt, and lemon zest and juice. Use immediately, or cover and refrigerate for up to one week or freeze for up to three months.

Makes 1 cup (8 oz/250 g).

# 184 Country-Style Gravy

Country-style makes for a good and reliable shortcut to gravy preparation. It starts with a seasoned roux (cooked flour and butter) to which pan juices are added, rather than gravy prepared from the long, slow simmering of the giblets. It's a lot easier to prepare than one might think—which is good, because no celebration turkey is truly complete without it.

- ½ cup (4 fl oz/125 ml) white wine
- ½ cup (4 fl oz/125 ml) water, chicken stock, or broth
- 2 tablespoons *each* unsalted butter and all-purpose flour
- Coarse salt and ground white pepper

**DEGLAZE & STRAIN** When turkey is finished roasting and is resting, mash roasted vegetables and herb sprigs remaining in roasting pan. Return pan to the grill over direct heat or to the stovetop on medium-high heat, and deglaze bottom of pan with white wine and water, using a wooden spoon to dislodge any brown bits. Strain through a sieve into a measuring cup with a spout or beaker; discard solids. Using a small ladle or spoon, skim grease off top, leaving 1–2 tablespoons in a cup with pan juices.

**COOK** In a saucepan over medium heat, melt butter until foam subsides. Stir in flour, season with salt and white pepper, and cook, stirring constantly, until golden brown, about 2 minutes. Add strained pan juices, ½ cup (4 fl oz/125 ml) at a time, and briefly remove pan from heat, whisking vigorously, after each addition. Simmer gravy until it is very smooth and thick enough to coat the back of a spoon, about 10 minutes. Taste and adjust seasonings.

Makes 4 servings.

# 185 Southern Louisiana-Style Smoked Turkey Breast

Bone-in breast halves are among the best and easiest turkey cuts for the grill—especially once you understand a few expert methods for maintaining the moisture of lean meat on the grill. Keeping meat on the bone is one easy method, and presoaking it in brine is another. For added protection against dryness, add water to the pan set underneath the indirect-heat cooking area, and don't overlook the reading of an accurate meat thermometer. Try it with this Southern-style recipe, with its tomato gravy pairing perfectly with the smoky meat.

- 3–4 tablespoons herb-and-spice rub (see item 251)
- 1 bone-in, skin-on turkey breast, 5–6 lb (2½–3 kg)
- 2 tablespoons canola oil
- 6–8 cups mixed hickory and applewood chips, soaked in water for 30 minutes
- ¼ cup (1½ oz/45 g) finely chopped shallots
- 2 cloves garlic, minced
- ½ cup (4 fl oz/125 ml) tomato sauce
- 1 tablespoon all-purpose flour
- 1 cup (8 fl oz/250 ml) low-sodium chicken broth
- ½ teaspoon dried thyme
- Kosher salt and freshly ground black pepper

**PREP** Make spice rub. Remove turkey from refrigerator at least 30 minutes before grilling. Brush the entire surface of the turkey breast with oil, then liberally season all sides with rub.

**PREHEAT** Prepare a smoker or a charcoal or gas grill for smoking over medium-low heat; the temperature inside the grill should be 300–325°F (150–165°C). If using charcoal, bank lit coals on either side of the grill bed, leaving a strip in the center without heat, then add about 2 cups wood chips to the fire just before grilling. If using gas, fill a smoker box with up to 2 cups wood chips, then preheat grill. Turn off one or more burners to create a cooler zone.

**GRILL** Place a roasting rack in an aluminum roasting pan, and put turkey breast on rack. Put pan over indirect-heat area of grill, and pour 1 cup (8 fl oz/250 ml) water into the pan. Cover the grill and smoke turkey until a rich golden brown and an instant-read thermometer inserted into the thickest part of the breast away from bone registers 165°F (74°C), 1½–2 hours, adding more wood chips every 30 minutes or so and more coals as needed.

**MAKE GRAVY** Transfer turkey to a cutting board, tent with aluminum foil, and let rest. Meanwhile, prepare gravy: Skim fat from drippings in turkey pan, then measure out ½ cup (4 fl oz/125 ml) of the drippings and pour into a sauté pan. Place over low heat, bring to a simmer, and simmer until reduced by about half. Add the shallots and garlic, and cook until softened, about 2 minutes. Stir in tomato sauce and cook 1 minute. Whisk in flour and cook, whisking occasionally, about 2 minutes. Slowly whisk in the broth. Continue to cook, stirring often, until thickened, 2–3 minutes. Stir in thyme and season with salt and pepper. Pour into a warmed bowl.

**SERVE** Slice turkey, arrange it on a platter, and serve at once with gravy.

Serves 6–8.

# 186 Try the Dry Brine

For anyone who has experimented with brining, there is little doubt that coating a bird with salty solutions improves both its flavor and moisture content. To understand the process, know that meat contains muscle proteins that are naturally dissolved by the salt in the brine solution, thereby decreasing the ability of muscle fibers to contract when cooking. This leads to less internal moisture being squeezed out, which in turn leads to juicier meat in the cooked bird. Wet brining—that is, in a salt-and-liquid solution—is perhaps the most popular choice, but dry brining with a salt-based rub is luring many grilling enthusiasts to its camp.

Champions of the dry brine applaud its ability to enhance flavor and retain moisture without introducing excess liquid. They also appreciate the enhanced crispiness and browning of the skin (thanks to the addition of baking powder). Last, dry brining can be a heck of a lot easier, principally for saving you the trouble of finding a tub large enough to submerge a whole turkey (that will still fit in your fridge).

To dry brine, combine ½ cup (4 oz/250 g) kosher salt (or 6 tablespoons table salt) with 2 tablespoons of baking powder. Carefully blot your turkey dry with paper towels. Generously sprinkle the salt mixture all over your bird, letting it shower down evenly over the surface. Place the turkey on a rack in a rimmed baking sheet and refrigerate fro 12–24 hours. Remove from the refrigerator at least 30 minutes before cooking—and don't add any extra salt during the seasoning or cooking process.

# 187 Compare Grill-Roasting vs. Smoking

The difference between grill-roasting and smoking a turkey is that for the latter the bird is put directly on the grill rack, rather than in an aluminum pan, and wood chips are added to the grill. The cooking time is about the same, but the result is a bird with firmer meat and a smokier flavor. Choose the wood chips according to how strong you want the smoky taste to be: Hickory is most pronounced, fruitwood is mellow, and mesquite adds a robust aroma.

# Spiced Turkey Burgers

Brines, rubs, and smoke are all well and good when it comes to adding flavor to poultry, but there's also something to be said for the quick addition of tasty enhancements and a custom grind to spice things up a bit. Turkey burgers are a case in point. Plain (especially when featuring dark meat), they're pretty good. But when you grind your own meat and add some favorite herbs and spices, the result can be sensational. Looking to save some time yet yield the same result? Ask your butcher to grind the meat for you.

- 2 lb (1 kg) bone-in turkey thighs
- ½ cup (3 oz/92 g) minced yellow onion
- ¼ cup (⅓ oz/10 g) chopped fresh cilantro
- 2 cloves garlic, minced
- 2 teaspoons chopped fresh jalapeño or serrano chile
- 1 teaspoon *each* ground coriander, ground cumin, and ground paprika
- ½ teaspoon freshly ground black pepper
- Burger toppings of choice
- 4–6 burger buns of choice
- Condiments of choice

**FREEZE** Cut turkey into 1-inch (2.5-cm) cubes. Place meat in a single layer on a rimmed baking sheet, cover with plastic wrap, and freeze until very cold, about 15 minutes.

**GRIND** Toss meat with seasonings and grind using a food processor (pulse until coarsely chopped) or the meat grinding attachment on an electric stand mixer (using the coarse attachment).

**PREP & PREHEAT** Form meat into four to six patties, each about ¾ inch (2 cm) thick. Layer patties between pieces of waxed paper, place stacks on a plate, cover, and refrigerate 30 minutes. Prepare a charcoal or gas grill for direct grilling over medium-high heat. Brush and oil grill grate.

**GRILL** Place burgers on grill and cook, turning once, until well marked and opaque in centers, 7–9 minutes total. Move burgers to grill sides to keep warm while you toast buns over the grill's remaining heat.

**SERVE** Place a warm burger on each toasted bun. Assemble toppings of choice on a platter and serve with condiments to add as desired.

Serves 4–6.

# 189 Marinated Duck Breasts with Orange Glaze

Duck prepared with orange has been pretty much at the core of "haute cuisine" since Catherine of Aragon, King Henry VIII's first wife, brought the dish to English high society from her home country of Spain back in the 16th century. It's no less elegant today, just refined with a range of grilling techniques. Crisp the breast, fat side down, over the flame first, then turn and finishing cooking until medium-rare.

- Grated zest and juice of 1 large orange
- ⅓ cup (3 fl oz/80 ml) *each* dry sherry and bourbon
- 1 tablespoon Worcestershire sauce
- 2 tablespoons grated shallot
- Kosher salt and freshly ground black pepper
- 4 boneless, skin-on duck breast halves, about 12 oz (340 g) each
- 1 cup (10 oz/315 g) orange marmalade, gently heated until liquid

**MARINATE** In a small bowl, stir together orange zest and juice, sherry, bourbon, Worcestershire sauce, shallot, ¼ teaspoon salt, and a few grinds of pepper. Place duck breasts in a large zip-top plastic bag and pour in marinade.

Seal bag closed, squish marinade around, and refrigerate overnight. Be sure to turn bag several times while duck is marinating.

**PREHEAT** Remove duck from refrigerator at least 30 minutes before grilling. Discard marinade and pat breasts dry with paper towels. Prepare a charcoal or gas grill for direct grilling over medium heat. Brush and oil grill grate.

**GRILL** Place duck breasts, skin side down, on the grill directly over the fire, and cook until the skin is nicely browned and crispy, about 6 minutes, checking occasionally for flare-ups and moving duck to a cooler part of the grill if needed. The skin should have a nice golden char and not be burned black. Turn breasts and brush with marmalade, then cook another 5–7 minutes to yield a perfect medium-rare duck breast. An instant-read thermometer inserted into the thickest part of the breast away from the bone should register 135–140°F (57–60°C).

**SERVE** Transfer duck breasts to a platter, brush once again with marmalade, and let rest about 5 minutes. Serve at once with any remaining marmalade on the side.

Serves 4.

# 190 Tea-Smoked Duck Breasts

Out of the teapot comes more than just a soothing cup. The Chinese have used tea leaves as a seasoning for centuries, and the leaves add a mellow flavor and golden color when used as a fuel for smoking. A traditional Chinese tea-smoking technique can be accomplished simply using a wok, but a classic smoking setup on a grill works even better. Look for bone-in, skin-on duck breasts for smoking; during the long, slow cooking, the bone adds flavor while the skin protects the meat from drying out and burning. In this recipe, the duck gets a double dose of tea: the first in a paste smeared onto the breasts, the second mixed in with the wood chips. Choose fresh tea for the best flavor and color. China black tea is a good all-around choice, but Lapsang souchong—with its already smoky flavor—is especially effective.

## FOR THE TEA PASTE

- ⅓ cup (1 oz/30g) loose tea leaves
- 5 whole cloves
- 3 whole star anise
- 1½ tablespoons grated orange zest
- ¼ cup (2 fl oz/60 ml) thawed, frozen orange juice concentrate
- 1 tablespoon *each* soy sauce and rice vinegar
- Salt
- ¼ teaspoon *each* red pepper flakes and ground cinnamon
- 6 bone-in, skin-on duck breast halves

## FOR THE SOAKING MIX

- 2 handfuls wood chips such as fruitwood or mesquite
- ⅓ cup (1 oz/30 g) loose tea leaves
- 1 cinnamon stick, broken in half
- 3 whole star anise
- 3 whole cloves

**MAKE PASTE** In a spice grinder or with a mortar and pestle, grind together tea leaves, cloves, star anise, and orange zest. Transfer to a small bowl. Add orange juice concentrate, soy sauce, vinegar, ½ teaspoon salt, red pepper flakes, and cinnamon, and mix well. Let stand 15 minutes, or cover and refrigerate up to 2 hours before using.

**MARINATE** Smear tea paste over duck breasts. Let duck breasts stand 20 minutes, or cover and refrigerate up to 2 hours. If refrigerated, remove from the refrigerator 25 minutes before grilling.

**SOAK** In a container, combine wood chips, tea leaves, cinnamon stick, star anise, and cloves. Add water just to cover and let soak at least 30 minutes. Drain, reserving soaking water.

**PREHEAT** Prepare a charcoal or gas grill for indirect grilling over medium heat: If using charcoal, bank lit coals on either side of the grill bed, leaving a strip in the center without heat. Place a drip pan in the center strip and fill with water from the smoking mixture to a depth of ¾ inch (2 cm). Sprinkle about half the smoking mixture over the coals. (Keep remaining chips in water, then drain and add to coals about halfway through smoking.) If using gas, fill smoker box with drained smoking mixture, then preheat grill. The wood chips should begin to smolder and release a steady stream of smoke. Turn off one or more burners to create an indirect-heat cooking zone. Place drip pan filled with ¾ inch (2 cm) of water from smoking mixture over indirect-heat area.

**SMOKE** Brush and oil grill grate. Place duck breasts on the grill rack away from heat elements. Cover the grill and smoke duck breasts until richly browned and cooked through, about 45 minutes. To check for doneness, insert an instant-read thermometer into the thickest part of breast away from the bone; it should register 150–160°F (65–71°C). The temperature will rise another few degrees while the duck is resting.

**SERVE** Serve hot or at room temperature, cut into serving sections if you like.

Makes 6 servings.

# 191 Cider-Glazed Quail

Halved quails can cook to perfection on the grill in just a few minutes, thanks to their petite size. Marinated in a simple apple cider and balsamic glaze, the quail crisp up on the outside while remaining tender and juicy in the center. They're delicious and perfect for a bite-size appetizer dish. Serve them with a salad of crisp greens, bacon, endive, and apple, or over a nubby barley or wild rice pilaf peppered with dried fruit and herbs. If you're preparing an appetizer-size portion, one quail per person should do the trick nicely.

- ¼ cup (2 fl oz/60 ml) apple juice concentrate, thawed
- ¼ cup (2 fl oz/60 ml) light agave syrup or honey
- 2 tablespoons balsamic vinegar
- 4 semiboned quail, about 1 lb (500 g) total weight
- Salt and freshly ground black pepper

**GLAZE** In a bowl, stir together apple juice concentrate, agave syrup, and vinegar. Pour half the glaze into a shallow non-reactive dish large enough to hold quail in a single layer. Pour the remaining half of glaze into a small bowl and set aside.

**PREP** Rinse quail, inside and out, under cold water, then pat dry with paper towels. Butterfly quail, opening it flat. (Follow directions for spatchcocking a chicken, see item 161). Cut each flattened bird in half lengthwise along center. You should have two halves, each with a leg, breast, and wing. Season quail halves with salt and pepper. Place in dish with glaze and turn to coat. Cover and refrigerate for at least 1 hour or up to 4 hours.

**PREHEAT** Prepare a charcoal or gas grill for direct grilling over medium-high heat. Brush and grease the grill grate with some duck fat.

**GRILL** Place quail, bone side down, directly over heat and cook until nicely charred, 1–2 minutes. Turn and move to edge of grill where heat is less intense. Brush with remaining marinade, cover, and grill until browned and cooked through, 2–3 minutes longer. Serve with reserved cider glaze spooned over the top.

Makes 4 servings.

# 192 Bacon-Wrapped Cornish Hens

If you're determined to cook whole chickens on the grill, Cornish hens may just be your target. Unlike whole chickens weighing in at 3–5 pounds (1.5–2.25 kg), these softball-size birds are compact enough to cook evenly when grill-roasted over indirect heat. Their only detractor is a slight tendency toward dryness—a common complaint of game birds—but it's easily remedied with a flavorful cloak of bacon.

- 8 slices bacon, about ½ lb (250 g) total
- 4 Cornish hens, about 1¼ lb (625 g) each
- Salt and freshly ground black pepper
- 4–8 fresh parsley sprigs
- 4–8 fresh thyme sprigs

**PREHEAT** Prepare charcoal or gas grill for indirect cooking over medium-high heat.

**PREP** Fill a large saucepan two-thirds full with water and bring to a boil over high heat. Add bacon and blanch for 3 minutes. Drain, rinse bacon with cold water, and pat dry with paper towels. Set aside. Pat hens dry with paper towels, sprinkle inside and out with salt and pepper, and tuck a sprig or two of parsley and thyme into each body cavity. Crisscross two slices of bacon across breast of each hen, and tie bacon securely to birds with kitchen string.

**GRILL** Place hens, breast side up, over indirect-heat part of grill. Cover and cook 30 minutes, then turn, breast side down. Continue cooking until birds are well browned, opaque throughout, and juices run clear, 20–25 minutes. An instant-read thermometer inserted into the thickest part of the breast should read 170°F (77°C), or inserted into the thickest part of a thigh should register 185°F (85°C).

**SERVE** Discard string and serve hot!

Serves 4.

# 193 Jalapeño Bird Poppers

Small game birds—dove, pheasant, quail, and grouse—don't offer much in the way of meat. The breast is really the most tender and best-tasting part and, in some game cooks' opinions, the only part worth keeping. But place most of these bite-size breasts on the grill rack and you'll lose them through the grate. Cook them up as poppers, however, and you'll have hit upon one of the best preparations for these tender morsels. With game bird popper and beer in hand, most guests will gladly pull up a chair to stake their claim around the barbecue for the rest of the night. Bacon is the not-so-secret ingredient. It grills best if it's on the thinner side; if you like it thick, precook it in the microwave for 3 minutes before using.

- 1 lb (16 oz/500 g) breast meat (pheasant, quail, dove, grouse, etc.), cut into 24 bite-size pieces
- 1 jar (4 oz/125 g) sliced or fresh jalapeño peppers
- 8 slices bacon, cut into thirds
- 4 bamboo skewers, soaked in water for 30 minutes
- 24 toothpicks

Place meat in a bowl. Pour brine from jalapeño jar over meat and let marinate 20 minutes (you can skip this step if using fresh peppers). Preheat for direct grilling over medium heat, and brush and oil grill grate. For each popper, layer meat and jalapeño on top of each piece of bacon. Wrap up the bacon to enclose filling and thread onto a skewer (loading six bundles per skewer). Place on the grill and cook, turning frequently, until bacon is crispy and meat is cooked, 15–20 minutes. Remove poppers from skewers and pierce with toothpicks to serve.

Makes 24 poppers.

SEAFOOD

# 194 Follow Foolproof Fish-Grilling Tips

The goal for perfectly cooked fish is a fillet that is tender, flaky, and moist. On the grill, the goal is the same but there's an extra challenge: preventing the fish from sticking to the grate. Once you've mastered that skill, you're well on your way to perfection.

You'll likely have the most luck with firm-fleshed fish such as tuna, swordfish, salmon, and halibut. As a general rule, count on about 8–10 minutes total for each 1-inch (2.5-cm) thickness of the fillet. Cutting fillets to an even size is a great way to make sure they cook evenly, and after cooking, let fish rest for 5 minutes or so to allow the juices to redistribute. Here are some of the best ways to make sure your fish makes it onto the grate and back again in one piece.

**BRUSH & OIL** Prepping the grill grate is always suggested; with tender fillets, it's a must.

**GREASE UP** Lubricate the fish in addition to the grate. Mayonnaise is the unexpected and unrivaled condiment for the job. Brush fillets on all sides before grilling for best no-stick results.

**BRING TO ROOM TEMP** Remove fish from the fridge and let sit at room temperature 5–10 minutes before placing it on the grill.

**HEAT THINGS UP** A hot grate will sear the fillet when it's placed on top. Don't force it—the fish should loosen somewhat when it's ready to be turned.

**HANDLE WITH CARE** Flip your fish only once. More than that and it may fall apart. Carefully shimmy a thin metal spatula under the fish to lift it from the grill.

**KEEP THE SKIN ON** Skin will help your fish hold together when it's cooked and turned on the grill grate. If you prefer fish without the skin, simply remove it after cooking.

**USE A BASKET** Another good way to prevent your fish from falling apart on the grill is to use a fish basket. It will hold your fish, however delicate, perfectly in place.

**GET A PLANK** Grill whole fish or a large fillet on a plank (such as wood or pineapple, see items 202, 205) to keep it in one piece on the grill.

# 195 Examine for Freshness

The nose knows when it comes to fish. Fresh fish should not smell fishy, but carry the mild, clean scent of the sea—and nothing more. Fish fillets or steaks should appear bright, lustrous, and moist, without signs of discoloration or drying. Whole fish will have bright, shiny, well-attached scales; bright pink or red gills; firm, elastic flesh that springs back to the touch; and eyes that are bright, clear and full—never cloudy, shriveled, or sunken. Check with your fishmonger or an app like Seafood Watch to learn about the best seasonal and locally sourced fish.

# 196 Select Shellfish

Aroma, or the lack of it, is an important indication of freshness in shellfish, too. Just like fish, shellfish should have a barely perceptible, mild, clean scent—not fishy, sour, or with whiffs of ammonia.

Clams, mussels, and oysters should be alive when purchased. Give them the tap test to check; if the shells don't close when touched, the shellfish is dead and should be discarded. Shells should be hard and free of cracks or other blemishes. Shrimp—the shellfish most often sold thawed from frozen—should have a firm texture and mild odor. Live lobsters should be active and will curl their tails when picked up.

When in doubt, always visit a reputable fishmonger with lots of customers (thus ensuring a quick turnover of inventory). Presentation is key, too. Go for the fishmongers with the crispest ice in their display—a good indication of their dedication to freshness and the proper storage methods.

# 197 Lemon & Herb–Stuffed Grilled Trout

Small fish grill quickly over the direct heat of a smoky fire, and trout has a delicate flavor that works well with many seasonings—in this recipe, applewood smoking chips intensify earthiness while the herbs and lemon lend a crisp freshness.

- 2 handfuls applewood chips, soaked in water for 30 minutes
- 8 fresh thyme sprigs
- 8 fresh oregano sprigs
- 4 fresh rosemary sprigs
- 8 lemon slices, each ¼ inch (6 mm) thick
- 1 tablespoon chopped garlic
- 4 small whole trout, about 12 oz (375 g) each, cleaned and heads removed, if desired
- ¼ cup (2 fl oz/60 ml) mayonnaise
- Extra-virgin olive oil for drizzling

**PREHEAT** Prepare a charcoal or gas grill for direct grilling over medium heat. If using charcoal, add the wood chips to the fire just before grilling. If using gas, fill smoker box with up to 2 handfuls wood chips, then preheat grill. Brush and oil grill grate.

**PREP** Stuff 2 thyme sprigs, 2 oregano sprigs, 1 rosemary sprig, 2 lemon slices, and one-fourth of the garlic in each trout cavity. Use a toothpick to secure each cavity closed, or tie closed with kitchen string. Brush outside of each trout with mayonnaise, coating evenly.

**GRILL** Wait until you see a good head of smoke rising from the grill, then place trout on the grill directly over the fire. Cover grill and cook, turning once, 5–6 minutes on each side. Two large spatulas will help with turning, and the mayonnaise will keep the trout from sticking to the grill. The fish is done when you can slide a paring knife into the thickest part of the flesh near the bone, pull it out, and touch it to your lip. If it's warm, you're ready to go. Don't wait too long and scald yourself.

**SERVE** Transfer trout to individual plates. Drizzle with the oil and serve at once.

Serves 4.

# 198 Gut Your Fish

You've been fishing all day long. You've finally reeled in a fat one. Now what? Time to dress the fish and get it ready for the grill. Once you know what you're doing, it won't be long until the fruit of your labor looks just like one you might purchase from the fishmonger—but better! First, you'll need a few simple tools and a little bit of know-how.

## YOU'LL NEED:

- A fish scaler (or try a butter knife, which works nearly as well)
- A sharp fillet knife
- Kitchen shears

## DIRECTIONS:

**STEP 1** Take your fish outside (if you aren't already there), set it down on a work surface, and scrape the fish scaler several times over the outside of the fish, around the fins and from head to tail, to remove all of the scales.

**STEP 2** Slip the tip of your fillet knife into the bottom of the belly near the tail and slice upward toward the head (moving along the belly).

**STEP 3** Force the knife through the bony portion that lies between the pelvic fins (the ones paired at the belly of the fish) and up toward the lower jaw.

**STEP 4** Remove the guts by reaching in and grabbing them at the base of the head where they connect. Pinch the connection spot and pull to dislodge and remove all of the guts. (For bigger fish, use the tip of your knife to sever the sinew at the connection site.)

**STEP 5** Scrape out the liver, which is attached to the backbone. Cut out any part that may remain of the swim bladder (the whitish sac that attaches itself to the cavity).

**STEP 6** Remove gills by lifting the flap with your fingers and snipping the gills with your kitchen shears where they attach at both ends of the arc.

**STEP 7** Rinse gutted fish in ice-cold water, then pack on a bed of crushed ice until the grill is fired and ready.

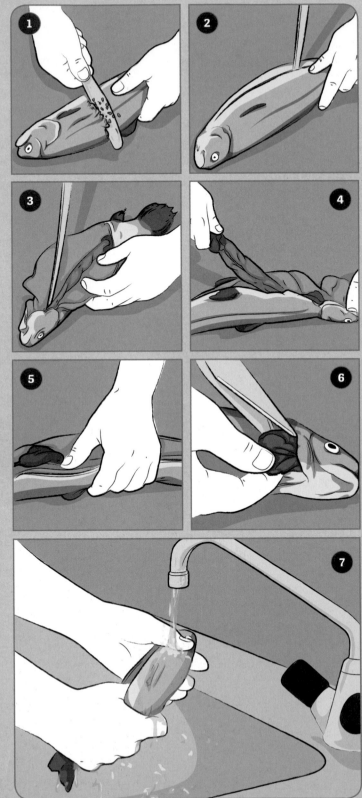

# 199 Citrus-Cilantro Snapper

Two quick techniques will take you most of the way toward success when cooking larger whole fish on the grill, like snapper or sea bass. First, score the meat to ensure even cooking. Second, resist the impulse to turn the fish before it's ready, keeping the skin intact and nicely browned when you pull it from the grill. Add to that a nice hot fire and a spritzy seasoning of lime juice and herbs, and your grilled fish will not disappoint.

- One 5-lb (2¼-kg) or two 2½-lb (1-kg) head-on whole fish (such as gray or pink snapper, black sea bass, or branzino), scaled and gutted
- Kosher salt
- ¼ cup (2 fl oz/60 ml) olive oil, plus more for serving
- 2 limes or 5 key limes, thinly sliced
- ¼ cup (2 fl oz/60 ml) key lime juice
- ½ bunch *each* basil and cilantro, stems and leaves separated

**PREHEAT** Prepare a charcoal or gas fire for direct-heat grilling over medium-high heat. Brush and oil grill grate.

**PREP** Score fish: Cut 1 slash lengthwise down to bone, then cut crosswise in two places, spaced evenly. Repeat to score other side. Season fish inside and out with salt, then drizzle with ¼ cup (2 fl oz/60 ml) olive oil. Stuff half the lime slices and all the herb stems inside fish.

**GRILL** Place fish on the grill and don't move it until the skin is nicely crisp and charred and the flesh is flaky and opaque down to the bone, 10–15 minutes depending on size. Place a metal spatula underneath the fish and, supporting it with tongs, lift and gently roll it over to other side. Continue to cook until flesh is flaky and opaque down to the bone, 10–15 minutes longer. Use the tip of a small knife to check for doneness; if it slides easily through the thickest part of the flesh, the fish is done. If not, move the fish to a cooler part of the grill or turn down the heat on a gas grill and continue to cook until opaque throughout.

**SERVE** Place fish on a serving platter, drizzle with oil and lime juice, then sprinkle basil and cilantro leaves over top.

## 200 Grilled Salmon Fillets with Herb Butter

Best fish for the grill? Definitely the meaty and oily varieties—thick-fleshed fish such as tuna, salmon, grouper, mackerel, sea bass, and striped bass. The fillets are firm enough to stand up to direct-heat cooking on a grill and, especially in the case of salmon, dense enough to encourage a nice crisp crust and enhanced flavor from grilling's dry heat. Don't forget to always clean the grate before cooking, and don't skimp on the mayonnaise—it helps prevent sticking.

- 1 tablespoon *each* finely chopped fresh chives, fresh dill, and fresh tarragon
- Kosher salt and freshly ground black pepper
- ½ cup (4 oz/125 g) unsalted butter, at room temperature
- ¼ lemon

- 6 skin-on center-cut salmon fillets, each about 8 oz (250 g) and 1 inch (2.5 cm) thick, pin bones removed
- ¼ cup (2 fl oz/60 ml) mayonnaise
- 2 teaspoons *each* ground cumin and ground coriander

**MAKE BUTTER** In a small bowl, mix chives, dill, tarragon, a pinch of salt, and a few grinds of pepper with butter. Squeeze juice from lemon into butter and mix in. Using a spatula, scrape butter out of the bowl onto a sheet of waxed paper. Roll paper over butter and press into a solid, uniform log. Twist both ends to seal securely. Refrigerate to harden. (Butter can be made up to five days in advance and refrigerated or frozen for up to a month.)

**PREHEAT & PREP** Prepare a charcoal or gas grill for direct grilling over high heat. Brush and oil grill grate. Brush salmon fillets on all sides with mayonnaise, coating evenly. Sprinkle cumin and coriander evenly over each fillet, then season with salt and pepper.

**GRILL** Place salmon fillets, skin side up, on grill directly over fire and cook for about 3 minutes. Turn and continue to cook until fish flakes when prodded gently with a fork, about 3 minutes longer. Salmon will be cooked to medium, which is perfect.

**SERVE** Transfer fillets to individual plates and top each fillet with a pat of herb butter. Serve at once.

Serves 6.

## 201 Pluck the Pin Bones

If cooking up a thick salmon fillet is in your game plan, then removing the tiny pin bones from the meat is the first part of your process. Here's how to do it in three easy steps.

**STEP 1** Locate the pin bones by laying your fillet flat on a work surface, then running your fingertips along the center of the fillet to feel for the prickly bone tips.

**STEP 2** When you find a bone, slide one hand under the fillet and lift it up under the bone so that the tip protrudes.

**STEP 3** Using fish tweezers or needle-nose pliers, grasp as much of the protruding bone tip as possible and pull slowly and steadily, wiggling it gently until it pulls free. Repeat to remove all the pin bones.

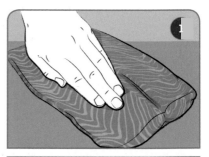

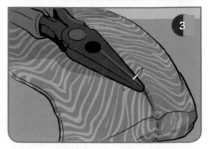

# 202 Plank-Grilled Salmon with Mustard-Dill Sauce

Native Americans of the Pacific Northwest transformed two of their greatest natural resources—salmon and cedar—into a grilling technique that has endured through centuries. Early cedar-grilling methods sandwiched a whole salmon fillet between two cedar planks for a slow smoke over an open fire. These days, fillet-size planks purchased in the grilling accessories aisle of most culinary retailers make for an easy smoke over direct heat on a grill. Soaking the wood first emits a slow-smoldering smoke for lingering smoky flavor, and dill-flecked honey mustard adds a modern finish to the age-old technique.

- Beer as needed for soaking (optional)
- 1 large or 4 small untreated cedar planks
- Olive oil for brushing
- Sea salt
- ½ cup (4 oz/125 g) unsalted butter
- ¼ cup (2 fl oz/60 ml) fresh lemon juice
- 2 tablespoons chopped fresh flat-leaf parsley
- 1 teaspoon reduced-sodium soy sauce or tamari
- 2 lb (1 kg) skin-on center-cut salmon fillet (either 1 large fillet or 4 small fillets), about 1 inch (2.5 cm) thick, pin bones removed
- ½ cup (4 oz/125 g) honey mustard
- ¼ cup (⅓ oz/10 g) chopped fresh dill

**SOAK** Soak cedar plank in water or beer to cover for at least 1 hour. (No matter what size you use, make sure your planks are big enough to hold your fillets.)

**PREHEAT** Prepare a charcoal or gas grill for direct grilling over high heat. Brush and oil grill grate. Remove plank from water. Brush one side with olive oil and sprinkle with salt. Place on grill directly over the fire, cover, and heat until it begins to crackle and smoke, about 5 minutes.

**PREP** In a small saucepan over medium heat, melt butter. Whisk in lemon juice, parsley, and soy sauce. Remove from the heat and keep warm.

**GRILL** Uncover grill and place salmon fillet on plank. Brush salmon generously with butter mixture. Cover again and cook, without turning fillet, until fish flakes when prodded gently with a fork, 10–12 minutes. Fillet should be cooked to medium. Check plank frequently to make sure it doesn't catch on fire, and have a spray bottle filled with water handy to extinguish any flames (but be careful—steam created from water can cause burns).

**SERVE** Using heavy-duty potholders, transfer plank to a heatproof work surface. Transfer salmon fillet to a warmed platter with a spatula. In a small bowl, stir together mustard and dill. Serve salmon with mustard sauce on side.

Serves 4.

# 203 Moroccan-Style Halibut

Halibut is a thick, meaty fish that has great texture and readily absorbs the flavors of all kinds of seasonings. In this recipe, the spices lend a North African accent, and the fillets are topped with a glaze of sweet and tart pomegranate molasses.

- 6 halibut fillets, each about 8 oz (250 g) and 1 inch (2.5 cm) thick
- 2 tablespoons mayonnaise
- 2 teaspoons ground cumin
- 1 teaspoon ground coriander
- ½ teaspoon ground cinnamon
- ½ teaspoon cayenne pepper
- Kosher salt and freshly ground black pepper
- ¼ cup (2½ oz/75 g) pomegranate molasses, warmed
- Chopped fresh cilantro for serving
- 6 lime wedges

**PREHEAT** Prepare a charcoal or gas grill for direct grilling over high heat. Brush and oil grill grate.

**PREP** Brush fish on both sides with mayonnaise, coating evenly. In a small bowl, stir together cumin, coriander, cinnamon, and cayenne. Sprinkle fish evenly on both sides with the spice mixture, then season with salt and black pepper.

**GRILL** Place fish on grill directly over fire and cook, turning once, until just opaque throughout and when it flakes when prodded gently with a fork, about 4 minutes on each side.

**SERVE** Transfer fish to a platter or individual plates. Brush each fillet with a thin coat of warm pomegranate molasses, then sprinkle with cilantro and serve with a lime wedge.

Serves 6.

# 204 Thai Sea Bass in Banana Leaves

In Thailand, banana leaves are pretty common when it comes to grill cooking—used the way Westerners might use aluminum foil. In addition to sealing in moisture and protecting delicate ingredients from the grill's harsh heat, banana leaves impart a very subtle grasslike flavor. A liberal dose of fresh herbs are the heavy flavor hitters in this preparation, adding to the leaf's mildness with a trifecta (basil, mint, cilantro) of Southeast Asian flavor. A simple red curry sauce is the coup de grâce for this special dish. Substitute it with a purchased peanut sauce if time is a consideration.

- ½ cup (¾ oz/20 g) *each* firmly packed chopped fresh basil, mint, and cilantro
- 4 banana leaves, cut to 12 inches (30 cm) square
- 4 sea bass fillets or steaks, each 4–6 oz (115–170 g)
- 1 lime, cut into 8 thin slices
- 2 tablespoons canola oil or spray
- Kosher salt and freshly ground pepper

**MAKE CURRY (OPTIONAL)** In a small saucepan over medium heat, bring 1 can (15 fl oz/450 ml) light coconut milk to a simmer. Stir in 3 tablespoons brown sugar, 2 tablespoons lime juice, 2 tablespoons peanut butter, 2 tablespoons curry paste, and 1½ tablespoons fish sauce. Simmer 10 minutes until thickened. Set aside until ready to serve. (Whisk in a little water, if needed, for the desired consistency.)

**PREHEAT** Prepare charcoal or gas grill for direct grilling over medium-high heat. Brush and oil grill grate.

**PREP** In a bowl, mix basil, mint, and cilantro. Lay banana leaves flat on a work surface, place 3 to 4 tablespoons herb mixture on center of each leaf, and top each mound of herbs with a piece of fish. Top each packet with 2 lime slices and ½ teaspoon canola oil (or some oil spray). Season with salt and pepper.

**FOLD** Fold sides of leaf inward, overlapping them like a letter. Fold top and bottom over center in same way, tucking ends underneath package. Secure with kitchen string. Brush or spray packet with more oil.

**GRILL** Place packets on grill directly over heat. Cover grill and cook, turning once, until interior of fish is opaque (unwrap a package and insert a knife into fish to test), 7–8 minutes per side. Transfer packets to individual plates, remove string, open tops, and offer curry sauce to add as desired. Serve hot.

Serves 4.

# 205 Swap in Some Pineapple

If you thought cedar-planked salmon was cool (see item 202), fish fillets on pineapple "bark" may just seem like the logical next step. The prickly exterior of whole pineapple has to be removed anyway, so why not use the thick slabs as flavorful grilling planks?

It's not a difficult procedure. Start with a thick fillet of meaty fish (mahi-mahi, halibut, or sea bass are good choices). The fillet should be ¾–1 inch (2–2.5 cm) thick and about the same size as a lengthwise slice of pineapple. (Trim the fillet to an even thickness if necessary.) From a fresh pineapple, simply cut two straight slabs of roughly the same size as the fillet. Sandwich the fillet between the two pieces of pineapple, season with salt and pepper, and secure with kitchen string. Grill over medium-high direct

heat on a gas or charcoal grill, turning frequently, until the pineapple is evenly browned and the fish is opaque throughout, about 12 minutes per side (depending on the thickness of your fillet and the thickness of the pineapple slab). Serve the fillet on its own with the pineapple or brush it with a little teriyaki sauce just before serving.

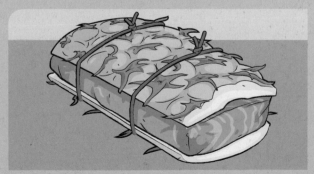

# 206 Sicilian-Style Swordfish

Swordfish is a great choice for the grill, as it has firm flesh and distinctive flavor—the perfect attributes for marrying grilling's hot, dry heat with robust sauces, marinades, and rubs. If you can't find swordfish, try grouper or cod in its place.

- 2 tomatoes, seeded and chopped
- 1 small yellow onion, chopped
- 2 celery stalks, chopped
- 2 tablespoons pitted, chopped green olives, plus 1 tablespoon brine
- ¼ cup (⅓ oz/10 g) chopped fresh flat-leaf (Italian) parsley
- 6 swordfish fillets, each 5–6 oz (155–185 g) and ¾–1 inch (2–2.5 cm) thick
- Balsamic vinegar and olive oil for brushing
- Salt and freshly ground black pepper

**MAKE SALSA** In a small bowl, mix tomatoes, onion, celery, olives and brine, and parsley. Season with pepper, then taste and adjust. Cover and refrigerate until serving, stirring lightly just before setting it out.

**PREP & PREHEAT** Prepare a charcoal or gas grill for direct grilling over medium-high heat. Brush and generously oil grill rack. Brush fillets on both sides with oil and vinegar. Sprinkle on both sides with salt and pepper. Grill fish over hottest part of fire, turning once, until it's opaque throughout and flakes when prodded with a fork, 4–5 minutes per side.

**SERVE** Transfer fillets to warmed plates. Spoon salsa evenly on top and serve immediately.

Makes 6 servings.

# 207 Tuna with Wasabi

Tuna is one of the best fish for cooking on a grill. As one of the few that is often preferred rare, thick slices of tuna can be perfectly seared over a hot fire, leaving the meaty centers pink and tender. Always use tuna from a good market when grilling it rare—ask for sashimi grade and serve it the same day you purchase it.

- ⅓ cup (3 fl oz/80 ml) *each* soy sauce and sake or dry sherry
- 1 teaspoon *each* Asian sesame oil and Asian chile oil
- 1 teaspoon sesame seeds, plus more for garnish
- 6 sashimi-grade ahi tuna steaks, each 5–6 oz (155–185 g) and ¾–1 inch (2–2.5 cm) thick
- 1 cup (8 fl oz/250 ml) crème fraîche
- 2 teaspoons wasabi powder, or to taste
- 2–4 whole fresh chives

**MARINATE** In a shallow, nonreactive dish, mix soy sauce, sake, sesame oil, chile oil, and sesame seeds. Add tuna in a single layer and turn to coat both sides. Cover and refrigerate 2 hours.

**PREHEAT & PREP** Prepare a charcoal or gas grill for direct grilling over medium-high heat. Brush and oil grill rack. In a small bowl, stir together crème fraîche and wasabi powder. Cover and refrigerate until ready to serve.

**GRILL** Remove tuna steaks from marinade and discard marinade. Grill fish over hottest part of fire, turning once, until seared on outside and rare in center when tested with a knife, 3–5 minutes per side. If you prefer your tuna cooked through, leave it on the grill for a minute or two longer on each side.

**SERVE** Transfer tuna steaks to warmed individual plates. Garnish the wasabi cream with the sesame seeds and chives, and pass it at the table.

Makes 6 servings.

# 208 Swordfish Kebabs with Romesco Sauce

*Romesco* is the ubiquitous sauce from the Catalonia region in southern Spain, where it's the classic partner to grilled meats and seafood. An earthy blend of tomatoes, roasted red peppers, and toasted almonds, the savory sauce is popular for a reason. Even the simplest of dishes becomes pretty darn amazing with even the smallest of dollops. Pair the crusty kebabs of tender swordfish with pineapple spears or papaya slices that have been brushed with melted butter and grilled to caramelized perfection over a hot fire.

## FOR THE ROMESCO SAUCE

- ¼ cup (1 oz /30 g) sliced (flaked) almonds, toasted
- 1 tomato, peeled and chopped
- 1 large red bell pepper, roasted, peeled, and seeded
- 2 cloves garlic, crushed
- ¼ cup (2 fl oz/60 ml) sherry vinegar
- 1 tablespoon dry sherry
- ⅓ cup (3 fl oz/80 ml) extra-virgin olive oil
- Smoked paprika and sea salt

## FOR THE KEBABS

- ½ cup (4 fl oz/125 ml) extra-virgin olive oil
- 2 tablespoons fresh lemon juice
- 2 cloves garlic, minced
- Freshly ground black pepper

- 2 lb (1 kg) total weight swordfish fillets, cut into 1–1½ inch (2.5–4 cm) cubes
- 2 large red bell peppers, seeded and cut into 1½-inch (4-cm) squares
- 6 bamboo skewers, soaked in water 30 minutes before use, or metal skewers

**MAKE SAUCE** In a food processor or blender, process almonds until finely ground. Add tomato, roasted pepper, garlic, vinegar, and sherry, and process until smooth. With motor running, slowly drizzle in oil, processing until thickened. Season to taste with salt and paprika. Pour into a bowl, cover, and set aside.

**PREHEAT & PREP** Prepare a charcoal or gas grill for direct grilling over medium-high heat. Brush and oil grill rack. In a bowl, stir together oil, lemon juice, garlic, and salt and pepper to taste. Generously brush the swordfish pieces on all sides with the oil mixture. Thread the swordfish cubes alternately with the red bell pepper squares onto bamboo or metal skewers.

**GRILL** Grill skewers over hottest part of fire, turning once, until the swordfish is opaque throughout but still moist at center when tested with a knife, 3–5 minutes per side. The peppers should be tender and lightly charred.

Makes 6 servings.

# 209 Shuck an Oyster

If you're grilling oysters on the half shell, you'll need to know how to shuck them. Don't let the task intimidate you. Here's how to do it.

**STEP 1** Using a sturdy brush, scrub oysters under running water to rid them of any sand and debris. Place them in ice for an hour to make sure they're well chilled.

**STEP 2** Hold oyster in gloved hand with the rounded side down and the peaked hinge pointing toward you.

**STEP 3** Pry it open by gently wiggling the tip of an oyster knife between the shells into the hinge. When you feel the knife point go in, twist the blade to pop open the shell.

**STEP 4** Run the knife underneath the oyster meat to sever the abductor muscle, being careful not to spill any of the oyster "liquor" inside. Discard the top shell.

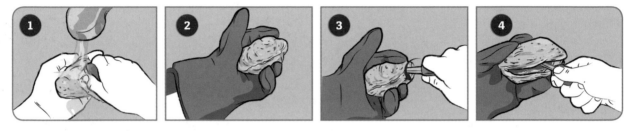

# 210 Grilled Mussels with Shallot Sauce

As for all shellfish, freshness is the name of the game when it comes to mussels. Give your purchased mussels a good sniff—they should smell just like the sea. Rinse them well (especially wild ones) under running water, discarding any that don't close to the touch. Most mussels sold these days are cultivated, so they're cleaner and have minimal "beards" attached to the shells. Any beards that do exist should be removed just before cooking, since doing so kills them, and you want your mussels as fresh as they can be when they hit the grill.

- ½ cup (4 fl oz/125 ml) lemon juice
- ⅓ cup (2½ fl oz/80 ml) red wine vinegar
- 2 tablespoons *each* olive oil and finely chopped shallots
- 2 lb (32 oz/1 kg) fresh mussels
- ⅛ teaspoon *each* salt and ground pepper
- ⅓ cup (½ oz/13 g) chopped fresh flat-leaf (Italian) parsley

**MAKE SAUCE** In a small bowl, whisk together ¼ cup (2 fl oz/60 ml) of the lemon juice, the red wine vinegar, the olive oil, and the shallots.

**PREHEAT & PREP** Lightly coat a grill wok, grill basket, or aluminum foil–lined grill rack with nonstick cooking spray. Prepare a charcoal or gas grill for direct grilling over medium-high heat. Scrub mussel shells with a stiff brush, removing beards. Discard any opened shells. Sprinkle mussels with salt, pepper, and remaining lemon juice. Transfer to grill wok, grill basket, or foil-lined rack.

**GRILL** Place mussels in pan on grill rack directly over the fire. Cover the grill and cook until shells open, 7–10 minutes. Discard any unopened shells.

**SERVE** Transfer mussels to a large dish and pour shallot mixture over top, stirring gently to coat. Sprinkle with parsley and serve hot. Makes 8 servings.

# 211 Grilled Oysters on a Bed of Salt

A thick layer of salt expertly dissipates heat from the grill, making it nearly impossible to overcook delicate oyster meat (and does double duty by preventing the open bivalves from toppling on the grill rack). A vinaigrette of charred lemons and fresh herbs adds to the smoky character.

- 2 lemons, halved, plus wedges for serving
- 2 sprigs fresh parsley
- 2 sprigs fresh thyme
- ¼ cup (2 fl oz/60 ml) olive oil
- Flaky sea salt and freshly ground black pepper, to taste
- 5 cups coarse salt
- 1 dozen large oysters, shucked, top shell removed (see item 209)

**PREHEAT** Prepare a charcoal or gas grill for direct grilling over medium-high heat.

**PREP** Place lemon halves, cut side down, on grill along with herb springs. Grill lemons until charred, 7–10 minutes. Squeeze juice from lemon halves into a bowl; add olive oil and season to taste with sea salt and pepper. Remove leaves from herb sprigs and mince finely; add to lemon mixture.

**GRILL** Spread coarse salt over heavy-bottomed baking sheet or roasting pan small enough to fit on your grill. Nestle oysters, oyster side up, into salt. Place pan with oysters on grill, cover, and cook until oysters are plump and edges are beginning to crisp, 2–3 minutes.

**SERVE** Transfer oysters to a serving platter and drizzle with lemon vinaigrette. Serve hot with lemon wedges for squeezing over tops.

Makes 6 servings.

# 212 BBQ Some Oysters

Shucked oysters cook beautifully when placed right on the grill rack, too. Serve them hot with a spritz of lemon and a spoonful of doctored-up barbecue sauce: Sauté 6 finely chopped garlic cloves in ½ cup (4 oz/125 g) *each* butter and BBQ sauce for 5 minutes to make the sauce, set aside, and carefully place your shucked oysters on the grill. Spoon a little sauce into each shell, cover, and grill about 5 minutes, or until done to your liking.

## 213 Grilled Clams with White Wine–Garlic Butter

There's nothing like fresh clams in a light wine sauce. If you're digging for clams yourself, make sure to soak them first before grilling (see item 214).

- 1 tablespoon *each* extra-virgin olive oil and butter
- 3 large cloves garlic, minced
- ½ cup (4 fl oz/125 ml) dry white wine
- Salt and freshly ground pepper to taste
- 3 lb (1½ kg) hard-shelled clams, cleaned and scrubbed
- Chopped fresh parsley for garnish
- Lemon wedges

**PREHEAT** Prepare a charcoal or gas grill for direct-heat grilling over medium-high heat.

**PREP** Heat oil and butter in a small saucepan over medium-low heat. Add garlic and sauté until fragrant, about 1 minute. Add wine and bring to a boil over high heat, then boil until reduced by about half. Remove from the heat and set aside.

**GRILL** Put clams in grill basket and place on hottest part of the grill. Cook until clams open, 6–8 minutes. Discard any that do not open.

**SERVE** Transfer clams to bowl. Drizzle garlic-wine butter over top and toss to mix. Sprinkle with chopped parsley and serve hot with lemon wedges on the side.

## 214 Purge your Clams

Wild clams and mussels, but especially clams, need a good seawater soaking before they hit the grill. Immerse them in a bucket of water for at least an hour (overnight is better) prior to cooking in order to rid them of any sand or grit they may have picked up while buried in the mud. Using water from the clams' native area is always best, as its salinity level matches that of the clams, keeping them happy and alive until they're reading for cooking. Keep the clams at the same temperature—usually somewhere between 35–78°F (2–25°C)—and cover the container (clams spit water, so you don't want them sprinkling the inside of your fridge or basement).

You may have heard rumors about adding cornmeal or pepper to the soaking water to better encourage the clams to purge their debris, but don't. Plain seawater will get the job done just right.

# 215 Source the Best Tools

When it comes to cooking shellfish on the grill, nothing does the trick like a perforated bowl, basket, or tray designed for that purpose. Efficient construction encourages even heat distribution to shellfish on the grill while keeping tiny mollusks contained and on top of the grill rack.

# 216

## Craft a Beach Bucket Barbecue

It doesn't get much better than digging a fire pit for grilling shellfish. But if you'd like a portable option, a bucket grill is tops. Stack it alongside buckets used for gathering the bivalves and tote it anywhere that looks prime for grilling. You can purchase a portable metal bucket grill, or make one yourself using these steps.

### YOU'LL NEED
- 2–3 gallon (7½–11 l) steel pail
- Hole maker (a ¾-inch/20-mm drill bit or large nails and a hammer)
- Metal grill rack that fits the top of the pail
- Charcoal

### DIRECTIONS

**STEP 1** Turn the pail upside down. Create airflow to feed the fire by drilling or hammering large, evenly-spaced holes along the bottom third of the pail.

**STEP 2** Light charcoal in the bottom of the pail.

**STEP 3** Place the grill rack on the top of the pail.

**STEP 4** When the charcoal is ash-gray, your bucket barbecue is ready for action.

# 217 Grilled Fish Tacos

They may seem rustic in essence, but grilled fish tacos are actually the more upscale version of what is widely considered the more prototypical fish taco—the battered and fried variety. These days, all you need is a few tender fillets of mahi-mahi or snapper doused in a quick bath of lime-spiked tequila and grilled to perfection—tuck them into soft corn tortillas and you'll get a sense of just how far tacos have come since their early days among the deep-fat fryers of beach stands along the Baja peninsula. Salsas run the gamut, with avocado, pineapple, and mango standing out as favorites. Grouper, halibut, or any other firm white fish works well on the grill, too. If you can find thick, fresh tortillas, you only need to use one per taco.

- Grated zest of 1 lime
- 2 tablespoons *each* fresh lime juice, tequila, and fresh orange juice
- 1 teaspoon agave nectar or honey
- 2 lb (1 kg) total weight skinless firm white fish fillets
- ¼ cup (2 fl oz/60 ml) mayonnaise
- 24 corn tortillas, about 6 inches (15 cm) in diameter
- 2 cups (6 oz/185 g) finely shredded green cabbage
- Salsa of your choice (see right), for serving
- ½ cup (¾ oz/20 g) coarsely chopped fresh cilantro

**MARINATE** In a small bowl, whisk together lime zest and juice, tequila, orange juice, and agave. Pour into a shallow baking dish large enough to accommodate fillets in a single layer. Add fillets, turn to coat, and marinate at room temperature for 30 minutes, flipping fish after 15 minutes.

**PREP & PREHEAT** Prepare a charcoal or gas grill for direct grilling over high heat. Brush and oil grill grate. Remove fish from marinade and discard marinade. Brush fish on both sides with mayonnaise, coating evenly.

**GRILL** Place fish on the grill directly over the fire and cook, turning once, until it's just opaque throughout and flakes when prodded gently with a fork. When it comes to timing, count on about 8 minutes total per 1 inch (2.5 cm) of thickness.

**SERVE** Transfer fish to a platter. Warm tortillas on grill, about 1 minute per side, then stack and wrap in a kitchen towel. Using a fork, break up fish into bite-size chunks. To assemble each taco, overlap 1–2 tortillas and top with fish, cabbage, a generous spoonful of salsa, and a sprinkle of cilantro. Serve at once.

Serves 4–6.

# 218 Creamy Avocado Salsa

- ½ cup (4 oz/125 g) sour cream
- 2 teaspoons *each* whole-grain mustard and white wine vinegar or Champagne vinegar
- 1 avocado, halved, pitted, peeled, and cut into small chunks
- Kosher salt and freshly ground pepper

In a bowl, whisk together sour cream, mustard, and vinegar. Carefully fold in avocado, then season with salt and pepper. Use right away, or cover and refrigerate for up to two days.

Makes about 1 cup (8 oz/250 g).

# 219 Fresh Mango Salsa

- ½ cup (4 oz/125 g) diced mango
- ¼ cup (2 oz/60 g) finely chopped red bell pepper
- 2 tablespoons finely sliced green (spring) onion
- 1 tablespoon finely chopped fresh cilantro
- 2 teaspoons fresh lime juice

Mix ingredients in a large bowl. Refrigerate for at least 30 minutes.

Makes about 1 cup (8 oz/250 ml).

# 220 Grill Perfect Shrimp

"Shrimp on the Barbie" is a favorite of many (not just the crowd from Down Under). Of all the varieties of shellfish, shrimp are perhaps the best to cook up on a grill—the shell protects the meat from overcooking and bumps up the flavor, to boot. Once you get the basic technique and timing down, the road to excellent shrimp is a short one. Here are a few tips to help you navigate it with ease.

**BUY BIG** The larger the shrimp, the longer they can stay on the grill and develop that delicious, flavor-enhancing smokiness. Browse the seafood counter and go for the ones that weigh in at 24 per pound (500 g).

**REMOVE THE VEIN** Most people prefer shrimp sans the dark vein that runs along its back. To remove it, use kitchen scissors to snip open the shell along the length of the back of the shrimp, then use the tip of a small knife to cut a shallow groove along the length of the vein and lift it out.

**KEEP THE SHELL ON** The shell protects the tender meat from the fire and lends a mellow toastiness to its flavor. Resist the temptation to remove it before grilling; it'll be easy to remove after, especially if the back has been cut to remove the vein.

**FIND (A LITTLE!) TIME TO BRINE** Brining adds the salt that helps protect shrimp from overcooking and adds to their overall flavor. But don't overdo it. Keep the brine time to no more than 1½ hours—any longer, and the salt with break down the muscles too much, leading to mushy shrimp.

# 221 Bacon-Wrapped Prawns

A nice, crispy piece of bacon wrapped around a perfectly grilled prawn makes for an appetizer you can't refuse. Poach the bacon before wrapping it around the shrimp, guaranteeing a crispy casing when the shrimp are done.

- 24 large shrimp (prawns) in the shell, about 1 lb (500 g) total weight, peeled and deveined, with tail segment intact
- Basic Shrimp Brine (see item 223)
- 6–8 metal or wooden skewers
- 12 slices thick-cut applewood-smoked bacon, cut in half
- 24 fresh basil leaves

**PREP & PREHEAT** Add shrimp to brine, cover, and refrigerate for 30 minutes. Prepare a charcoal or gas grill for direct grilling over high heat. Brush and oil grill grate. If using wooden skewers, soak them in water for at least 30 minutes.

**POACH** Bring a saucepan three-quarters full of water to a boil over high heat. Drop in bacon slices, reduce heat to medium, and simmer 5 minutes. Drain on paper towels.

**WRAP** Remove shrimp and discard brine. Pat dry with paper towels and wrap a basil leaf tightly around middle of each shrimp, then wrap a half slice of bacon around basil. Slide wrapped shrimp onto a skewer, piercing it through the middle to secure all layers.

**GRILL** Place shrimp skewers on the grill and cook, turning once, until the bacon is crispy and shrimp turn creamy white, 3–5 minutes per side.

**SERVE** Slide shrimp off skewers onto a platter. Serve at once.

Serves 4–6.

## 222 Cocktail Sauce

In a small bowl, whisk together 1 cup (8 oz/250 g) ketchup, 1 tablespoon grated fresh or jarred horseradish, 1 teaspoon Worcestershire sauce, 1 teaspoon sugar, and a squeeze of fresh lemon juice. Set aside at room temperature and serve with everything!

## 223 Basic Shrimp Brine

In a large bowl, combine 6 cups (48 fl oz/1½ l) water with ½ cup (4 oz/125 g) kosher salt, 2 tablespoons sugar, 1 teaspoon ground cumin, and 1 teaspoon ground coriander, and stir to dissolve. Use right away. Makes enough for 2 lb (1 kg) shrimp (prawns).

## 224 Grilled Shrimp Cocktail

**This recipe will be your new go-to for those times when you have a bundle of fresh shrimp on hand.**

- Cocktail Sauce (see item 222)
- Basic Shrimp Brine (see item 223)
- 10 wooden or metal skewers
- 48 large shrimp (prawns) in shell, about 2 lb (1 kg) total weight, deveined
- 2 tablespoons canola oil

**PREHEAT & PREP** Make cocktail sauce and set aside at room temperature. Add shrimp to brine, cover, and refrigerate 1½ hours. If using wooden skewers, soak for at least 30 minutes before grilling. Prepare a charcoal or gas grill for direct grilling over high heat. Brush and oil grill grate.

**GRILL** Place shrimp on grill directly over fire and cook for 3 minutes. Turn and cook until shrimp turn creamy white, 2–3 minutes longer.

**SERVE** Transfer shrimp to a platter. Slide shrimp from skewers onto platter. Everybody gets to peel their own shrimp. Offer cocktail sauce for dipping.

# 225 Lobster Tails on the Grill

If you want to impress your guests, grilled lobster tails are an excellent choice. Add a little something extra with a flavored butter applied right on the grill. The result is rich, restaurant-worthy decadence.

**PREHEAT** Prepare charcoal or gas grill for direct cooking over medium-high heat. If using bamboo skewers, soak them in water for at least 30 minutes before grilling.

**PREP** Make the flavored butter of your choice (see item 227) and set aside. Using shears, butterfly lobster tails straight down the middle of the softer underside of the shell. Cut the meat down the center without cutting all the way through. Insert a metal skewer down the tail so it stands straight. Brush tails with olive oil and season with salt.

**GRILL** Grill lobsters, cut side down, until shells are bright in color, about 5 minutes. Turn over and spoon a generous tablespoon of butter onto butterflied meat. Continue to grill until meat is an opaque white color, about 4 minutes longer.

**SERVE** Remove lobster tails from grill and serve with more flavored butter and lemon wedges.

- 4 lobster tails, each about 7 oz (200 g)
- Olive oil
- Kosher salt
- Flavored butter (see item 227)
- Lemon wedges, for garnish
- 4 metal or bamboo skewers

# 226 Cook 'Em Whole

It can feel downright impossible to walk by a tank of live lobsters in season and avoid making a purchase. When that's the case, you'll likely want to grill your prized catch whole. Slay them first by plunging them headfirst into a pot of boiling water for 1 minute (keep the lid on in case of a struggle). Remove them from the pot and drain, then grill them over a medium-hot fire, turning often to avoid burning the shells, until the meat is opaque, 8–10 minutes. (You'll have to crack a claw to check.)

# 227 Dip It in Butter

There's no limit to the variety of savory butters to be whipped together as delicious dipping sauces. These are a few of the tried-and-true favorites. Substitute in any of your favorite herbs or flavorings when the mood strikes.

**HERB-GARLIC BUTTER**
In a small bowl, blend 1 stick (4 oz/125 g) room-temperature salted butter with 2 tablespoons chopped chives, 1 tablespoon chopped tarragon leaves, and 1 minced garlic clove, a dash of hot sauce, and freshly ground black pepper.

**GARLIC-SHALLOT BUTTER**
In a small saucepan over low heat, melt 1 stick (4 oz/125 g) unsalted butter. Stir in 2 cloves minced garlic, 1 tablespoon finely chopped shallot, and the finely grated zest of 1 lemon. Remove from heat. Stir in 1 teaspoon chopped fresh parsley and season with salt.

**CILANTRO-CHILE BUTTER**
In a small bowl, blend 1 stick (4 oz/125 g) room-temperature unsalted butter, 3 tablespoons minced fresh cilantro, 4 fresh chiles (stemmed, seeded, and minced), and the zest from 1 lime.

# 228 Chicken, Shrimp & Sausage Paella

Paella has been cooked in the coastal city of Valencia, Spain, since the 13th century. Those first incarnations were slowly simmered over open fires; modern adaptations still cook up best over a grill's high heat, building the signature golden crust along the bottom. The process remains much the same, simmering on the grill for quite a while, offering plenty of time to open a bottle of good Spanish wine.

- ¼ teaspoon saffron threads
- 6 bone-in, skin-on chicken thighs
- Kosher salt and freshly ground black pepper
- 1 Spanish-style chorizo sausage
- ¼ cup (2 fl oz/60 ml) olive oil
- 3 tomatoes, finely chopped
- 1 yellow onion, finely chopped
- 4 cloves garlic, minced
- 1 tablespoon chopped fresh thyme
- ½ teaspoon smoked paprika
- 1 cup (7 oz/220 g) short-grain paella rice such as bomba
- 4 cups (32 fl oz/1 l) low-sodium chicken broth, or as needed
- 1 jar (7 oz/220 g) roasted red peppers, drained
- ½ cup (2½ oz/75 g) fresh or frozen English peas
- 1 lb (500 g) shrimp in the shell, deveined
- Chopped fresh flat-leaf (Italian) parsley leaves for garnish
- 1 lemon, cut into 6 wedges

**PREP & PREHEAT** In a small bowl, add saffron threads to ¼ cup (2 fl oz/60 ml) hot water and set aside. Prepare a charcoal or gas grill for direct grilling over high heat. Brush and oil grill grate. Season chicken with salt and pepper, and slice up chorizo.

**GRILL** Place a 15-inch (38-cm) paella pan on the grill directly over the fire, let it heat for a few minutes, then add oil. When oil is hot, add chicken thighs, skin side down, and sear, turning once, until nicely browned, about 5 minutes on each side. Add chorizo and cook, turning often, until browned, about 5 minutes. Transfer chicken and chorizo to a platter and set aside. Add tomatoes, onion, garlic, thyme, and paprika to oil remaining in pan and cook, stirring often, until softened, about 5 minutes. Season with salt and pepper, add rice, and cook, stirring, until lightly toasted, 2–3 minutes. Pour in 2 cups (16 fl oz/500 ml) broth and bring to a boil. Cover grill and cook for about 10 minutes.

**COMBINE** Arrange reserved chicken and chorizo evenly over rice, nestling chicken into rice until almost covered. Add 1 cup (8 fl oz/250 ml) of remaining broth, cover the grill, and cook for another 20 minutes. Cut roasted peppers into strips. Top rice evenly with peas, roasted pepper strips, and shrimp. If rice looks dry, add as much of remaining broth as needed to moisten. Cover and cook until shrimp are opaque, 7–10 minutes.

**SERVE** Remove paella from grill and sprinkle with parsley. Serve at once with lemon wedges.

Serves 6.

> ### QUICK TIP
> Resist the urge to stir the paella as it cooks—it should have a nice crust on the bottom.

# 229 Pick a Paella Pan

Paella is actually named for the pan in which it is made. A good paella pan is key, as it multitasks as griddle, cooking pot, and serving platter. Placed right on the grill rack over a searing hot fire, it delivers a charred exterior to meats and a nice golden brown crust to the casserole bottom. Choose the largest size that will fit inside your grill and take your pick of materials. Carbon steel is the most traditional and conducts heat well, but it requires some maintenance to keep the surface clean and rust-free. Stainless steel is the easiest to maintain but also the most expensive. Enameled steel is carbon steel coated with a speckled enamel finish. The enameled steel pans are easy on the wallet and a breeze to clean but can chip if banged around in the cupboard or on the grill.

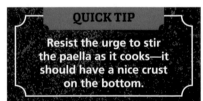

# SIDES & DRINKS

# 230 Grill Up Veggie Side Dishes

Once the grill is fired up, fresh cut and whole vegetables are a natural addition, producing some of the most simple yet delicious sides for your barbecue favorites—and all within just a few minutes of hitting the grates.

Stick with what's in season and watch your timing—don't stray too far when your vegetables are on the rack, as some will burn easily. Brush vegetables with a little bit of plain or flavored olive oil, and sprinkle with salt and pepper before you start cooking. Or toss them in a sauce or marinade for added flavor.

Nearly any vegetable cooks well on the grill, but a few tried-and-true favorites include the following: sliced sweet potato, zucchini, eggplant, and summer squash, whole corn, whole asparagus, halved leeks, quartered onions, halved and seeded bell peppers, halved or quartered tomatoes, whole portobello mushrooms, and whole radicchio leaves.

# 231 Sauce It Up

Plain grilled vegetables really benefit from a little bit of snazzing up post-grill. Try romesco (see item 208), chimichurri (see item 070), or any of the following, which can work well as a marinade or basting sauce. Keep in mind that sauces with fresh herbs retain their refreshing character better if drizzled on the veggies just after they're removed from the heat.

## ON THE GRILL

**SOY-SESAME SAUCE** In a small bowl, whisk together ½ cup (4 fl oz/125 ml) soy sauce, 2 tablespoons rice wine or dry sherry, 1 tablespoon bottled oyster sauce, ½ teaspoon Asian sesame oil, and 1½ teaspoons peeled and finely minced fresh ginger.

**BALSAMIC GLAZE** Combine ½ cup (4 fl oz/125 ml) balsamic vinegar, ½ cup (4 fl oz/125 ml) olive oil, ¼ cup (2 fl oz/60 ml) lemon juice, ¼ cup (⅓ oz/10 g) fresh flat-leaf (Italian) parsley, and 2 minced garlic cloves.

## AFTER THE GRILL

**MINT VINAIGRETTE** In a small bowl, whisk together 2 tablespoons olive oil, 2 tablespoons rice vinegar, and ½ cup (¾ oz/20 g) finely chopped fresh mint leaves.

**SALSA VERDE** In a food processor, blend 2 anchovy fillets, ⅓ cup (½ oz/15 g) chopped fresh flat-leaf (Italian) parsley, 6 fresh basil leaves, 1 teaspoon capers, 1 tablespoon caper brine, and ¼ cup (2 fl oz/60 ml) olive oil until finely minced.

# 232 Toast Some Corncobs

Fresh corn is the ultimate partner for a summertime barbecue, and everyone seems to have their own favorite method. Naked corncobs (that is, ones with the husks and silk removed) borrow lots of the grill's smoky flavor, char nicely over direct heat, and cook up quickly. Wrapped corncobs (either with husks intact or encased in foil) steam and grill at the same time, staying plump and moist and infusing the cobs with the flavor of any butter or spice enclosed in the wrapping. Try a dab of compound butter (see item 227), a drizzle of flavored oil, or any of your favorite herb or spice rubs. Here is a quick rundown of the top three corn-grilling techniques.

**NAKED** Remove the husks and silk. Brush with butter or oil, and place on a medium-hot grill, turning often, until evenly charred and tender, 10–12 minutes.

**IN HUSKS** Peel back the husks (leaving them attached at the stem) and remove the corn silk. Soak cobs with husks in heavily salted water for about 10 minutes. Drain, shaking off any excess water. Secure husks over corn with kitchen string. Grill, turning often, until evenly cooked and tender, 15–20 minutes.

**IN FOIL** Remove husks and silk from corncobs. Wrap each one in an individual piece of aluminum foil, allowing a little bit of room for the corn to plump. Grill, turning often, until evenly cooked and tender, 15–20 minutes.

# 233

## Perfect Mashed Potatoes

Fire up some hefty cuts on the barbecue and a side of equal substance is the only one to satisfy. Mashed potatoes are obviously a classic. Add any of your favorite flourishes to customize—chives, Parmesan, bacon bits—or instantly whip up the garlic-mashed variety by simmering the milk with 5 or 6 cloves of fresh garlic before adding it.

- 3 large russet potatoes, peeled and cut lengthwise in half
- ¼ cup (2 oz/60 g) unsalted butter
- ½ cup (4 fl oz/125 g) whole milk
- Salt and freshly ground black pepper

**COOK** Place potatoes in a large pot and cover with salted water. Bring to a boil over high heat. Reduce heat to medium-low, cover, and simmer until tender, 20–25 minutes. Drain and return to pot. Place over high heat and allow potatoes to dry for about 30 seconds. Turn off heat.

**MASH** Using a potato masher, mash potatoes twice around the pot, then add butter and milk. Continue to mash until smooth and fluffy. Mix in salt and black pepper.

# 234 Quick Coleslaw

Good coleslaw doesn't need to be fancy—especially when it comes to barbecue. Served alongside grilled chicken or crowning a sandwich of pulled pork, a creamy coleslaw will seldom disappoint. Take advantage of prepackaged coleslaw mix to cut out the chopping and keep prep time to a minimum. In a large bowl, mix ¾ cup (6 fl oz/180 ml) mayonnaise, ⅓ cup (3 oz/05 g) sour cream, ¼ cup (2 oz/60 g) sugar, ½ teaspoon *each* seasoned salt and ground mustard, and ¼ teaspoon celery salt. Add 1 package (14 oz/400 g) coleslaw mix and toss to coat.

# 235 Zesty Coconut Rice

Whether your main dish hails from Southeast Asia, Japan, China, South America, or the tropics, coconut-infused rice is a perfect side. Vary the recipe according to theme or whim: Add in some chopped, toasted macadamia nuts or almonds, or stir in diced bits of fresh pineapple or chopped fresh cilantro.

- 1 tablespoon canola oil
- 1 large shallot, minced
- 1 teaspoon peeled and grated fresh ginger
- 2 cups (14 oz/440 g) jasmine rice
- 1 cup (8 fl oz/250 ml) coconut milk
- Kosher salt
- ½ cup (2 oz/60 g) toasted flaked coconut

**COOK** In a large saucepan over medium-high heat, warm canola oil. Add shallot and ginger, and sauté until fragrant, about 30 seconds. Add rice and stir to mix well. Add 2 cups (16 fl oz/500 ml) water, the coconut milk, and 1 teaspoon salt, and bring to a boil. Reduce heat to low, cover, and simmer for 20 minutes.

**SERVE** Remove pan from heat. Let stand, covered, until tender, about 10 minutes longer. Fluff rice with a fork, stir in flaked coconut, and serve. Serves 6.

# 236 Arugula Salad with Grilled Peaches

Stone fruits are ace when it comes to grilling. The cut fruits love the grill's searing heat, sizzling to caramelized perfection, and are firm enough to hold their shape. In salad, they partner well with greens that offer a counterpoint to their charred sweetness—like the acerbic bite of peppery arugula. Add a liberal dose of creamy cheese and a sprinkle of crunchy pecans for a study in culinary harmony. Try any of your favorite stone fruits here; peaches are the most classic choice.

- 3 peaches, plums, or nectarines, pitted, peeled, and each cut into six wedges
- 10 cups (about 10 oz/285 g) arugula, rinsed and spun dry
- 2 oz (125 ml) thinly sliced prosciutto, cut into ¼-inch (6-mm) strips
- 2 tablespoons crumbled Gorgonzola, goat, or feta cheese
- 2 tablespoons chopped candied pecans
- ¼ cup (2 fl oz/60 ml) homemade or store-bought balsamic vinaigrette

Prepare charcoal or gas grill for direct grilling over medium heat. Brush and oil grill grate. Grill peaches 30 seconds on each side until slightly charred, but still firm, and set aside. In a large bowl, toss arugula, prosciutto, cheese, pecans, and balsamic vinaigrette; top with peaches and serve.

# 237 Prosciutto-Wrapped Figs

Cooked up until hot, sweet, and gushy, figs from the grill taste downright sinful. Add a stuffing of heat-softened goat cheese, a blanket of salty prosciutto, a drizzle of honey and balsamic, and the result is nothing short of pure bliss.

- 4 Mission figs
- 4–6 slices Parma prosciutto
- ¼ cup (1¼ oz/30 g) fresh goat cheese, at room temperature
- Olive oil for brushing
- Salt and freshly ground black pepper
- 2 tablespoons balsamic vinegar or balsamic syrup (see item 238)
- Honey for drizzling

**PREP** Trim off stem ends of figs and cut figs lengthwise into quarters. Lay prosciutto slices flat on a work surface. Cut each slice crosswise into four pieces. Spoon 1 teaspoonful of goat cheese on top of each fig and tightly wrap with a piece of prosciutto. Secure bundles with toothpicks, if necessary.

**HEAT** Prepare a charcoal or gas grill for direct grilling over medium-high heat. Brush and oil grill grate.

**GRILL** Brush fig bundles with oil and season with salt and pepper. Grill over direct heat, turning often, until evenly marked, 4–6 minutes. Move bundles to indirect heat and drizzle with balsamic vinegar. Grill, covered, until figs are cooked through and cheese is melted, about 3 minutes longer.

**SERVE** Arrange bundles on serving platter, drizzle with honey, and serve piping hot.

# 238 Try a Hit of Balsamic

When it comes to flavor boosts for grilled fruits and vegetables, balsamic syrup is in the tried-and-true category. The syrup slides on like a sparkly coating, doing double duty as flavor enhancer and finishing glaze. Even plain sliced fruits like peaches and pineapples ratchet up the wow factor when hit with a splash of the good stuff.

Look for it in well-stocked markets or make your own by combining 1 cup (8 fl oz/250 ml) balsamic vinegar and 2 tablespoons light agave syrup in a small saucepan and bringing to a boil over medium-high heat. Reduce heat to low and simmer until thickened, about 2 minutes. Let cool and serve.

# 239 Chile-Lime Pineapple Skewers

Pineapples are grilling superstars—their cut edges caramelize perfectly in the searing heat while their flesh stays juicy and sweet. As an unexpected appetizer, grilled pineapple pops go a long way towards setting the mood for an Asian- or island-inspired menu. (You can also load up the skewers to serve alongside the main course.) Serve these sweet and savory pineapple bites alongside a chilled pitcher of mai tais or floral-festooned piña coladas.

- 2 tablespoons coarse sea salt
- ¼ teaspoon cayenne pepper
- Finely grated zest of 1 lime
- 16–20 wooden skewers
- 1 pineapple
- Olive oil for drizzling

**MIX** Make a chile-lime salt by mixing salt, cayenne, and lime zest in a small bowl. Mash ingredients with the back of a spoon, then let flavors meld for at least 30 minutes.

**PREP** Soak wooden skewers in water for at least 30 minutes ahead of time. Prepare charcoal or gas grill for direct grilling over medium heat. Brush and oil grill grate.

**THREAD** Using a serrated knife, cut off the top and bottom of the pineapple. Stand it upright on a cutting board and slice off the skin in long strips, then cut the pineapple lengthwise into pieces, slicing along the outer edge of the tough core. Discard core. Cut pieces lengthwise into 1-inch (2.5-cm) slices, then crosswise into 1-inch (2.5-cm) chunks. Place chunks in a bowl, sprinkle with 2 teaspoons of the chile-lime salt, and toss to coat evenly. Thread a few chunks onto skewer ends and drizzle on all sides with oil.

**GRILL** Grill skewers over direct heat, turning as needed, until all sides are equally charred, about 8 minutes.

**SERVE** Place on a platter and sprinkle with remaining chile-lime salt. Serve hot.

## QUICK TIP

To prevent wooden skewers from burning on the grill, build a heat shield using a doubled-up piece of heavy-duty aluminum foil (see item 083 for instructions). The folded foil acts as a skewer rest—just preheat the grill first, then place your crafty contraption on the grate and rest a fruit-free portion of each skewer on the foil, allowing the fruit to sear without torching the wood.

WS

# 240 Flash-Grilled Asparagus

Flash-grilled asparagus can serve as the base for a range of easy appetizers. Start with a small bunch—about ½ lb (8 oz/250 g)—of fresh spears. Toss in a drizzle of olive oil and season well. Grill on a hot grate over direct medium heat until charred in places but still firm—about 6 minutes depending upon thickness. If you're at all nervous about spears slipping through the grate and into the coals, skewer a few stalks crosswise in two places to make a "raft." If your next quandary is about how to serve them, try sprucing up plain grilled asparagus with a simple vinaigrette, romesco sauce (see item 208), lemony mayonnaise, or one of these simple preparations.

**PARMESAN** Marinate with olive oil, grated Parmesan, minced garlic, and salt and pepper, then grill until charred in places but still firm.

**SESAME** Marinate asparagus with 2 tablespoons sesame oil, 1 tablespoon soy sauce, and 1 crushed garlic clove. Grill until charred but firm, sprinkling on 1 tablespoon sesame seeds during the last minute or so of grilling.

**PROSCIUTTO** Wrap each asparagus spear in a single slice of prosciutto (or, if the spears are pencil-thin, group three or four at a time). Brush with olive oil and sprinkle with salt and pepper. Grill until prosciutto is crispy but spears are still firm to the touch.

**MOZZARELLA** Marinate spears in a lemony vinaigrette, grill them until charred but firm, then top them with a slice of fresh mozzarella, a drizzle of vinaigrette, and a sprinkle of fresh parsley.

**SMOKY SPICED** Whisk together ¼ cup (2 fl oz/60 ml) mayonnaise, 2 tablespoons olive oil, 1½ tablespoons fresh lemon juice, 1 crushed garlic clove, 1½ teaspoons smoked paprika, 1 teaspoon salt, and ½ teaspoon ground cumin. Marinate asparagus for at least 30 minutes, then grill.

# 241
## Marinated Baby Artichokes

- ½ cup (4 fl oz/125 ml) extra-virgin olive oil
- 3 cloves garlic, minced
- 2 tablespoons fresh lemon juice
- ⅛ teaspoon red pepper flakes
- 1–2 dashes hot pepper sauce
- Salt and freshly ground black pepper
- 20 baby artichokes, about 1 lb (500 g) total

Artichokes are at their best when they're "babies"—wonderfully supple and nearly free of the fuzzy, prickly centers at the heart of mature chokes. They're perfect marinated and charred and hot off the grill—eat them plain, or whip up a lemon and garlic–infused mayonnaise to serve alongside.

**MIX** In a shallow bowl, mix together all ingredients except the artichokes.

**PREP** Whack each artichoke on a countertop a couple of times to loosen the leaves. Trim away the stem's rough outer layer and cut each artichoke lengthwise into quarters. Scoop out any hairy chokes.

**MARINATE** Toss artichokes in vinaigrette and marinate for 30 minutes.

**GRILL** Place on grill rack, cut sides down. Grill, turning every 5 minutes and brushing with remaining marinade, until evenly charred and tender, about 20 minutes total.

**SERVE** Dish them up hot from the grill.

Serves 4–6.

# 242 Charred Padrón Peppers

- 12–16 Padrón peppers
- 1–2 tablespoons extra-virgin olive oil
- Flaky sea salt, such as French grey

Little Padrón peppers pack a serious flavor punch. They're perfectly bite-size and usually blessedly mild (although some have a bit of an angry side). Coating them with a crispy grilled-on char brings out their natural sweetness and makes them nice and tender. Best of all, they couldn't be easier to cook. Throw the peppers on the grate while your grill is warming up, then munch on them while the main course cooks.

**OIL** Toss peppers in a drizzle of olive oil until evenly coated. Sprinkle on some flaky sea salt and toss again.

**GRILL** Preheat a grill to medium-high heat. Place peppers on grill rack and, using tongs, turn often until evenly charred, 3–5 minutes.

**SERVE** Sprinkle with more sea salt and serve.

# 243 Seared Salad with Asiago

Leave yourself open to new ideas in grilling and you will seldom be disappointed. Grilled salad is a case in point. Searing heat brings out the natural sweetness of romaine's crisp leaves.

**BLEND** In a blender or food processor, combine vinegar, anchovy paste, mustard, lemon juice, oregano, and roasted garlic. Pulse to blend. With machine running, slowly add both oils and process until emulsified. Transfer to a bowl. Stir in honey and season with salt and pepper. You should have 1¼ cups (10 fl oz/310 ml); store extra in an airtight container in the refrigerator for up to one week.

**HEAT** Prepare charcoal or gas grill for direct grilling over medium heat. Brush and oil the grill rack.

**PREP** Cut each romaine head in half lengthwise. Trim base of stem on each half, leaving remainder attached to hold leaves together. Drizzle cut side of each half with olive oil.

**GRILL** Place romaine halves, cut sides down, on grill rack. Cook until leaves develop a little char and begin to wilt, 2–3 minutes. Turn and cook 2 minutes longer. Romaine should be a little wilted but still hold its shape.

**SERVE** Turn the romaine halves cut side up and serve on individual plates. Garnish each one with a quarter of the tomatoes and avocado. Use a vegetable peeler to shave cheese over salads. Spoon some vinaigrette over the top and serve.

Serves 4.

- ¼ cup (2 fl oz/60 ml) white wine vinegar
- ½ teaspoon *each* anchovy paste and whole-grain mustard
- 1 tablespoon fresh lemon juice
- 1 tablespoon fresh oregano
- ¼ teaspoon granulated garlic
- ½ cup (4 fl oz/125 ml) *each* canola oil and extra-virgin olive oil, plus more for drizzling
- 1 teaspoon honey
- Kosher salt and freshly ground black pepper
- 2 heads romaine lettuce, outer leaves removed
- 1 cup (6 oz/185 g) cherry tomatoes, halved
- 1 avocado, pitted, peeled, and sliced
- ¼ lb (125 g) Asiago cheese

# 244 Grilled Gazpacho

- 6 plum (Roma) tomatoes
- 4 heirloom tomatoes
- Salt and ground pepper
- Olive oil for brushing
- 2 small zucchini, sliced lengthwise into ¼-inch (6-mm) thick strips
- 2 red bell peppers, halved lengthwise and seeded
- 2 jalapeño chiles, halved lengthwise and seeded
- 2 English (hothouse) cucumbers, peeled, seeded, and chopped
- 1 tablespoon hot pepper sauce
- 4 cups (32 fl oz/1 l) tomato soup
- Extra-virgin olive oil for drizzling
- 1 tablespoon each fresh chives, French parsley, flat-leaf (Italian) parsley, and tarragon

If you think fresh gazpacho is good, then this unusual grilled variation will knock your socks off—the grill adds an unexpected depth of flavor that will leave you hankering for more. Whip up this summer soup at least a few hours in advance; it's best when you let the flavors meld before serving. Snip a few fresh garden herbs over each bowlful for a refreshing final touch.

**PREP** Core, quarter, and seed the tomatoes. Place in a colander over a bowl and sprinkle with salt. Let stand 10 minutes. Transfer drained tomato water to a sealed container, cover, and refrigerate.

**HEAT** Prepare a charcoal or gas grill for direct grilling over medium-high heat. Brush and oil grill grate or vegetable grilling basket.

**OIL** Brush tomatoes, zucchini, bell peppers, and chiles with olive oil. Season with salt and pepper.

**GRILL** Grill vegetables, turning often, until soft and nicely charred on all sides, 2–4 minutes for zucchini and 10 minutes for tomatoes, peppers, and chiles. Transfer to a platter and let cool slightly.

**BLEND** Working in batches, combine the grilled vegetables, half the cucumbers, and the hot pepper sauce in a blender or food processor and blend until puréed. Add ½ cup (4 fl oz/125 ml) of the tomato soup (or as much as needed for a nice consistency). Taste and adjust seasonings as desired. Transfer to a glass pitcher, cover, and refrigerate at least 2 hours or overnight.

**SERVE** Fill chilled shot glasses or espresso cups three-quarters full with soup. Top each with 1 teaspoon of remaining cucumbers, 1 tablespoon of reserved tomato water, 3 drips of extra-virgin olive oil, and a pinch of fresh herbs. Serve at once.

Makes 8–10 servings.

# 245 Top Bruschetta 10 Ways

Bruschetta is proof that the greatest pleasures in life are often the simplest—sometimes it's nothing more than toast with a rub of garlic. Bruschetta served right from the grill is an easy and memorable dinner party food, and, like most straightforwardly delicious dishes, it's all about focusing on great ingredients and pairing them with panache.

Classic bruschetta begins with a slice of bread; dense, country-style varieties or artisanal loaves are good options. Brush each slice with good-quality extra-virgin olive oil and arrange in a single layer on a hot grill. Grill, turning once, until crispy and nicely charred. Rub the grilled slices with the cut side of a garlic clove and add an extra drizzle of olive oil. You can stop there to enjoy traditional bruschetta in its purest form, or opt for the addition of any one of these awesome toppings.

**TOMATO & BASIL** Combine diced ripe tomatoes with chopped fresh basil, minced garlic, salt and pepper, and a glug of olive oil.

**LEMON & RICOTTA** Top with fresh ricotta and lemon zest or a drizzle of creamy honey.

**BUTTER & RADISH** Smear toast with butter and top with thin radish slices and sea salt.

**AVOCADO & SPICES** Combine fresh sliced avocado with an extra drizzle of olive oil, a sprinkle of flaky sea salt, and crushed red pepper flakes.

**MUSHROOMS & GARLIC** Sauté some cremini mushrooms in olive oil with minced shallots and garlic until crisp and browned. Add a healthy dash of red wine vinegar and a half cup of vegetable broth and cook down until almost evaporated. Sprinkle with fresh thyme leaves.

**BALSAMIC ONIONS & CHEESE** Grill thick slices of red onion on a medium-hot grill until nicely charred, then toss with balsamic vinegar. Place a slice of fresh mozzarella cheese on each hot toast and spoon grilled onions on top. Sprinkle with fresh chopped parsley.

**FIGS & HONEY** Spread mascarpone or cream cheese on toasts. Top with sliced fresh figs, a drizzle of honey, and a sprinkle of flaky sea salt.

**SMASHED PEAS & MINT** Mash cooked fresh peas with roasted garlic, fresh lemon juice, and chopped preserved lemon peel to taste. Stir in enough extra-virgin olive oil to yield a good, spreadable consistency. Season to taste with salt, pepper, and more lemon juice as needed. Garnish with torn mint.

**GORGONZOLA, PROSCIUTTO & PEARS** Spread gorgonzola on toasts. Top with sliced pears, thinly sliced prosciutto, and a drizzle of walnut oil.

# 246 Pick Your Pizza Method

Perfecting pizza-grilling technique is the holy grail to many pie-loving enthusiasts. Like most passionate pursuits, everyone has a different idea about the best way to go about it. Although a pizza stone best mimics the charring effects of a traditional pizza oven, some cooks prefer pizza cooked right on the grill rack.

To make use of this method, prepare a charcoal or gas grill for direct-heat grilling over medium-high heat or indirect-heat grilling over high heat. (Direct heat cooks dough more quickly, so any toppings should be precooked. Use indirect heat when adding toppings that need some

time to cook.) Shape the dough into a round and brush it with olive oil. Next, brush and oil the grill rack and flip the dough onto it. Cover and cook until browned on the bottom, 1–2 minutes over direct heat, 3 minutes over indirect. Brush the top with olive oil. Using a pizza peel, flip dough round over to cook the other side. Place toppings on pizza, cover, and cook until browned on the bottom, 1–2 minutes longer over direct heat, 3 minutes over indirect. Use the peel to transfer pizza to a cutting board.

Specialty grills can also do wonders for pizza baking—like ceramic kamado-style grills. Their domed ceramic interior, hardwood charcoal, and custom-fit pizza stones are best at producing the same extreme heat and smoky flavor forged in classic brick ovens.

# 247 Top Pizza Like a Pro

Choose toppings that improve with the caramelizing effects of searing heat, then pair up complementary ingredients and flavors.

### SAUCES

Marinara
Basil pesto
Sun-dried tomato pesto
Alfredo

### CHEESES

Melty: Mozzarella, fontina, provolone
Creamy: Goat, cream cheese
Piquant: Feta, blue, Gorgonzola
Hard: Grated Parmesan, Romano

### MEATS

Sliced salami, pepperoni, prosciutto
Sautéed pancetta or bacon
Sliced or crumbled sausage
Shredded chicken
Diced ham

### VEGGIES

Spinach
Kale or chard
Thinly sliced zucchini
Sliced baby artichokes
Shaved brussels sprouts
Thinly sliced radicchio
Coarsely chopped broccoli
Roasted bell peppers
Sliced onion (red, green, and/or white)
Very thinly sliced Yukon gold potatoes

### FRUITS

Sliced pear
Sliced peach
Cut figs
Diced pineapple

### EXTRAS

Pitted Kalamata olives
Roasted garlic
Fresh arugula (add just before serving)
Red chile flakes
Basil, thyme, rosemary

# 248 Accessorize Your Setup

Wish you had a pizza oven but don't want to fork over the small fortune required to satisfy the hefty price tag? No worries! There are plenty of grill accessories (at varying levels of cost and effectiveness) that will transform your regular gas or charcoal grill into the high-heat pizza oven you might be hankering for.

**PIZZA STONES** One pizza stone is good; two is better. Since most of a grill's heat comes from the bottom, using only one stone (especially with the thinner ones) may lead to some charring on the crust's bottom. Setting a second stone atop the first will prevent burning and help the pizza cook more evenly. You can also look for extra-thick pizza stones in raised metal frames made especially for the grill.

**PIZZA OVEN BOX** These portable boxes for gas or rectangular charcoal grills feature stone baking chambers in enameled steel housing. Preheated atop a grill rack, they reach interior cooking temperatures of up to 750°F (400°C), turning out nicely charred crust in a brief 2–4 minutes of grill time.

**KETTLE GRILL PIZZA FRAME**
A heavy-duty metal band frames a pizza stone while keeping the lid of a charcoal kettle grill lifted so you can slide the pies in and out with ease. With lots of charcoal burning underneath, the frame traps heat and provides smoky flavor all at once.

# 249 Master the Peel

You can spend hours babying your dough to perfection, topping your round like a master chef, then find that the most difficult part of the whole process is sliding the dough from the pizza peel onto the hot stone.

Here's how to do it like a pro. First, bring the topped pizza on the cornmeal-dusted peel to the hot pizza stone. Maneuver the peel over the stone, and gently shift the peel with a sliding motion to get the leading edge of the pizza crust just off the end of the peel. Touch the crust down to the stone, then quickly and smoothly slide the peel back from under the crust—like a magician pulling the tablecloth out from under the plates. It may take a few tries, but you'll get the hang of it.

# 250 Pizza Party Dough

For fun, casual gatherings that involve a bit of guest participation, try a pizza-making party. Make the dough in advance (or use the store-bought variety), set out an array of toppings, preheat the grill, and let your guests take care of themselves.

Making pizza dough at home is easier than one might think, especially if you use an electric mixer or stand mixer (to help with mixing and kneading). This recipe makes enough for eight small pizzas. If you don't use all the dough, simply seal it in a zip-top plastic bag and refrigerate for up to a day, or freeze for up to three weeks. Bring to room temperature before using.

- 3 cups (24 fl oz/750 ml) lukewarm water (about 110°F/43°C)
- 2 packages (2½ teaspoons) active dry yeast
- 1 teaspoon salt
- 2 tablespoons olive oil, plus oil for greasing bowls
- 8 cups (6 lb/3 kg) all-purpose flour

**MIX** Pour water into a large bowl and sprinkle yeast over the top. Let stand until foamy, about 5 minutes. Add salt, olive oil, and 5 cups (25 oz/785 g) flour. Beat with an electric stand mixer, using paddle attachment if you have one, until dough is glossy and stretchy, about 5 minutes. Beat in 2½ cups (1½ oz/390 g) more flour.

**KNEAD** If kneading with a dough hook, place hook on mixer and beat on medium speed, gradually adding up to ¼ cup (1½ oz/45 g) more flour if needed, until dough is springy and pulls cleanly from the sides of the bowl, 5–7 minutes. If kneading by hand, turn out dough onto floured work surface and knead until smooth and springy, 10–15 minutes, adding as little flour as possible to prevent sticking.

**LET RISE** Generously grease a large bowl with olive oil. Place dough in bowl and turn to grease top. Cover with plastic wrap and let rise until doubled, about 45 minutes. (Or cover and refrigerate for up to 12 hours.)

**PREHEAT** Prepare charcoal or gas grill for indirect grilling over high heat. Place a thick pizza stone (or stack 2 stones) in the center of the grill rack. Make the grill as hot as you can get it (about 500°F/260°C for gas or 700°F/370°C for charcoal). Grill should preheat at least 30 minutes before you cook.

**SHAPE** Punch down dough and turn out onto lightly floured board. Press dough flat to release any excess air. (If it has risen in the refrigerator, cover with a kitchen towel and bring to room temperature—about 1½ hours—before continuing.) Cut dough in half and cut each half into four equal pieces. Let guests press and stretch dough into rounds about 9 inches (23 cm) in diameter, being careful not to knead too much, as it will activate the gluten and make it difficult to stretch into a round.

**TOP** Place dough round on a pizza peel well dusted with cornmeal. Top with choice of toppings.

**GRILL** Sprinkle cornmeal on pizza stone. Slide topped round from pizza peel onto hot stone (see item 249). Cover and grill until crust is slightly charred and toppings are browned, 4–12 minutes depending on temperature of your grill. (Use peel to turn pizza during cooking time if browning unevenly.)

**SERVE** Slip peel under pizza and transfer it from grill to cutting board. Let cool briefly, then cut into pieces.

Makes eight 10-inch (25-cm) pizzas.

# 251 Add Some Flavor

Even the best cut of meat tastes just that much better when paired with the right spice rub, marinade, or sauce. A vast collection of flavorful seasonings is sprinkled liberally throughout the pages of this book, yet there is always more to share. These are among the best of the basics—each one lending its own regional nuance to the finished dish.

## LATIN SPICE RUB

- ¼ cup (1 oz/30 g) ground cumin
- 3 tablespoons freshly ground black pepper
- 2 tablespoons sugar
- 1 tablespoon ground coriander
- 1½ teaspoons kosher salt

In a small container with a tight-fitting lid, combine all ingredients. Shake to mix. Store for up to one month. Goes great with skirt, hanger, or flank steak; pork tenderloin; or fish.

Makes about ½ cup (4 oz/125 g).

## CLASSIC BARBECUE SAUCE

- 1 cup (8 oz/250 g) ketchup
- 2 tablespoons yellow mustard
- 1 tablespoon cider vinegar
- 2 teaspoons *each* ground pepper and firmly packed dark brown sugar
- ½ cup (4 fl oz/125 ml) low-sodium chicken broth
- Pinch of salt, plus salt to taste

In a saucepan over medium heat, combine all ingredients and bring to a simmer, stirring to dissolve sugar. Simmer 5 minutes for a relatively thin sauce or 10–15 minutes for a thicker one. Taste and adjust seasoning with salt.

Makes about 2 cups (16 fl oz/500 ml).

## BEST PEANUT SAUCE

- 1 can (14 fl oz/430 ml) full-fat, unsweetened coconut milk
- ¾ cup (8 oz/230 g) unsweetened, all-natural creamy peanut butter
- ¾ cup (6 oz/185 g) sugar
- ½ cup (4 fl oz/125 ml) water
- 2 tablespoons apple cider vinegar
- 3–4 tablespoons Thai red curry paste
- ½ tablespoon salt
- Juice of ½ lime

In a saucepan over medium heat, combine all ingredients except lime juice and bring to a very gentle boil. Reduce heat to low and simmer, stirring often to prevent scorching, 3–5 minutes. Let cool. Squeeze in a lime juice and stir to blend. Serve at room temperature.

Makes about 3½ cups (28 fl oz/830 ml).

## HERB-AND-SPICE RUB

- ¼ cup (2 oz/60 g) paprika
- 6 tablespoons (1½ oz/45 g) kosher salt and granulated garlic
- 5 tablespoons ground pepper
- 3 tablespoons *each* granulated onion and cayenne pepper
- 2 tablespoons *each* dried oregano and dried thyme
- 1 tablespoon smoked paprika

In a small container with a tight-fitting lid, combine all ingredients. Shake to mix. Store for up to 1 month.
Makes about 1 cup (8 oz/250 g).

## BALSAMIC-MUSTARD MARINADE

- ¼ cup (2 fl oz/60 ml) *each* tamari or reduced-sodium soy sauce, extra-virgin olive oil, and balsamic vinegar
- 6 cloves garlic, finely minced or pressed
- 2 tablespoons whole-grain mustard
- 1 tablespoon *each* Dijon mustard and yellow or brown mustard seeds
- 2 teaspoons peeled and grated fresh ginger
- 1 teaspoon freshly ground black pepper
- Pinch of salt

In a bowl, combine all ingredients. Mix well. Use right away, or cover and refrigerate for up to one day before using.

Makes about ¾ cup (6 fl oz/180 ml).

# 252 Classic Sangria

Any fruity, full-bodied red wine will do the trick for a traditional Spanish-style sangria—it makes for an excellent make-ahead party drink, a perfect cocktail on a summer afternoon, or a great accompaniment to fish tacos hot off the grill.

- 1 apple, cored, skin on, sliced into thin wedges
- 1 orange, rind on, sliced into thin wedges, large seeds removed
- 3–4 tablespoons firmly packed brown sugar
- ¾ cup (6 fl oz/180 ml) orange juice
- ⅓ cup (3 fl oz/80 ml) brandy
- 1 bottle (24 oz/750 ml) dry Spanish red wine
- Ice to chill

**MUDDLE** Add apple, orange, and sugar to a large glass pitcher, setting aside a few segments for garnish, and muddle (use the back of a wooden spoon if you don't have a muddler). Put some muscle into it for a solid 30 seconds or so. Add orange juice and brandy, and muddle again to combine.

**MIX** Add red wine and stir, then taste and adjust the flavor as desired.

**SERVE** Add ice and stir once more to chill. Garnish with orange or apple segments to serve.

# 253 Rosé Spritzer

For a fruity, bubbly option, slice a pint of strawberries and combine with 1 bottle (24 oz/750 ml) rosé wine, then chill 3 hours. When ready to serve, stir in 2 cups (16 fl oz/ 500 ml) sparkling water, ⅓ cup (3 fl oz/80 ml) Aperol, and 2 tablespoons fresh lemon juice, then divide over ice and garnish with a few strawberry slices on each glass. There are oodles of excellent rosé and rosato options these days, so pick your favorite and then doctor it up for the party.

# 254 Apple Limeade

To vary this quick and refreshing nonalcoholic drink, add ½ cup (½ oz/15 g) fresh mint leaves or 1 tablespoon peeled and finely grated fresh ginger to the juice mixture before refrigerating.

- 12 limes
- 4 cups (32 fl oz/1 l) unfiltered cold-pressed apple juice
- Ice cubes
- 1 bottle (24 fl oz/750 ml) sparkling water
- 2 small Granny Smith apples, halved, cored, and sliced

**PREP** Cut 10 of the limes in half and squeeze the juice from them. You should have about 1 cup (8 fl oz/250 ml) juice. Reserve 6 squeezed lime halves and discard the rest.

**MIX** In a large glass jar or pitcher, combine the lime juice, apple juice, and the reserved lime halves. Cover and refrigerate at least 1 hour or up to 12 hours to blend the flavors.

**SERVE** When ready to serve, slice the remaining limes and fill a large serving pitcher half full with ice, then add the sparkling water, lime slices, and apple slices. Strain the apple juice mixture through a fine-mesh sieve into the pitcher and stir. Pour over ice into tall chilled glasses and serve at once.

# 255 Plum & Nectarine Sangria

For a twist on the classic apples-and-oranges recipe, look for plums and nectarines that are ripe but still firm (if they're too soft, they'll get floppy when soaked in the wine).

- 3 plums and 3 nectarines, halved, pitted, and cut into thin wedges
- 1 can (12 fl oz/375 ml) nectarine nectar
- ¼ cup (2 fl oz/60 ml) orange liqueur
- 1 bottle (24 fl oz/750 ml) dry white wine
- Ice cubes
- 1 bottle (24 fl oz/750 ml) sparkling water, chilled

**MIX** In a large pitcher, combine the plum and nectarine wedges, nectar, orange liqueur, and white wine. Stir well, cover, and refrigerate for at least 2 hours or up to 12 hours to blend the flavors.

**SERVE** Fill glasses with ice cubes and add the sangria, then top with sparkling water. Serve at once.

# 256 Caribbean Rum Punch

Among their repertoire of rip-roaring sea chanteys, colonial-era seamen had this rhyme committed to memory: "One of sour, two of sweet, three of strong, four of weak." It's the singsong formula for the classic rum punch—a favorite of both early pirates and British sailors in thriving port towns along the Caribbean. Ale didn't take well to the tropical environment, paving the way for a fruity punch that made the most of the region's fresh fruit and amber-hued local spirit. To make, combine 1 cup (8 fl oz/250 ml) lime juice, 2 cups (16 fl oz/500 ml) simple syrup, 3 cups (24 fl oz/750 ml) amber rum, and 4 cups (32 fl oz/1 l) orange juice in a pitcher, then pour over ice and garnish with lime slices to serve.

# 257 Try a White Sangria

To pair with lighter dishes like fish, seafood, and chicken—or for those who avoid red wine—white sangria is a delectable alternative. Combine 2 thinly sliced plums, 1 orange (rind on, sliced into thin wedges), 1 cup (6 oz/185 g) green grapes, a handful of blueberries, and ¼ cup (1 fl oz/60 ml) orange liqueur in a large pitcher. Muddle the fruits to release their juices, add 1 bottle (24 oz/750 ml) crisp white wine, and stir. Cover and refrigerate at least 8 hours. To serve, divide over ice and garnish with orange slices.

# 258 Honeydew and Mint Agua Fresca

This easy Latin drink of sweetened crushed fruit mixed with sparkling water is a nice alternative to soft drinks.

- 2 honeydew melons, about 12 lb (6 kg) total weight
- Juice of 4 lemons plus 3 additional lemons, thinly sliced
- ¾ cup (6 oz/185 g) sugar
- 1 cup (1 oz/30 g) crushed fresh mint leaves
- 3 cups (24 fl oz/750 ml) sparkling water, chilled
- Ice cubes
- 10–12 fresh mint sprigs for garnish

**PREP** Cut the honeydew melons in half and discard the seeds. Using a metal spoon, scoop out the flesh into a large bowl. Working in batches, puree the melon in a blender or food processor.

**MIX** Add the lemon juice, sugar, and mint leaves to the puree in a large bowl and stir to combine until the sugar is dissolved. Cover and set aside at room temperature for at least 1 hour or up to 4 hours to blend the flavors.

**SERVE** Pour the melon mixture through a medium-mesh sieve into a large pitcher or jar. Add the sparkling water, lemon slices, and ice, and stir well. Pour into glasses and garnish with mint sprigs.

## 259 The Perfect Margarita

Crafting a taco from fresh mahi-mahi and washing it down with a regular old beer might not seem quite right. A frothy, chilled, and tart margarita is the logical alternative. Serve it shaken over ice or "up" in a martini glass. Like a little salt on the glass? Rub the rim with a cut lime before dipping it in a saucer of nubby kosher, sea, or margarita salt before pouring in the cocktail.

- 1½ parts tequila (100 percent agave a must, preferably *reposado*)
- 1½ parts triple sec or Cointreau
- 1¼ parts lime juice
- Salt for the rim of the glass, optional
- Slice of lime, optional

Shake all ingredients with crushed ice in a cocktail shaker until the exterior frosts. Salt the rim of the glass, if desired. Strain into a glass over rocks, or into a cocktail glass. Add a slice of lime as a garnish—while not strictly necessary, it's a nice touch.

## 260 Pair Beer and Wine

All that fire and smoke and a person can start to get thirsty! When that's the case—and in the case of barbecue, it always is—nothing quite hits the spot like a frosty brew or perfectly partnered vino.

**BEER** With so many beers to choose from, try matching intensity rather than flavor. Meaty, char-grilled steak is nicely accented with a rich porter, stout, or full-bodied IPA. Grilled pork tenderloin or chops also partner well with stout, as well as the spicy, peppery, and herbal notes of Belgian farmhouse ales. Lamb likes beer with a bit of tang—dark lagers like German *schwarzbier* and Bavarian *märzen*. Pair poultry in accordance with preparation: Robustly prepared chicken, game birds, and turkey go well with dark and rich porters or malty German *dunkels*, whereas lighter dishes are best with effervescent Mexican lagers. The same rules apply for fish: Go light for tender fish fillets, but try pairing meatier fish like salmon and tuna with stronger IPAs and pale ales. The brininess of shellfish is an ideal counterpoint to the burned-toast quality of an Irish dry stout.

**WINE** The incredible diversity of wine makes for some excellent pairing capabilities. Like beer, wine is best matched to flavor intensity. Char-grilled beef works well alongside full-flavored reds, like Cabernet Sauvignon or Meritage. Grilled pork tenderloin is nicely matched to a jammy Zinfandel or Beaujolais, and you can cut rich lamb with a peppery Shiraz. When it comes to chicken, white wine is the go-to for simplicity. Poultry with a gamey edge, such as quail and duck, benefits from the fruitier notes of Viognier. Pairing turkey, on the other hand, can be a challenge: Try wines that bolster its flavor, such as a German Riesling or spice-driven Zinfandel. Seafood marries well with wines that are light but not overpowering—Champagne is a natural partner, as is the citrusy and herbaceous crispness of Sauvignon Blanc. For full-flavored fish, go for a smoky Pinot Noir, especially those with notes of berry and plum. Crab shines with the grapefruit acidity of Sancerre, oysters with soft and mellow citrus notes. For summer parties, rosé wine is a reliable choice: It goes with everything, even dishes slathered in barbecue sauce.

# 261 Grilled Peaches with Butter Rum Sauce

Peaches and rum are like an "a-ha!" moment, so perfectly do their flavors go together. Brush peach halves with a basting sauce of sweetened, cinnamon-flecked, rum-spiked butter, and they grill to perfection—sticky and caramelized on the outside, juicy and sweet throughout.

- ¼ cup (2 oz/60 g) *each* unsalted butter and firmly packed brown sugar
- ¼ cup (2 fl oz/60 ml) amber rum
- ½ teaspoon ground cinnamon
- ¼ teaspoon salt
- 4 peaches, halved and pitted
- Olive or grapeseed oil for brushing
- Vanilla ice cream for serving

**PREHEAT & PREP**  Prepare a gas or charcoal grill for direct cooking over medium-high heat. Brush and oil grill grate. In a small saucepan over medium-high heat, combine butter, brown sugar, rum, cinnamon, and salt. Bring to a boil, then reduce heat to low and simmer, stirring often, until sugar is melted and mixture is syrupy, 2–3 minutes. Set aside.

**GRILL**  Brush cut sides of peaches with oil. Place peaches, cut sides down, over direct heat on grill. Grill, basting once with rum sauce, until nicely browned, 3–4 minutes. Turn peaches and baste with glaze. Cover grill, and cook until browned on second side and fruit is tender, 3–4 minutes longer.

**SERVE**  Top peaches with equal portions vanilla ice cream and remaining sauce.

Serves 4.

## 262 Grilled Figs with Honeyed Mascarpone & Mint

- 12 ripe, plump Mission figs
- ¾ cup (3 oz/90 g) plus 1 tablespoon honey
- ¼ lb (4 oz/125 g) mascarpone cheese
- ½ teaspoon vanilla extract
- Zest of 1 lemon
- Fresh mint leaves for garnish

Dunk fresh fig halves into warmed honey before toasting them on the grill and the result is at once crisp and gushy, caramelized and fabulous. Lemony mascarpone and a sprinkle of mint balances out the sweetness.

**PREHEAT & PREP** Prepare a charcoal or gas grill for indirect cooking over medium heat. Brush and oil grill grate. Cut figs lengthwise into halves and place on a platter. In a small saucepan over medium heat, heat honey, stirring often, until liquid, about 1 minute. (Or heat honey in a small bowl in a microwave on high for 30 seconds.) Quickly but carefully dip fig halves into hot honey and return to platter. Set aside.

**WHIP** In a bowl, combine mascarpone, vanilla, and lemon zest. Using an immersion blender or hand mixer, whip until frothy and light, 1–2 minutes. Cover and refrigerate until ready to use.

**GRILL** Place figs on grill, cut sides down, over indirect heat. Grill just until browned, about 1 minute. Turn and continue grilling for a minute or so longer, until browned on the second side, nicely caramelized, and warmed through.

**SERVE** Arrange 2–4 fig halves atop individual serving plates with a few dollops of mascarpone and a sprinkle of mint leaves.

## 263

# Grilled Apricots with Chocolate & Almonds

You can plate these sweet grilled apricots or allow guests to assemble their own treats—just put out a platter of the grilled fruits with bowls of melted chocolate and toasted, chopped almonds for dipping.

- 10 fresh apricots, halved and pitted
- Vegetable oil or grapeseed oil for brushing
- ¼ lb (4 oz/125 g) bittersweet chocolate, melted
- ¼ cup (2½ oz/40 g) toasted slivered almonds, chopped

**PREHEAT & PREP** Prepare a gas or charcoal grill for direct cooking over high heat. Brush and oil grill grate. Brush apricots with oil.

**GRILL** Grill apricots, cut sides down, over direct heat until well marked, 1–2 minutes. Turn and continue grilling until well marked and tender, about 1 minute longer.

**SERVE** Divide apricots evenly among plates. Drizzle chocolate over apricots, sprinkle with almonds, and serve.

Serves 4.

# 264 Grilled Specialty S'mores

Turns out s'mores aren't just a campfire treat. They can be cooked over a grill fire, too. You can even set a hibachi in the center of the table, surrounded by cookies, candies, and marshmallows, for a dessert your guests won't soon forget. Approach the classic graham cracker combo with a little bit of outside-the-box thinking and you may discover a toasted delicacy all your own.

**KNOW THE BASICS** Unless you've been living on the moon, you're likely acquainted with the nuts and bolts of s'more preparation. Toasting a marshmallow over charcoal or gas isn't much different from roasting one over a campfire. For charcoal toasting, the coals should be well covered with gray ash and burning with low, hot flames. For toasting over gas, remove the grill grates and turn the heat to medium-high. When the fire is hot, stick a marshmallow on the end of a long stick or skewer and brown over the heat, turning to color evenly, until crisp on the outside and soft in the center. Sandwich between two graham cracker squares, add a square of chocolate, and you're good to go!

**GET CREATIVE** Once you have the basic technique down, you can start getting creative. When it comes to pairing possibilities, the sky's the limit. Along with plenty of marshmallows for toasting, mix and match some of these scrumptious additions.

### COOKIES

Graham crackers, chocolate graham crackers, oreos or wafer cookies, chocolate chip cookies, peanut butter cookies, crispy-rice treats, ginger cookies, waffle cookies, snickerdoodles, French macarons

### FILLINGS

Chocolate, Nutella, peanut butter, *dulce de leche*, caramel, thin mint-filled chocolates, thin caramel-filled chocolates, toasted coconut, candied bacon, sliced bananas, sweetened sliced berries, peanut butter cups, KitKat bars, chocolate-covered pretzels, sliced candy bars, lemon curd

### POSSIBLE COMBOS

Peanut butter cookies + Nutella + banana

Chocolate graham crackers + mint-filled chocolate

Ginger cookies + lemon curd

Graham crackers + dark chocolate + salted caramel + candied bacon

Chocolate wafers + peanut butter cup

Graham crackers + caramel + toasted coconut + dark chocolate

Waffle cookies + sweetened fresh strawberries + Nutella

INDEX

**Lisa Chaney Atwood** spent the formative moments of her childhood at the elbow of her father in a halo of charbroil grill heat. The first grill of her own was a 14-inch Smokey Joe, which led to a long succession of barbecues, grills, and smokers, as well as a love of cooking that endures today. As an editor, writer, and publisher for Weldon Owen in San Francisco, Lisa has produced numerous cookbooks and authored three of her own, including *The Art of Preserving* (2010), *The Cookbook for Kids* (2010), and *Kids Parties* (2008).

# Credits

All illustrations by Conor Buckley.

All images courtesy Shutterstock with the following exceptions:

*Maren Caruso:* 35; The Companion Group: 3 (quesadilla maker); *Ray Kachatorian:* Cover, Half Title, Page 8, Front Matter (poultry), 002 (bottom left, bottom middle), 013 (left), 034, 055, 056, 060, 062–063, 066 (main image), 067, 069, 073, 077¬–078, 080, 085, 103 (both images), 107–109, 112, 114, 125, 133, 139, 145, 148, 149 (main image), 152–153, 157, 165, 171, 174, 178, 181, 185, 197, 200, 202–203, 212, 217, 221, 224–226, 228, 230, 232, 236, 244, 239–241, 243, 245 (main image, left page), 250 (4 inset images, excepting middle left), 259, 260 (main image, right page), 263; *Jason Lowe:* 162, 169, 189–190, 206–208; *Iain Morris:* 001 (smoker); *Nordic Ware:* 003 (popcorn popper); *Rome Industries, Inc.:* 003 (s'more roaster, sandwich iron); *Stock Food:* 002 (fish basket, rotisserie), 059, 066 (bottom inset), 086, 089, 090, 091 (main image), 092, 110, 124, 141 (Greek Marinade), 149 (inset), 180, 184, 192, 216, 219, 246, 250 (bottom, right page), 251 (Herb and Spice Rub, Balsamic Mustard Marinade), 252, 253, 257, 258, 262

# weldon**owen**

**President & Publisher** Roger Shaw
**Associate Publisher** Mariah Bear
**SVP, Sales & Marketing** Amy Kaneko
**Finance Manager** Philip Paulick
**Editor** Bridget Fitzgerald
**Editorial Assistant** Ian Cannon
**Creative Director** Kelly Booth
**Art Director** William Mack
**Senior Production Designer** Rachel Lopez Metzger
**Illustration Coordinator** Conor Buckley
**Production Director** Chris Hemesath
**Associate Production Director** Michelle Duggan
**Production Manager** Michelle Woo
**Director of Enterprise Systems** Shawn Macey
**Imaging Manager** Don Hill

Weldon Owen would also like to thank Marisa Solís for editorial assistance and Kevin Broccoli for the index.

**DESIGN BY CAMERON + COMPANY**
**Publisher** Chris Gruener
**Creative Director** Iain R. Morris
**Designer** Suzi Hutsell

Library of Congress Control Number
on file with the publisher

ISBN 978-1-68188-047-1
10 9 8 7 6 5 4 3 2 1
2016 2017 2018 2019 2020

Printed in China by 1010 Printing International